A small government unit, say, is moving across a long stretch of flooded rice paddies. The only high ground on which to walk is a straight, narrow road atop a wide paddy dyke, the nearest tree line a mile or more away. Suddenly, heavy machine-gun fire starts coming in from the right side, 400 or 500 yards away.

The enemy machine gun is too far away to destroy the column. All the troops are in position to fire at the lone enemy gun, which is not far enough away that it can be ignored. Slugs are snapping overhead or thumping into the right back of the dyke. So the main force does the instinctively correct thing: it jumps off the left side of the dyke into the paddy, so as to get maximum cover and to use the road as a firing parapet.

But as in so many aspects of this war, the instinctively right thing is the wrong thing in practice. The left side of the dyke turns out to be studded with spiked foot traps, booby traps, and mines. And another enemy machine gun, only 100 yards ahead and almost up against the left bank of the dyke, opens fire. This gun has the government troops in what is known as enfilade. This means that only the few troops at the head of the line can fire on the enemy, while the enemy can cover the entire group without changing aim.

This is the type of ambush in which the Viet Cong does not need overwhelming superiority of numbers to win. Twenty-five guerrillas stand a reasonable chance of wiping out 100 government troops.

THE NEW FACE OF WAR

MALCOLM W. BROWNE

Revised Edition

BANTAM BOOKS

TORONTO • NEW YORK • LONDON • SYDNEY • AUCKLAND

THE NEW FACE OF WAR
A Bantam Book / published by arrangement with
Macmillan Publishing Company

PRINTING HISTORY
Macmillan edition published 1965
Bantam edition / June 1986

Drawings by Greg Beecham.

Maps by Alan McKnight.

Bantam Books are published by Bantam Books, Inc. Its trademark, consisting of the words "Bantam Books" and the por-
trayal of a rooster, is Registered in U.S. Patent and Trademark
Office and in other countries. Marca Registrada. Bantam
Books, Inc., 666 Fifth Avenue, New York, New York 10103.

PRINTED IN THE UNITED STATES OF AMERICA

O   0 9 8 7 6 5 4 3 2 1

TO LE LIEU

CONTENTS

AUTHOR'S PREFACE

Every war in history, whatever its cause or justification, has been filthy, agonizing and degrading to all concerned. The spectrum of horrors perpetrated in Viet Nam represents nothing new in human experience.

In several important respects, however, the war in Viet Nam has been something new in America's experience.

We have won our other wars of this century according to Voltaire's dictum that "God is always for the big battalions."

In World War I, vast armies were bled white, and the Allies' greater numbers outlasted the Central Powers. In World War II, thousand-bomber raids blackened European skies, and as the American industrial potential got into gear, the Allies had more of everything than the Axis. In the end, the Japanese will to resist was pulverized in a nuclear fireball. In Korea, the firepower was all on America's side.

In Viet Nam, the United States and its Saigon ally have outnumbered and outgunned the enemy from the start. Vast quantities of blood, bullets and treasure were spent to crush the Viet Cong. But as the years wore on, each American blow was like a sledgehammer landing on a floating cork. Somehow the cork refused to stay down.

Americans began dying in Viet Nam in 1961, and after seven years, they were still dying there. Viet Nam has been a far longer war for America than either of the World Wars or Korea.

In terms of its cost to America, the Viet Nam war could easily become chronic without being too disturbing.

True, it was extremely expensive. The spending rate shot past one million dollars an hour years ago, and the American taxpayer picks up the check. But cars are also expensive, and Americans continue to buy them, even though they kill more than 50,000 of us every year—more than three times the number of GIs killed in six years of war in Viet Nam.

The difficulty for Americans in Viet Nam is perhaps more one of intangibles than of simple bloodletting and spending. There are both moral and intellectual issues involved. In a way, the entire American approach to existence has been subjected to a severe test in Viet Nam.

There are reasons to suppose that Viet Nam may prove the prototype for future American wars, and our country-men should examine it in that light. We went into Viet Nam ill prepared in every way, and it has seemed to me since that America as a nation has learned virtually nothing as the years wore on.

This book is not intended as a lecture. It is based on the experiences of my senses during a five-year tour as a reporter in Viet Nam, and my object is to share these experiences with as many people as possible.

For me, there was a deadly fascination with the little country and its people. I cannot pretend to be entirely detached from Viet Nam, nor would I choose to be. Only a psychotic can view war at close range with real detachment.

I owe thanks to thousands of people of many nationalities for whatever insights I have been able to put into this book. As the second edition of a book written originally in 1964, it has undergone some significant changes. These changes represent changes in my own views of the war, and I am indebted to all those who have helped make my vision clearer.

My special gratitude is reserved for Wes Gallagher, General Manager of The Associated Press, who sent me to Viet Nam in the first place.

The war has had many heroes. But none, in my eyes, have made a greater contribution to humanity than those newsmen who reported things as they were, even at their physical and professional peril.

May our society and its newsman never lose touch with each other.

MWB

THE NEW FACE OF WAR

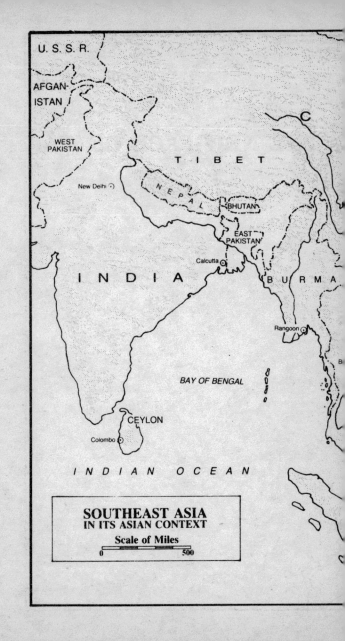

SOUTHEAST ASIA
IN ITS ASIAN CONTEXT

Scale of Miles

0   500

1

PADDY WAR

Colonel Pham Ngoc Thao *was* South Viet Nam, both in the best sense and in the worst.

He could be both idealist and materialist.

He could be a devious, Byzantine plotter, or disarmingly frank.

He loved his wife and family, but he also loved pretty girls and movie stars, and enjoyed being photographed with actress Sandra Dee on a trip to Hollywood.

He could be kind and gentle, and he could kill without mercy.

His family, Roman Catholic for many generations, was split down the middle, half on the communist side and the other with the anticommunists.

He was short and slightly built, he kept his hair cropped short, he usually wore jungle fatigues camouflaged in a mottled green and black pattern, and he moved like a cat. He spoke excellent English and French, and his colorful style attracted American correspondents and writers in droves. He loved impressing them, particularly when he stood to make political gain by it. Like correspondent Joe Alsop, he loved strong black coffee.

He had a walleye that always seemed to be watching for enemies while the other one twinkled right at you. He had some of the style and dash of the Chinese warlords whose day ended in 1949, when Mao Tse-tung swept over a crumbling continent.

But Thao knew the other side, since it had once been his own. During the Indochina War against the French he was a colonel in the Viet Minh and had commanded an infantry regiment. Later, he was placed in charge of the superlative Viet Minh intelligence apparatus for Cochin China, what is now most of South Viet Nam.

He loved to reminisce about those days of conspiracy and courage. There was a constant shortage of equipment in the Viet Minh, just as there is today in the Viet Cong, its historic successor. Thao's job, besides collecting intelligence from the enemy, was to get the enemy's equipment as well.

Within the French puppet cabinet there were Vietnamese ministers who actually sympathized with the Viet Minh cause, just as there were cabinet ministers in Saigon during the 1960s who secretly sympathized with the Viet Cong.

These ministers were Thao's special targets, because they could usually be pressured into leaking government equipment or information to the Viet Minh. Thao used to chuckle as he told of sneaking into ministerial villas in Saigon waiting for officials to return home from fancy dress balls given by the French colonialists.

"I'd wait in the dark facing the door, with a pistol on the table," he told me once. "When the minister walked in, I'd tell him what I wanted, and let him know that he could easily call the police, but if he did, both he and I would be dead. They usually cooperated."

Sometimes they didn't cooperate. Once, Thao was delivered a secret shipment of pistols and radios, but the pistols' barrels had been sabotaged with acid, and the radios didn't work. The Viet Minh never let betrayals like that go unpunished.

But when Viet Nam won its war against France in 1954, Thao decided not to remain with the communists in the North, but to make a new life in the newly independent, noncommunist Republic of Viet Nam in the South.

President Ngo Dinh Diem decided Thao would be useful, and Thao was given colonel's rank in the new Saigon army. He was assigned as the Province Chief of Kien Hoa Province in the Mekong River Delta, where he ruled vigorously for years, battling one of the strongest Viet Cong machines in the country.

In 1963, the last year in the reign and life of Diem and his family, Thao was pulled out of his province job for "special assignments" with the government. Thao had close contacts with the American CIA, and he also had close contacts in Hanoi.

One of his brothers was serving as Hanoi's ambassador to East Germany, and other members of his family held impor-

tant jobs in the Democratic Republic of Viet Nam in the
North.

In 1963, there were a lot of noncommunist Vietnamese
in Saigon who hated Americans worse than the Viet Cong and
Hanoi. Among these were President Diem, his brilliant
opium-smoking brother, Ngo Dinh Nhu, and Nhu's dragon
lady wife, Madame Nhu. The family was overthrown and
destroyed in the military coup of November 1, 1963, and
Madame Nhu, who survived, blamed the whole thing on the
United States. She wrote later from her villa near Rome that
her family had been secretly negotiating with President Ho
Chi Minh in Hanoi at the time of the coup. The idea, she
said, was to form a united Saigon-Hanoi front to throw the
American imperialists out of the country.

The truth of what was happening then may never be
known publicly. Certainly there were rumors in the diplomatic corps and ministries of Saigon at the time that Colonel
Thao's "special assignments" were in Hanoi as a kind of secret
ambassador from Diem. Thao would never deny or confirm
anything he was doing. Unfortunately, everyone involved
except Ho and possibly the CIA is dead now, and neither Ho
nor the CIA is likely to shed much light.

In the chaos following the coup, Thao quickly fell out
with the new military masters of the country, but in a second
coup a few months later, Thao suddenly was thrust into the
councils of state. Major General Nguyen Khanh, the new
strongman, knew Thao and his talents, both as conspirator
and as a man with the gift of gab with newsmen. Accordingly,
Thao was placed in charge of the Prime Minister's press office
and at the same time given a clandestine intelligence role.

Alas for Thao, he never lost his almost childish taste for
plots and counterplots. Perhaps it is all part of being Vietnamese.

In any case, Thao fell in with a clique of army officers,
including General Lam Van Phat, who had ideas about seizing power. Phat, who had been Interior Minister in Khanh's
government, had just been kicked out for plotting. And on
September 13, 1964, a task force of tanks and troops headed
by Phat, Subbrigadier General Duong Van Duc, and Colonel
Thao entered Saigon in apparent triumph, to depose Khanh
and seize power.

Unfortunately for them, the air force commander, Air

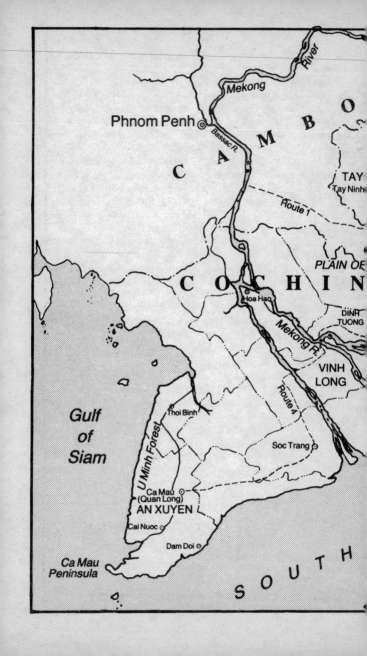

Commodore Nguyen Cao Ky (who eventually became premier himself), decided not to join the rebels but to defend Khanh against them. Maintaining control of Saigon Airport and all its planes, Ky threatened to bomb Saigon if the rebels refused to give up. They gave up.

But they were not through, even though the rebel commanders now were sought as criminals. Five months laater, on February 19, 1965, Phat and Thao made another try. Again, the rebels poured into Saigon without firing a shot. Thao, sitting in a tank and sipping soda pop, joked with newsmen about coups and plots, and then delivered a triumphant speech over the newly captured government radio station.

But again, Air Commodore Ky decided against the rebels, and again he managed to control the air force. By threatening again to bomb Saigon, he forced the rebels to capitulate. A day later, Ky quietly went on himself to oust Khanh, who was forced into exile February 25.

Most of the rebel officers escaped into exile, and some, including Phat and his German wife, opened restaurants.

On May 7, a military tribunal set up by Ky tried all the leaders of the attempted coup against Khanh. Since Ky's coup had succeeded, there was naturally no trial for Ky.

General Phat and Colonel Thao were sentenced *in absentia* to death. Phat was safely away, but Thao was still living in Saigon.

Thao, at first, took the news of the sentence lightly. He was living in an American CIA "safe house" (an official hiding place) and felt he was secure from arrest. He traveled around the city quite openly in a bicycle-taxi "cyclo," and would have the driver stop from time to time so he could talk to friends. He attended parties given by officials and the diplomatic corps, and the death sentence seemed like a joke.

But Ky did not intend it as a joke, and he was waiting only until he could consolidate enough power to act.

Eventually, the public firing squad executions in front of the National Railroad Building in downtown Saigon began, and Thao was forced to leave the CIA safe house. He took refuge in a suburb of Saigon and, for the first time, was forced really to hide.

On June 19, Ky installed his new "war cabinet" and

announced tough controls over the nation. His new Chief of National Police, Air Force Colonel (later General) Nguyen Ngoc Loan, became his chief secret policeman and executioner.

Loan's men tracked Colonel Thao down to his hiding place on July 16, and machine-gunned him to death. They refused later to return the body to Thao's family. Thao's widow took up teaching Vietnamese to American soldiers in the United States at various military posts. She narrowly escaped expulsion from the United States after publicly criticizing Premier Ky.

Such are the officers who have led South Viet Nam's forces against the Viet Cong over the years.

I personally liked Thao despite his plots, and his death has always seemed to me little short of murder. Those who speak of America bringing freedom, democracy and civil liberties to Viet Nam know nothing of the country and its people. Somehow, America has always ended up on the side of the police state in Viet Nam.

I first met Thao in 1961, when he was Province Chief of Kien Hoa, a rich, fertile rice bowl fifty miles south of Saigon, noted for its ardent communists and beautiful girls.

He put me up in his white-walled Province Chief's Mansion, which had several military orderlies, very high ceilings on which squeaky electric fans were mounted (a switch on the wall controlled their speed), and a fine view across one of the little estuaries of the Mekong. On the other side of the waterway were the jungle and the Viet Cong, which occasionally snipes through the windows.

Thao was having one of his bouts with malaria, but was up and eager for the big theater opening that night.

In common with one of his illustrious French predecessors, Colonel Le Roi, Thao believed that a province chief had a responsibility to turn off long, hot summers with entertainment. Le Roi, back in colonial days, had built a splendid lake in Ben Tre, the provincial capital, and surrounded it with beautiful gardens, restaurants, gambling casinos and theaters. When people are being entertained, they're not fighting, Le Roi reasoned. As a matter of fact, Le Roi succeeded, both with his bread-and-games policy and by being merciless to rebels, in vastly reducing Viet Minh activity in Kien Hoa Province.

Thao meant to do the same thing. The Lake and its amusement park area had fallen into total disrepair since the French
collapse in 1954, but Thao had built a new theater.

The gathering was festive. Loudspeakers blared popular
Vietnamese songs into the streets, the lights of downtown
Ben Tre were blazing, and Thao and his entourage (including,
for the moment, myself) took seats in the balcony, like a
Roman emperor and his party. Bottled orangeade and Xa-xi
(pronounced "sah-see," the Vietnamese version of sarsaparil-
la) were passed out to the audience of several hundred, girls
in their party dresses giggled, children chattered, and the
show began.

There were jugglers, comedians, and some classical
Vietnamese opera-ballet-drama. The actors in glittering traditional costumes postured in the styles that have dominated
the Vietnamese theater for many centuries; the stylized medi-
eval themes always are both courtly and tragic.

Halfway through the evening, one of the actors on stage
had just been beheaded, and the audience was weeping and
applauding. Thao turned to me and said,

"By the way, my troops are going out in the morning.
We have intelligence that a battalion of Viet Cong is moving
through one of my districts. I'm not going, but would you be
interested?" I was.

At about four o'clock the following morning, a drenching
predawn dew had made the pavements of Ben Tre slick. The
French used to call it "spitting rain," because it makes
everything slippery. I felt tired and cold, which is the way
one always feels at the beginning of all operations in Viet
Nam.

The landing craft were tied up at a little dock on the
estuary behind the province chief's house, and their sloping
steel decks were slimy with dew. I slipped several times
climbing aboard in the inky blackness. Soldiers cursed sleepi-
ly as they heaved heavy mortar base plates and machine guns
from the pier onto their field packs on deck.

The 300 or so troops on the pier that morning were an
odd-looking bunch, a mixture of civil guards and self-defense
corpsmen. Some were in neat fatigue uniforms with helmets,
others in the loose black garb of the Vietnamese peasant,
topped with old French bush hats. There were no troops
from the regular army on this operation. The commander was

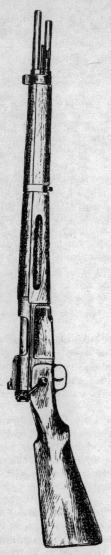

French MAS-36 7.5 mm.

a crusty French-trained captain with several rows of combat ribbons on his faded olive drab uniform.

The diesel engines of the three landing craft carrying our makeshift task force belched oily smoke and we were moving, the black silhouettes of palm trees sliding past along the edges of the narrow canal. Here and there a dot of light glimmered through the trees from some concealed cluster of huts.

For a few minutes, the commander studied a map with a neat plastic overlay, making marks with red and black grease pencils, under the light of a pocket flashlight.

One of the few things Western military men have taught Vietnamese officers to do really well is mark up maps. The Vietnamese officer studies his sector map like a chessboard. Even if he has only a squad or two of men under his command, he uses all the ornate symbols of the field commander in marking his deployment on maps. This love of maps has often infuriated American advisors, who feel more time should be spent acting and less on planning.

After a while the light flicked out. A few of the troops were smoking silently, but most had arranged their field packs as pillows and had gone to sleep amid the clutter of weapons. We were not scheduled to reach our objective until several hours after sunrise.

I finally dropped off to sleep, and must have been asleep about an hour when a grinding lurch and the sound of splintering wood roused me.

It was still pitch dark, but people were screaming, and on the deck of the landing craft, troops were rushing around. In the darkness, we had somehow collided with and sunk a large, crowded sampan. Twenty or thirty sleeping occupants had been thrown into the canal, with all their worldly possessions. A few of them apparently were hurt.

The two other landing craft were chugging on down the canal, but we had stopped. Troops holding ropes were helping swing the people in the water over to the shore. When everyone had reached safety, we started up again, people still yelling at us in the distance. We must have destituted several large families at a blow, but there was no thought of getting their names so that they could be compensated by the government. I couldn't help feeling that their feelings for the government must be less than cordial.

The sky began to turn gray, and at last we left the maze of narrow canals and turned into a branch of the great Mekong itself.

The sun rose hot and red, its reflection glaring from the sluggish expanse of muddy water. We were moving slowly ("We don't want to make too much engine noise or the Viet Cong will hear us coming," the commander told me), and the dense wall of palm trees on both banks scarcely seemed to move at all.

It was nearly 9 A.M. when our little flotilla abruptly turned at right angles to the left, each vessel gunning its engines. We had reached the objective and were charging in for the beach. As we neared the shore we could see that the beach actually was a mud flat leading back about fifty yards to the palm trees, and it would be arduous hiking getting ashore.

The other two landing craft were going ashore about one mile farther down the river. The idea of this exercise, it was explained to me, was to seize two sets of hamlets running back from the river front, trapping the reported Viet Cong battalion in the wide expanse of rice fields in between.

We slammed into the mud, and the prow of our clumsy ship clanked down to form a ramp. We leapt into waist-deep water and mud and began the charge toward higher ground.

If the Viet Cong had even one machine gun somewhere in the tree line, they certainly could have killed most of us with no danger of encountering serious fire from us. Each step in that smelly ooze was agonizingly slow, and at times both feet would get mired. Little soldiers carrying heavy mortars and machine guns sank nearly to their necks. It happened that no one was shooting at us that day.

The first squads clambered up to high ground and began firing. Two light machine guns began thumping tracers across the open rice field, and mortars began lobbing shells at random. Individual soldiers with Tommy guns (I was surprised how many of our group were equipped with submachine guns) were emptying their magazines into a string of huts or into the field. Off a mile or so to our right, noises told us that our companion party was similarly employed. It really sounded like a war.

I was standing on a high path running parallel to the river near a machine-gun position, looking out over the field where our Viet Cong battalion was supposed to be trapped. The green rice was nearly waist-high, and there might easily be a battalion concealed in this field for all anyone knew.

Suddenly, a man leapt up about fifty yards away and began to run. This was it!

Every machine gun, Tommy gun, rifle and pistol in our sector poured fire at that man, and I was amazed at how long he continued to run. But finally he went down, silently, without a scream.

Our little army continued to pour intense fire into the field and several huts until it occurred to someone that no one was shooting back and it might be safe to move forward a little.

Some of the troops began to move into the huts, shooting as they went.

Near me was a cluster of five Dan Ve (local self-defense corpsmen) dressed in ragged black uniforms with American pistol belts and rusty French rifles. The group was detailed to go into the field to look for the man we had seen go down, and I went with them.

We found him on his back in the mud, four bullet holes

stitched across the top of his naked chest. He was wearing only black shorts. He was alive and conscious, moving his legs and arms, his head lolling back and forth. There was blood on his lips.

The Dan Ve squad, all young peasant boys, looked down at the man and laughed, perhaps in embarrassment. Laughter in Viet Nam does not always signify amusement.

Perhaps as an act of mercy, perhaps as sheer cruelty, one of the men picked up a heavy stake lying in the mud and rammed one end of it into the ground next to the wounded man's throat. Then he forced the stake down over the throat, trying to throttle the man. The man continued to move. Someone stamped on the free end of the stake to break the wounded man's neck, but the stake broke instead. Then another man tried stamping on the man's throat, but somehow the spark of life still was too strong. Finally, the whole group laughed, and walked back to the path.

The firing had stopped altogether, and several old peasant men were talking to the officers of our party. Two of the old men had a pole and a large fish net.

The peasants—I think they were hamlet elders—walked out to the wounded man, rolled him into the fish net, and with the net slung between them on the pole, carried him back to the path. As they laid him out on the ground, two women, both dressed in baggy black trousers and blouses, ran up from one of the huts. One of them put a hand to her mouth as she saw the wounded man, whom she recognized as her husband.

She dashed back to her hut and returned in a moment carrying a bucket, which she filled with black water from the rice field. Sitting down with her husband's head cradled in her lap, she poured paddy water over his wounds to clean off the clotting blood. Occasionally she would stroke his forehead, muttering something.

He died about ten minutes later. The woman remained seated, one hand over her husband's eyes. Slowly, she looked around at the troops, and then she spotted me. Her eyes fixed on me in an expression that still haunts me sometimes. She was not weeping, and her face showed neither grief nor fury; it was unfathomably blank.

I moved away some distance to where the operation commander was jabbering into a field telephone. When his conversation ended, I handed him a 500-piastre note (worth about $5.00), asking him to give it to the widow as some small compensation.

"Monsieur Browne, please do not be sentimental. That man undoubtedly was a Viet Cong agent, since these hamlets have been Viet Cong strongholds for years. This is war. However, I will give her the money, if you like."

I don't know what happened to that money, and I didn't go near the place where the woman was sitting, but I walked into the hut I had seen her leave.

It was typical of thousands of Mekong Delta huts I have seen. The framework was bamboo, and the sides and roof were made of dried, interlaced palm fronds with a layer of rice straw thatch on top. The floor was hardened earth. A large, highly polished wooden table stood near the door. Peasants eat their meals on these tables, sleep on them and work on them. There were four austerely simple chairs. In a corner were several knee-high earthen crocks filled with drinking water. Just inside the door was the family altar, extending all the way to the ceiling. Pinned to it were yellowed photographs and some fancy Chinese calligraphy. On a little shelf incense sticks smoldered in a sand pot, giving off fragrant fumes.

To the right, from behind a woven bamboo curtain, two children were peering with wide eyes. The eyes were the only expressive elements in their blank, silent little faces. Incongruously, one of them was standing next to a gaily painted yellow rocking horse, one rocker of which was freshly splintered by a bullet hole.

I walked out of the hut and down the path. By now, troops were strung all along the path between the two hamlets, about a mile apart, and they were stringing telephone wire and performing other military chores.

Snaking through the palm trees, a water-filled ditch about twenty feet across obstructed my progress. But a few yards away, a soldier had commandeered a small sampan from an old woman and was ferrying troops back and forth. I went across with him. As I continued down the path, scores of mud walls about five feet high obstructed progress. All were obviously freshly built, and most had gun slots. It was strange that no one had decided to defend these good emplacements against us.

I came to a small hut straddling the path, consisting only of upright bamboo spars and a roof. The little building was festooned with painted banners, the largest of which read *"Da Dao My-Diem"* ("Down with U.S.-Diem"). A group of young women were dismantling the hut as soldiers trained rifles at them. I was told that this was a Viet Cong "information center."

Finally, the troops began moving out from the tree line into the field itself, converging from three sides: the two hamlets and the path itself. The battle would come now, if ever.

We moved single file along the tops of the dykes that divided the field into an immense checkerboard. The thought struck me that if there were guerrillas hiding in the tall rice we would make fine targets as we moved along, but no one seemed worried.

Progress was slow. The mud dykes were slippery as grease, and every time a solder toppled into the muddy paddy, the whole column halted as he was pulled out. I was reminded somehow of the White Knight in Lewis Carroll's *Through the Looking Glass*. Superficially, we combed the field from one end to the other, our various forces finally meeting in the middle.

A little L19 spotter plane droned overhead, radioing what was no doubt useful information to the ground commander.

It would be difficult to search that field more completely than we did, and we found not the slightest trace of a human being. Of course, the rice could easily have concealed a thousand or even ten thousand guerrillas, without our knowing.

Viet Cong guerrillas have developed the art of camouflage to an incredible degree. In rice fields, they often remain completely submerged under the muddy waters for hours, breathing through straws.

But by now the sun stood like a blast furnace in the sky, and the troops were tired. A few had tied to their packs live ducks and chickens they had pilfered from the hamlets and were looking around for level ground on which to prepare lunch.

"It looks as though the Viet Cong got away again," the commander told me. "It's time to go. It's not a good idea to be moving around out here when the sun starts going down."

By noon, 300 mud-drenched, tired troops were boarding

the landing craft, and silence had settled over the hamlets again. We had suffered one wounded—a civil guard who had stepped on a spike trap, which had pierced his foot.

The three landing craft churned their way out into deep water, and the tension disappeared. Soldiers lighted cigarettes, talked and laughed, and spread their sopping clothing on the deck to dry.

All of them had a warm feeling of accomplishment, of having done a hard day's work under the cruel sun. The irregularity in the palm-lined shore that marked our hamlet receded into the distance.

And I couldn't help thinking of the old travelogues that end, "And so we leave the picturesque Mekong River Delta, palm trees glimmering under a tropic sun, and happy natives on the shore bidding us 'aloha.'"

2

MECHANIZED PADDY WAR

Marshy rice fields for years were the bane of South Vietnamese government forces and a blessing for the Viet Cong. Somehow the guerrillas could always move swiftly across this terrible terrain, while government troops loaded with tons of heavy weapons got hopelessly mired down. Even helicopters were only a partial answer.

The Viet Cong for years had used a little one-man boat shaped like a saucer and made of woven palm fronds and bamboo. A man with one knee on the little saucer could scoot across the gooiest mud, propelling himself with his free leg.

In late 1962, the United States began introducing its own answer to paddy warfare—the M113.

The M113 looks superficially like a tank, and travels on tracks. Called an amphibious armored personnel carrier, it weighs only about five tons (a medium tank weighs about forty tons), and it is supposed to be equally mobile on land and water. Its armored hull is made of thick aluminum instead of steel, and it floats. A crew of two operates the squat slab-sided vehicle: a driver and a man to operate the heavy .50-caliber machine gun on top. There is a large hatch in the upper deck in which ten or twelve men can stand with their heads and shoulders sticking out. If the vehicle is fired on, the troops can sit inside on steel benches, holding on with nylon straps suspended from the ceiling. It is not unlike the inside of a New York City subway car.

The first thirty M113s arrived in Viet Nam in mid-1962 and were promptly sent to war in the Mekong River Delta.

This time, American advisors were sure, the Vietnamese army would be the match of the wily Viet Cong.

It happened that I went along with one of the first M113

16

combat operations, and by coincidence the operation was in
almost exactly the same part of Kien Hoa Province where I
had witnessed my first operation a year earlier.

The battle plan for this particular exercise was an enormous pincers—two salients of fifteen vehicles each—converging
from north and south on the target area. Troops on foot, some
fifteen hundred of them as I recall, were to set up blocking
forces to the east and west, to complete the trap.

I went with the southern group of M113s. They had
been traveling and maneuvering for several days to get into
the jumping-off position, and when I joined them, they were
clustered in a thicket of palms and young bamboo.

The crews, young and freshly trained, were eager for
combat. Several American advisors were chanting warlike
Vietnamese slogans they had learned, acting like college
cheerleaders. Crew-cut American Army captains leapt in the
air, waving their arms and yelling *"Sat cong!"* ("Slaughter
communists!") as their Vietnamese trainees took up the chant.

The M113s themselves had been "spit shined," and
looked as beautiful in their fresh olive brown paint as they
ever can be. There was scarcely a speck of mud in the tracks.

As the sun set, troops were still making last-minute
adjustments and checks on their machines. We were to start
before dawn.

We headed out of the thicket with running lights on but
headlights off. We were moving along a narrow dirt road, and
drivers were taking it easy, even though there was a bright
moon. This road, like many others in the Mekong Delta, had
no shoulders and dropped off sharply into paddies on both
sides. The rainy season had nearly ended, but the paddies
were still flooded.

It struck me at the time as a little ominous that the
drivers were being so careful to stay on the road. After all,
this vehicle was designed to go on any kind of terrain.

We traveled about fifteen miles, and the sky began to
brighten. Viet Nam is only a few degrees north of the
Equator, and sunrises and sunsets are abrupt.

The whole column clanked to a stop. We had reached the
point at which we were to leave the road and cut across country.

Paralleling the road to our right was an irrigation ditch
some thirty feet wide with rather steep sides dropping about

L-19 (O1F Birddog)

five feet to the water level. The water itself was probably about neck deep.

We paused perhaps ten minutes while the column commander surveyed the situation through field glasses. At length, the first M113 nosed down into the ditch, sliding sideways as it went. Tracks churning wildly, it made for the other shore, momentum carrying it about halfway up the opposite bank. Then it stopped. The tracks were still going full speed, but they were only hacking deep furrows into the soft mudbank.

The driver finally gave up and backed out for another try. The same thing happened. And again and again.

The sun was higher, and troops on the other fourteen waiting vehicles had stretched out on the top decks for a snooze. The driver now was trying to make the stranded

M113 climb back the bank he had come down, but with no more success than he had had on the opposite bank.

The column commander (and his irritated American advisor) finally decided some kind of remedial action was necessary, and headed off down the road to try to find a more propitious fording place. In forty minutes or so they were back on the other side of the ditch. Evidently they had found the spot.

The column started off down the road, and we reached a place where the banks were almost level with the water. Spray flying, we plunged into the ditch, and the whole column made it across.

By now we were badly behind schedule, and the column commander ordered more speed as we headed across the flooded paddies.

Incidentally, M113s are probably the most uncomfortable vehicles ever devised. They do not ride along smoothly like tanks, which are usually longer and weigh up to eight times as much. Edges and corners on M113s are sharp and hard, and the nylon hand straps with which troops hang on begin to cut the skin after a while. The comfort quotient reaches its lowest point when you are moving at high speed (about twenty-five miles an hour) across a rice field.

Paddies are laid out with dykes every hundred yards or so, and slamming into one of these dykes nearly halts the M113 and upends it, all in one shattering movement. Then the nose swoops down and slams into the paddy on the other side, usually at an oblique angle. A man standing in the hatch is easily caught unaware by one of these maneuvers and is banged into all kinds of sharp objects before he recovers his balance. I have seen seasoned personnel-carrier troopers lose eight inches of flesh off legs and arms as the result of such encounters.

A moving M113, by the way, also makes a very unstable platform for the .50-caliber machine gun mounted on top. It is possible to fire a long burst under such conditions and miss a target only 100 yards distant. I will come back to this deficiency in a later chapter which tells how the lives of two children were saved as the result of poor gunnery.

But at any rate we were charging now, no longer in a column but in a ragged scrimmage line.

The commander of the operation, meanwhile, had radioed our troop that he was not pleased with our slow progress.
The northern pincer, it seemed, was ready for the final
charge, and we were still nowhere in range.

It was probably with this message in mind that our
plucky little commander decided we should not waste time
reconnoitering when we came to another canal, about fifty
feet wide.

Delta canals in Viet Nam, all of them man-made, are
straight as arrows. Even from the air, they stretch all the way
to the horizon, like glittering slashes across the verdant plain.

Like the first big obstacle we had come to, this canal had
steep banks that looked solid enough but were actually
merely coagulated ooze. Like lemmings racing for the sea,
our little armada charged into the canal.

That, as far as I was concerned, was the end of the
operation.

M113

I waited around for a few hours while drivers churned at the banks on both sides, without success. But by now the crews and our troops had begun to lose interest in the operation. With typical Vietnamese fatalism, some drivers had given up altogether and were idly smoking. A few crew members, including the commander, had climbed into the water and were knowingly poking at the bottom with sticks. The American advisor with us was hurling obscenities.

In due course, the radio message came that the operation had decided to go on without us, and we were to go somewhere else if the M113s were finally rescued from the canal. A helicopter arrived after a while with some angry Vietnamese officers on board, and I talked them into giving me a seat.

I understand the M113s finally got out of the canal, although I was not informed how or when.

As a matter of fact, the northern force got to its objective only an hour or two behind schedule, partly, I suppose, because it had fewer difficult canals to cross. They found no Viet Cong, however.

I don't want to imply that the M113s were a complete fiasco. In fact, more and more were put into service in the Vietnamese army, and U.S. forces coming to join the war in later years leaned heavily on the M113. It has no doubt been useful.

Since the early operations there have been improvements in the machines themselves and in techniques for using them. For one thing, most M113s now are equipped with cable winches that are useful in pulling themselves out of mire.

For another, drivers and commanders both have a more realistic idea of the limitations of the M113. They know that the M113 runs very well on dry ground or in deep water, but has trouble in mud of a certain depth. Drivers look for good fording places, as a rule, and generally cross one at a time. Often the first vehicle across a canal becomes a belaying point for the others, which are towed across by cable. Still, progress across rain-soaked delta terrain is often painfully slow.

The personnel carrier has another defect: it is very vulnerable to heavy weapons fire. Its aluminum armor will stop little more than rifle bullets. Heavy machine-gun slugs will penetrate the slab sides, and recoilless cannon shells easily demolish vehicles.

The first M113s sent to Viet Nam lacked any kind of armor for the machine gunner, who was exposed from the waist up to fire.

It didn't take the Viet Cong long to begin capitalizing on these things.

On January 2, 1963, near a cluster of huts called Ap Bac ("Northern Hamlet") in the delta forty miles southwest of Saigon, the Viet Cong decided to try its strength against the best gadgets the Free World had to offer—including the M113.

The communist force involved was, at the time, probably the most dangerous fighting unit in the country—the notorious 514th Battalion. Word that the 514th is operating nearby is considered very bad news. American GIs have written and sung rambling folk songs, including one called "On Top of Old Ap Bac," in which the 514th is prominently mentioned.

The 514th had prepared its positions at Ap Bac well. The guerrillas had dug good fortifications behind a tree line, looking out over a wide expanse of rice field. They had a number of machine guns in positions to lay grazing fire across the muddy field. And, most important, the Viet Cong had received orders for the first time in the war to stand and fight a major government operation.

Troops of nearly every description were involved on the government side; there were regular army troops, paratroopers, civil guards, self-defense corpsmen and others. There were American advisors and pilots, three of whom were killed during the day.

There were fifteen helicopters carrying troops into the assault, fourteen of which were hit by Viet Cong fire. Several were downed.

There also was a troop of M113s which arrived appallingly late for the fight because of problems negotiating a canal.

As has happened so many times since, the M113s were sent into the fray as tanks—a role for which they were not designed. The big machines charged up to the tree line and moved along it, firing into the Viet Cong positions.

Eight of the unprotected M113 machine gunners were killed outright by the fusillade that met them, and the whole troop of M113s was forced back.

The foot soldiers were pinned down, and it was apparent the government forces were in serious trouble. Several hundred paratroopers were dropped into the area from Saigon at about sunset, but missed the drop zone.

The next day, government forces cleaned up the carnage in the rice field and "liberated" Ap Bac without a shot. The Viet Cong had melted away in the night.

For the Viet Cong, Ap Bac became the victory cry. The hamlet's name, in gold letters, was affixed to the 514th's battle flags. Communist propaganda posters, professionally printed in four colors, bloomed throughout the delta, all glorifying the fighters at Ap Bac.

Statistically, Ap Bac could hardly be considered a real victory or defeat for either side. Government fatalities ran to more than sixty, but numbers like that have become common.

Ap Bac was closely studied, however. A section of the U.S. Military Assistance Command responsible for battle research was turned loose on the M113 and its flaws.

This section, headed by a brigadier general, reached the conclusion that M113 gunners should have some armor. Field engineers in Saigon soon designed and built makeshift armored cupolas for nearly all the M113s in the country, and the death rate of gunners dropped sharply.

New helicopter landing tactics were devised, with variable success.

Still seeking the ideal paddy vehicle, the United States began bringing hundreds of Fiberglas dinghies to Viet Nam.

These little watercraft, called "swimmer support boats," could hold about twelve men, were equipped with large outboard motors, and were unsinkable. They worked fine in shallow canals and ditches and brought a new dimension to amphibious warfare. Of course, they still could not travel across paddies.

With the massive introduction of U.S. combat forces after February 7, 1965, American research and development of paddy warfare techniques were redoubled.

One of the innovations was the Air Boat, a very shallow-draft vehicle with an air propeller, similar to the "swamp buggies" used in Florida and Georgia. The new Air Boats could zip around on mere puddles, since they had no water propellers or other protuberances underneath to catch in the mud, weeds and underwater roots.

SK-5 Air Cushion Vehicle

The trouble with an Air Boat is that since it has an airplane propeller it sounds like an airplane and can be heard from great distances. In a war of stealth, this can be a fatal flaw.

One of the most spectacular later arrivals in Viet Nam, the Hovercraft, has a similar disadvantage.

The Hovercraft, an English concept produced in the United States by Bell Aerosystems, is a cross between an aircraft and a boat and will travel over flat land, including paddies, with no difficulty.

Although the Hovercraft weighs eight tons, it rides along on a cushion of air. A huge engine drives a ducted fan that blasts air straight down. This raises the machine a few inches above the water or ground. Forward motion is provided by a pusher-type aircraft propeller, and the thing is steered by an airplane-type rudder. The Hovercraft is armored and heavily armed with machine guns, and it cruises around the waterways of the Mekong River Delta at about fifty miles an hour. Obviously, the pilot of such a machine must be an expert.

The Hovercraft makes a noise that can be heard from

several miles away. However fast it may be, its roar always precedes it enough to give the Viet Cong ample warning.

Of course, the United States has yet to find a surface vehicle that will move over paddies with anything like the facility of a helicopter. Meanwhile, the M113 remained the primary all-terrain surface carrier, imperfect though it was.

New uses were found for the M113s.

Someone discovered that they are useful in crushing concealed guerrillas. By driving fifteen M113s in an irregular zigzag pattern across a flooded paddy a few hundred yards square, a commander can be fairly sure there are no living enemies left in the field. On several occasions, I have seen blood oozing into muddy track marks as the big machines swiveled through fields, and have even seen pieces of bodies thrust to the surface. South Viet Nam's former Premier, Major General Nguyen Khanh, narrowly escaped death in 1964 when an M113 near him ran over a mine in just such a field.

Another and unexpected use for the M113s evolved. They turned out to be very good for use in Saigon during coups, both by rebel forces and by loyalists.

As a matter of fact, the M113s got practical experience in the Saigon coups that later was to be applied in the United States. The big vehicles proved successful in throwing scares into urban mobs in Saigon, and this same type of machine was later used for similar purposes during the big 1967 Negro rebellions in Newark, Detroit and elsewhere. There's nothing like a big tracked vehicle to dampen crowd spirit.

3

VIET CONG GADGETS

Among my souvenirs of the war is an object that seems to me an almost perfect symbol of the factors that have made the Viet Cong a potent and feared fighting force.

It is a brass cartridge case about one-half inch in diameter and three inches long. I picked it up after a clash in the Mekong River Delta near the riddled body of a government soldier, and it is probable that this cartridge was the instrument of his death.

It is no ordinary cartridge case. The cylindrical part of the case is made of brass plumber's tubing. The base of the case, soldered to the tube, is an old French ten-centime coin, the kind with a hole in the middle. A percussion cap was crimped into the hole, and the whole thing made an effective shotgun shell. The cartridge was made to fit a weapon the Viet Cong calls the "sky horse gun," made of scraps of plumbing and wood. These guns often blow up, killing their users. But more often they project a deadly hail of buckshot into some hapless squad of government troops.

I wonder how many of those old French colonial coins found their way into communist ammunition factories in the jungle for use against first the French and then the Amercians?

Viet Cong armament plants are marvels of ingenuity and "field expediency," to use an American military phrase. Occasionally government forces find them, and I have seen several.

One such factory, a long hut with a thatched roof, contained a homemade lathe turned by an ancient Japanese marine diesel engine. Electric power for the plant came from a generator hooked to the motor of a Vespa motor scooter. In one corner, near a brick chimney, was a charcoal-fired forge, to which was connected a system of bellows. The big bellows were operated by bicycle pedals, and three small boys pedaling at top speed could easily keep the forge glowing brightly.

This plant had only two products—rifle grenade launchers and 60-millimeter mortars. Finished or partly finished products were neatly crated in one corner of the hut when the government unit I was with seized the plant.

The grenade launchers were ingenious and effective. They were steel cups exactly the diameter of an American hand grenade, each fitted with a threaded hole into which a rifle muzzle could be screwed. A steel loop was welded to the outside of the cup. To fire one, the user puts a blank cartridge in his rifle, screws the cup to the barrel, and puts an ordinary grenade in the cup, with the grenade's safety handle stuck through the cup's steel loop. The pin of the grenade is then pulled, and the guerrilla aims and fires. The gas from the cartridge drives the grenade forward, and as it leaves the cup, the safety handle is automatically released. Compared with American grenade launchers, the thing is remarkably simple and cheap. Best of all, it is perfectly adapted to the use of captured equipment.

Over the years, this plant had turned out tens of thousands of grenade launchers.

The mortar works were more complicated. The mortar tubes themselves were precisely bored from heavy steel tubing legally purchased in Saigon. Each tube was reinforced by welded bands of steel. Mortar bipods and base plates were made of scrap steel, all welded neatly together. Finished mortars were professionally painted and oiled.

American 60-millimeter mortar shells are abundant in Viet Nam and easy to capture, and that was why this was the caliber of choice for the homemade guns.

The former chief of An Xuyen Province, Lieutenant Colonel Pham Van Ut, thought so highly of these Viet Cong mortars that he issued them to his own troops whenever they were captured.

'They're every bit as good as American or French mortars," he told me. "They lack optical sighting devices, but good mortarmen don't need gadgets like that. We can't afford to be proud about using enemy weapons, even if they're homemade."

Viet Cong armorers are notoriously poor chemists and

prefer whenever possible to use captured explosives rather than make their own. But they can and do make effective explosives.

Nitroglycerin, TNT, plastic, blasting gelatin and so on are beyond the competence of jungle factories. But explosives chemically akin to gunpowder are not. The basic ingredient, called an oxidizing agent, is normally sodium or potassium chlorate or nitrate.

To these are added substances called reducing agents, such as sulfur and powdered charcoal.

The great advantage of these materials, from the Viet Cong standpoint, is the fact that they are all legal to buy and possess. Sodium nitrate is extensively used by the Saigon meat processing industry as a preservative, for example.

On February 16, 1964, terrorists placed a bomb in the lobby of Saigon's Capital Kinh-Do Theater, the "Americans-only" movie theater. The front wall of the building was demolished, two American servicemen were killed, and fifty-one other Americans were injured—many of them women and children.

U.S security agents analyzed fragments of the bomb, and found that the explosive was a mixture of potassium chlorate and arsenic sulfide. Potassium chlorate can be purchased legally at Western-style pharmacies in Saigon, and arsenic sulfide is available at Chinese pharmacies.

Most of the terrorist explosions in South Viet Nam are caused by such improvised bombs.

Despite the Viet Cong's difficulties with making reliable explosives themselves, no one can fault them for lack of ingenuity in turning seemingly innocent substances into deadly weapons.

One of the standard types of footgear for men in Viet Nam is the tennis shoe. Until the mid-1960s, many Vietnamese regular troops and practically all the uniformed militia wore tennis shoes, not combat boots. The tennis shoes, made of olive-drab canvas and composition rubber soles, are cheap and light. They are also popular among civilian men, especially poor ones.

Viet Nam makes it own tennis shoes. There are several moderately large factories, the largest run by the "Bata" firm.

To help out this local industry and to assist Viet Nam along the road to self-sufficiency, the U.S. AID Mission provided money, through the counterpart funding program, to buy materials for tennis shoe manufacture. The main material provided was a composition produced by E. I. Du Pont de Nemours Company called Unicel 100. Unicel 100, a synthetic rubber, was found suitable for Vietnamese tennis shoes.

But once Unicel 100 began arriving in Viet Nam, the Viet Cong research men went to work. As usual, their object was to turn plowshares into swords.

In the spring of 1966, someone at the U.S Mission noticed that enough Unicel 100 had been shipped to Viet Nam to make eight or nine million pairs of shoes, but that only about half a million pairs actually had been manufactured.

An investigation was begun to find out what had happened to the missing shoe-sole compound, and the U.S. Naval Ordnance Laboratory was quickly involved. That laboratory found that Unicel 100 has roughly the same explosive qualities as TNT when set off with a standard detonator cap.

Secretary of State Dean Rusk personally ordered an instant halt in shipments of Unicel 100 to Viet Nam. But the mind boggles at how many powerful mines and booby traps were made from that Unicel 100. How many American lives may have been lost as the result of Viet Cong ingenuity coupled with stupid American aid practices?

Viet Cong bombs and booby traps take an infinite number of forms, all based on clever concealment and powerful effect.

I have seen miniature bombs installed in cigarette lighters and fountain pens, designed to blow the hands off their American users.

There are bombs and booby traps concealed in cucumbers and other kinds of vegetables and fruits. And more than one bar patronized by Americans has been blasted by bombs concealed in loaves of bread.

For large explosions, the Viet Cong often puts its charge in five-, ten- and twenty-five-gallon drums used normally for powdered milk. These usually carry the U.S. handclasp emblem affixed to all American aid products, and can be carried around in Saigon without attracting attention. Timer-detonators are mounted in the bottoms of the cans, out of sight.

In the field, mines and booby traps are rigged in all kinds of ingenious ways. Viet Cong battle flags are sometimes left around, hooked to booby traps. The enemy guerrillas are fully aware that Viet Cong battle flags are valuable to U.S. troops as war souvenirs and bring as much as $200 each in stores in New York City. I have heard that many of these flags have been manufactured by both the Viet Cong and private entrepreneurs for purely commercial purposes.

Some explosive booby traps are made from ordinary cartridges. The Viet Cong makes one, for instance, out of a bamboo tube, into one end of which a nail is driven. The guerrilla finds a rifle cartridge and very carefully files the metal on its percussion cap as thin as possible, to make it ultrasensitive to shock. This is very dangerous, of course, and guerrillas often are seriously wounded or killed filing the caps. When the cartridge is prepared, it is carefully inserted, cap first, into the open end of the bamboo tube, with the bullet sticking out a fraction of an inch and the cap resting against the point of the nail.

The assembly is then buried in a trail or other appropriate place, bullet-end up, with the bullet protruding aboveground just enough that it can be stepped on. The least pressure from a foot sets the cartridge off, firing the bullet through the foot at the least, or at worst killing the victim.

Lacking explosives, the Viet Cong use all kinds of traps and snares based on pits, sharpened stakes and heavy weights. Their "jungle bomb" is nothing more than a massive weight made by tying short wooden logs together (weighing around 500 pounds), usually with the addition of wooden daggers that protrude at all angles. The thing is mounted with a snare release cable high in a tree over a trail.

The famous "Saigon bicycle bomb" described in Graham Greene's novel *The Quiet American* is worth special mention. The lethal potency of these specially modified bicycles led to a law under which any purchaser of an electric timing device must register the device and obtain a license for it. The law even extends to the little self-timers built into some electric stoves, and to the timers used on photographic enlargers.

The standard Viet Cong bicycle bomb is made by filling the entire frame tubing with explosive. In French colonial days, plastic was the explosive of choice, but in recent years this has become hard to get.

Wires attached to blasting caps inside the frame are led out small holes and tied to the brake cables, which camouflage them. The wires lead to the electric headlamp, in which has been mounted a stopwatch which has an electric contact attached to one of the hands. A small flashlight battery furnishes the detonating power.

A bicycle bomb parked with hundreds of other bicycles is very difficult to spot. A policeman must either notice extra wires connected to the brake cables, or he must take the headlamp apart—an operation that may cost him his life.

Workmanship on these bombs is sometimes slipshod, of course. Every month or so, a man is mysteriously blown to fragments while peacefully pedaling along. Whenever this happens it is presumed the Viet Cong has lost another agent.

Somewhere in the Mekong Delta, a Viet Cong plant has been turning out tens of thousands of hand grenade cases for years. These cases are made of cast aluminum and are very effective.

For years, the Viet Cong has laid special stress on the capture of American 105-millimeter howitzer shells. At this writing, the guerrillas are not believed to own any 105 guns, but the shells are put to another use. The nose fuse of these shells is easily unscrewed, and an electric blasting cap can be tamped into the fuse well instead.

Thus rigged, the 105 shell becomes an excellent mine that can be concealed in a pile of rice straw on the shoulder of a road, with wires running back several hundred yards to a foxhole or tree line. The first American combat death in Viet Nam in 1961 resulted from one of these mines, and many other Americans have been killed or wounded by them since.

Viet Cong gadgetry extends to fortifications as well. The communist guerrilla in Viet Nam probably spends more time on digging than on any other military pursuit.

About twenty miles north of Saigon is an area covered mostly with jungle and rubber plantations which Americans have dubbed "the Iron Triangle." It is roughly triangular tract of wilderness about a hundred square miles in area in which all efforts to drive out the Viet Cong so far have proved ineffective.

One of the reasons is a vast network of tunnels the guerrillas have dug throughout the area. The tunnels are interconnected in a huge maze, with camouflaged ventilation holes extending to the surface every fifty yards or so.

All efforts to wipe out this tunnel system have failed.

Tanks have sometimes crushed sections of tunnel, but never all the tunnels. Smoke generators operated by diesel engines have been ducted into the tunnel works, but they never seem to smoke out all the enemy. Demolition charges have blown out long stretches of tunnel. Entrance holes have been found under stoves in peasants' huts and sealed.

But with molelike perspicacity, the guerrillas go on digging, and the tunnels continue to expand.

"It wouldn't surprise me to learn," an American officer told me, "that one of these damn tunnels leads right under my desk in Saigon."

The idea is farfetched, but not so impossible as it sounds.

At the end of World War II, French colonial forces reoccupied the North Vietnamese capital of Hanoi, which, they had every reason to believe, was militarily secure. But Ho Chi Minh's guerrillas had an ugly surprise for the French. One day, the guerrillas came pouring into the heart of Hanoi from a tunnel system the French had never known existed, and all at once Hanoi was at war. The French quickly crushed the city insurrection, and it was to be nine years before the guerrillas again took the city—this time for good.

The digging philosophy of the Vietnamese guerrilla extends to any area through which he passes, even if he is not

A1E "Skyraider"

fighting. Over the years, the Viet Cong has built solid, cleverly concealed fortifications in many thousands of hamlets, against the day when it may have to use them. Innocent-seeming paddy dykes are studded with gun ports; apparently accidental holes in the corners of fields actually are machine-gun emplacements; tall trees contain snipers' nests, and even graveyards become enormous bunker systems.

More often than not today, government operations chase enemy guerrillas into areas where they feel the Viet Cong is cornered, only to find the Viet Cong has moved into one of its own bastions.

At this point the Viet Cong fights with the terrain all on his side. As a rule, government forces then react by hurling artillery, aerial bombs, rockets and napalm at the enemy fortification. Finally, government troops move into the hamlet or thicket (often the following day) and find no Viet Cong anywhere. Sometimes enemy bodies or evidence of casualties have been left behind, but more often there is nothing.

Meanwhile, the young American pilots of the helicopters and fighter bombers return to their bases with rosy reports of the havoc they have wrought on the enemy.

"Nothing could have lived down there," a young Skyraider pilot said once as he stepped from his cockpit. "Considering the concentration of the enemy down there and the sheer volume of stuff we threw at him, we must have killed at least two hundred. That's my estimate, and I think it's a good one."

Seasoned infantrymen rarely agree with these reports, which often are submitted in the form of official enemy casualty statistics.

"I was at Tarawa," an old marine officer told me once. "All of us thought there couldn't be a Jap left alive on that little island after all the shells and bombs we poured in to soften it up. But I guess you can remember what happened when we hit the beach. You'd think people would have learned from that that bombs and shells and napalm don't necessarily knock out a well-prepared enemy."

Assaulting a Viet Cong tunnel network is normally an exhausting and bloody business, resulting in heavy friendly casualties. The ground over and near the tunnels is invariably studded with thousands of concealed spike foot traps—another specialty of Viet Cong ingenuity. These traps, made of upright nails with barbed points, easily penetrate the sole of a combat boot, and painfully incapacitate a soldier stepping on one. Sometimes they are treated with tetanus-infected buffalo urine to make their wounds even more dangerous.

The Viet Cong usually posts snipers at tunnel ventilation holes.

"One of them stood up and shot at me," a wounded American captain told me once. "I saw him and drew a bead, but he ducked down just as I fired. I started moving cautiously toward the place I saw him disappear, when another shot came from another spot about fifty yards away. That was the one that got me. I believe it was the same sniper, using another hole."

Entrance holes to tunnels or weapons depots are sometimes underwater in the bank of a canal or water hole, and are accessible only to swimmers who know where to look.

Viet Cong weaponry tends to harmonize with terrain and the soldiers who use the weapons.

In the jungle-covered mountain range extending from fifty miles north of Saigon all the way to North Viet Nam, the war is combat by stealth, characterized by privation and discomfort.

Conventional weapons and ammunition are hard to capture or make in the desolate rain forest, but the primitive tribesmen of the area know well the uses of simpler weapons.

The mountain crossbow is native to the area, and kills silently. This can be important when ambushing with only a small force of guerrillas. The Vietnamese mountain crossbow is very small and light. The bow is about two and a half feet long, but a pull of about a hundred pounds is required to cock its leather string. Its arrows are short spikes of bamboo fletched with palm fronds. Crossbow arrows have enormous penetration at short range, and often are tipped with a poison chemically similar to curare.

I have heard of cases in which Viet Cong tribesmen carried as many as ten crossbows laced together to make one weapon, firing ten arrows at a single shot.

The Viet Cong in the mountains also have built spear catapults, which they sometimes use even as antiaircraft weapons. In 1963, a U.S. Army helicopter operating in the mountains staggered back to its base with a spear in its belly.

For the disciplined and intelligent Viet Cong guerrilla,

any material object is a potential weapon. Slivers of scrap steel are fashioned into daggers and swords. Viet Cong squads frequently used to precede assaults on government outposts by hurling thirty or more hornets' nests into the fortifications. American forces, especially the 25th and 9th Infantry Divisions, have been encountering Viet Cong hornets in these and other forms, especially in cleverly laid booby traps along trails. Sometimes a trip wire is connected to a firecracker which explodes against a hornets' nest on a trail, resulting in thousands of painful stings for the GIs marching along.

As the Viet Cong has grown and been supplemented by fighting forces from North Viet Nam, the needs of its arsenal have expanded.

This has meant a need for weapons superior to the ingenious homemade jungle products. While most of the Viet Cong's modern weapons are captured American types, there has also been a need for infiltrated communist-made arms.

Very few experts agree exactly on how extensive the infiltration of weapons into South Viet Nam has been.

There have been some impressive incidents indicating a stream of infiltrated weapons.

On February 16, 1965, a U.S. Army helicopter pilot flying over the South China Sea just off the rugged coast of South Viet Nam was blown off course. As he flew close to the densely wooded coast of remote Vung Ro Bay between Tuy Hoa and Nha Trang, he spotted a very peculiar island.

There were a few trees on the island and some other foliage, and in all respects it looked like thousands of other tiny coastal outcroppings. The great difference was that this one was moving.

The helicopter pilot reported his find, and in minutes a Vietnamese Air Force single-seat Skyraider fighter-bomber was on its way. The Skyraider poured cannon fire, rockets, and bombs into the island, drawing heavy machine-gun fire in exchange. The island caught fire and quickly revealed itself as a boat. It keeled over and sank in shallow water, its side sticking up.

Three days later, Vietnamese land forces accompanied by American intelligence experts completed their assault on the area.

The camouflaged boat turned out to be a steel-hulled

motor vessel 135 feet long which had evidently come down very recently from North Viet Nam. There were fresh Haiphong newspapers and other documents aboard the hulk.

But the most interesting find was a group of giant piles of crates, hastily hidden in the jungle just beyond a clearing at the water's edge. Saigon and Washington experts found in them about 100 tons of communist-made arms and ammunition, including 4,000 rifles, light machine guns, rockets and other field weapons.

The rifles, carbines, "assault rifles" and light machine guns all were of Soviet or Chinese manufacture and chambered to take the Soviet-type short 7.62-millimeter cartridge. This copper-wash cartridge is intermediate in size between an American rifle cartridge and a carbine cartridge, and does not fit any Western weapon.

Vung Ro was a colossal propaganda windfall both to the Washington and Saigon governments, and to several individuals. I happened to be with General Nguyen Khanh, the Vietnamese strongman at that time, when the Vung Ro cache was discovered.

Khanh was jubilant. He was in serious political trouble (in fact, he was overthrown by a coup several days later) and saw Vung Ro as a crisis around which he might build desperately needed support from his fellow officers and, at the very least, from the Americans. It was too late to do him any good, however.

Subsequent Saigon leaders have found Vung Ro a perfect excuse for the terrible showing their forces have made against the Viet Cong. By implying that the Viet Cong gets all its muscle from a foreign country (North Viet Nam), Saigon argues that it can't really be expected to carry on the war unaided. Consequently, more American troops, more American weapons, and more American economic aid are needed to make up the difference.

There was also quiet jubilation in Washington. Twelve days prior to the finding of the Vung Ro cache, on February 7, 1965, the United States had begun bombing North Viet Nam, sending U.S. combat troops to fight in South Viet Nam, and escalating what had been a Vietnamese conflict into an American war.

Washington contended that this was being done to counter the massive introduction of arms and troops from North

Viet Nam into the South, with the consequent danger of an imminent Southern collapse.

The danger of an imminent Southern collapse was obvious to all of us who were there, but that this collapse was mainly the result of infiltration was far from obvious. In fact, it was obvious in most cases that the Viet Cong was reliant on what it could capture on the battlefield and on the men it could recruit in the South, not on an invading North Vietnamese army. I shall return to this in a later chapter.

It has been Washington's contention ever since that the introduction of 7.62-millimeter communist ammunition had enormously sinister implications. It meant, the Pentagon said, that the Viet Cong felt so confident about supply channels from the North that it intended to standardize on communist weapons rather than captured U.S. equipment. The inference was that unless the infiltration could be halted swiftly, the war would be lost for the West.

A halt could only be achieved, it was argued, by intensive bombing of infiltration routes in North Viet Nam, Laos, Cambodia, and South Viet Nam, along with massive blockade patrolling by 7th Fleet and other naval units to protect the coast. The advocates of interdiction bombing further argued that the United States should bomb not only the trails, junction points and depots, but also certain hostage targets in North Viet Nam. Indeed, the opening raids of February 7 were specifically represented by Washington as reprisals for a series of Viet Cong ground attacks during the preceding twenty-four hours.

In any event, communist arms and ammunititon *were* coming into South Viet Nam.

In 1964, U.S. intelligence experts estimated that something in the neighborhood of 2 per cent of the Viet Cong's arsenal was made up of infiltrated communist-made weapons. This percentage rose substantially when North Viet Nam began introducing combat units into South Viet Nam in 1965 after America began its escalation. In North Vietnamese units the weaponry is often nearly or entirely communist-made.

But for the Viet Cong guerrilla, the standard service rifle remained the M-1, the U.S. carbine, or the later American service rifles such as the M-16. Mountains of American equipment had been captured over the years, and there was no reason why the Viet Cong should not go on using it.

Nevertheless, the Viet Cong did begin using increasing numbers of heavy weapons made in China, Russia or other communist nations. In heaviest use were the Red Chinese infantry rocket launchers (with projectiles capable of destroying tanks), the Chinese 82-millimeter mortar and 75-millimeter recoilless cannon, and Chinese and Soviet 12.7-millimeter (slightly larger than American .50-caliber) heavy antiaircraft machine guns.

But even North Vietnamese units rely to a large extent on field ingenuity. It is well to remember that the North Vietnamese army started out as a guerrilla force like the Viet Cong, and has never completely lost its guerrilla characteristics. It is still commanded by the father of Vietnamese guerrilla warfare, General Vo Nguyen Giap, who smashed the French army in 1954.

Thus, there is a blend of weapons even in regular North Vietnamese forces fighting in the South. I remember seeing one government outpost that had been heavily attacked by a reinforced North Vietnamese regiment. The attack had been beaten off, and the bodies of enemy troops (mostly teenagers) and their gear were strewn everywhere. The weapons included Soviet-made AK (Avtomat Kalashnikov) "assault rifles" (a cross between a rifle and a submachine gun), American carbines and M-1s, and some Chinese rocket launchers.

But there also were great numbers of bangalore torpedoes the attackers had used to blast through the curtains of barbed wire surrounding the post. These torpedoes were obviously improvised in the jungle, made of long bamboo logs stuffed with whatever explosives were at hand, possibly taken from American dud shells.

According to the Pentagon, the Viet Cong required imports of between five and six tons of supplies and arms from the outside world per day during the early war years. By early 1966, this requirement, according to the Pentagon, had risen to about twelve tons per day.

In terms of conventional military logistics, twelve tons per day of supplies is a negligibly tiny percentage of the requirement one would expect for an army estimated at somewhere near a quarter million men and women. If this is all the Viet Cong needed in early 1966, it's obvious that the Viet Cong was very largely self-sufficient. I have seen nothing to indicate this general pattern has changed since early 1966.

Of course, as the Viet Cong fighting organization has grown, it has needed better weapons. Some of these, notably carbines of Russian design, a few Chinese communist SKZ recoilless cannon, machine guns and Czech or Chinese ammunition, have reached the Viet Cong by infiltration from North Viet Nam.

Some communist weapons used by the Viet Minh during the Indochina War were left in secret caches when the war ended in 1954, and capture of a communist-made weapon from a Viet Cong guerrilla is not necessarily proof of recent infiltration. Communist-made weapons rarely carry proof marks that would positively identify the year in which they were made.

But substantial quantities of Czech submachine-gun ammunition have turned up in Viet Cong hands near the southern tip of Viet Nam, and ammunition normally is dated. The bases of many of these cartridges are dated 1962 and 1963, furnishing absolute proof of infiltration.

Nevertheless, intelligence experts feel that less than 10 per cent and probably more like 2 per cent of the Viet Cong's stock of modern weapons is communist-made. The rest are all captured American weapons.

In his memoirs of the Indochina War, General Giap (who is now Deputy Premier of North Viet Nam and its supreme military commander) wrote:

"The sole source of supply could only be the battle front: to take the material from the enemy and turn it against him. While carrying on the aggression against Viet Nam the French Expeditionary Corps fulfilled another task: it became, unwittingly, the supplier of the Viet Nam People's Army with French, even U.S. arms."

Giap's philosophy has not changed.

Apart from hardware, the most important aspect of Viet Cong gadgetry is the art of camouflage.

Many writers on Indochina have discussed the proficiency of Vietnamese guerrillas at camouflage, and many of these writings are standard texts read by senior Vietnamese and American military officials.

It is probably safe to say, nonetheless, that camouflage continues to receive more lip service than application by the Saigon and U.S. forces.

It is difficult, of course, to camouflage a modern conven-

tional army on the move. Conventional troop units move in
masses even when their columns are stretched out, and they
cannot avoid detection. Guerrilla units move only in groups
of two or three men each, coalescing into battalions and
regiments only at the precise time and place at which they
have decided to do battle.

The American-equipped and -trained soldier (including
the Vietnamese government soldier) wears a steel helmet
covered with a camouflage net, and his uniform is sometimes
printed in a camouflage pattern. But compared with a well-
camouflaged Viet Cong guerrilla, he is a sitting duck.

The Viet Cong often wears a helmet made of wicker and
plastic sheeting that looks like an inverted pie tin. It is a
much better platform for camouflage foliage than the American helmet. But the guerrilla is not content to pin a few
leaves to his hat. His whole body is very often swathed in
foliage, and he changes his foliage as he moves from one type
of terrain to another.

The black clothing worn by most regional guerrillas is
exactly the same clothing as that worn by all Vietnamese
peasants, and is, in itself, a form of camouflage.

Guerrillas sometimes dress as women selling fruit and
vegetables when infiltrating a hamlet or post.

"When you're not sure, grab 'em between the legs," a
U.S. Army Special Forces man told a Vietnamese guard at the
gate of one of these hamlets.

Good camouflage is the most important factor in setting
up ambushes.

The pilot of a U.S. Army L19* spotting plane once
watched in horror as the Viet Cong ambushed a large government unit moving along a road.

"I was flying low over the convoy, and could see everything
perfectly. Everything looked normal, and the fields on the
side of the road seemed empty," he said.

"All at once, the whole shoulder of the road, about a half
mile long, seemed to lift up and turn into about two hundred
men, all of them shooting into the convoy at point-blank
range. After the first volley of shots, they charged in and

---

*This aircraft was later renamed the O1F Birddog, in keeping with the military
policy of keeping everyone confused. I still call it the L19.

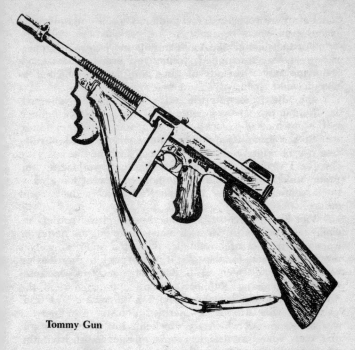

Tommy Gun

mixed up with the government troops in such close hand-to-hand fighting it all looked like one group. I couldn't have strafed them even if I'd been armed, because I'd have killed government troops too. It was all over quickly, long before reinforcements even got rolling."

The experts agree there is no magic or genius involved in camouflage. Camouflage, they say, is the infinite capacity for taking pains and a psychological outlook that thinks of concealment before anything else. These qualities, in turn, are dependent on military discipline. A unit must be so well disciplined that it does the right things instinctively, without requiring separate orders each time.

More than anything else, this, I believe, is what often gives the Viet Cong the edge over government troops. The Viet Cong regular has many deficiencies as a fighting man, but I believe there can be no argument that he is, in general, a much better disciplined soldier than his government counterpart.

For that matter, the Viet Cong, in my judgment, generally are better disciplined, willing to endure greater hardships for longer periods of time, and more dedicated to winning the war than are most American combat troops. This is not to slight the American GIs. The Viet Cong, after all, are fighting in their own country and have a special interest in the outcome of things.

Both communist and anticommunist troops make extensive use of military gadgetry in Viet Nam. In the following chapter, I shall discuss some of the gadgets working for the Free World. But I would like to note here what I regard as the essential difference between Viet Cong gadgetry and ours.

Viet Cong gadgetry begins and ends on the battlefield, while ours begins in America and is adapted, for better or worse, to the Vietnamese jungle. When the American gadget proves inadequate for the task, it is sent back to the drawing boards, some of which are in Saigon but most of which are 10,000 miles away. Supply lines are attenuated, and the American military designer lives in a different world from Viet Nam. This is in no way a criticism of American guerrilla weapons, some of which are excellent. But it seems to me that men who can design Polaris missiles must have the greatest difficulty adjusting their frames of reference to crossbows. And, unfortunately for us, the crossbow is an eminently more practical weapon in Viet Nam than the ballistic missile.

There is another dangerous aspect to the differences between our gadgetries.

Viewed through guerrilla eyes, a complicated weapon like the American Thompson submachine gun is a work of art. Its many precision-made parts work smoothly together as a lethal masterpiece of the Industrial Revolution: a revolution that never reached Viet Nam. If the reader has never examined a Tommy gun close up, I can assure him that it is a very impressive mechanism indeed—the more so if the beholder has spent the past five years making shotguns out of pieces of pipe.

Consider the guerrilla who has nothing but a water canteen made from a bamboo log, a cloth sleeve over his shoulder containing rice, a pair of cloth shorts, a coolie hat made of palm fronds, sandals made of slabs cut from a rubber tire and fitted with leather thongs, and a dagger made from an old butcher knife.

This guerrilla is a man who must live by his wits and who knows the uses of everything he carries as well as he knows his own body. He cherishes all his possessions.

He may, if he is a clever machinist or has a good friend in the party organization, have obtained a "sky horse gun." If so, he regards it as a wonderful weapon—much more effective than the dagger. It is also a matter of prestige to own a firearm, since only about one out of every three Viet Cong guerrillas has his own gun.

It is not difficult to imagine how this guerrilla would feel if, in the heat of a battle, he managed to capture a Tommy gun and were allowed by his squad leader to keep it. All at once, our guerrilla would have a superb weapon and the prestige of owning the best of all possible battle trophies.

The Tommy gun in his hands becomes a treasured object, to be used against the enemy, but most of all, to be cleaned and cared for, and never, under any circumstances, to be lost.

The Viet Cong do, in fact, take excellent care of the weapons they capture, and use them with the skill that speaks of unstinting practice. In short, they treat their weapons the way all soldiers are supposed to.

Guerrilla gadgetry moves from privation and necessity through ingenuity, and finally to sophisticated weapons.

The tendency in an American-trained and -equipped army is exactly the reverse. When a soldier is issued a weapon, he knows that it is exactly like the weapons issued to everyone else. It would never occur to him to marvel at its efficiency, because he has never been faced with the necessity of making weapons on primitive lathes.

He is trained to take care of his gun, and is theoretically subject to discipline if he breaks it or loses it. But he knows that if something does happen to it, he will merely get a scolding and another weapon will come from America to replace it.

It is not surprising, therefore, that Vietnamese government troops have lost staggering numbers of American weapons and ammunition to the Viet Cong. Vietnamese units, unless they have unusually tough officers (or tough American advisors), often carry new weapons that already are pitted with rust, full of sand, and filthy. A heavy weapon is a heavy burden for a small Vietnamese soldier, and he is apt to dislike it, especially after lugging it for years over waist-deep mud, across canals and through jungle.

In summary, I feel that Viet Cong gadgetry has evolved as part of its fighting spirit and is ideally suited to its human materiel. The guerrillas have learned to take on American helicopters—at first, by putting up millions of bamboo helicopter traps in likely landing areas, later by antiaircraft batteries of captured .50-caliber machine guns.

But even with the captured machine guns, the guerrillas have taught themselves, building mock-up helicopters towed along cables between trees, for gunnery practice.

The whole training and equipping of the communist force is a naturally evolving process, carried on continuously under fire.

Our program, on the other hand, has been geared to adapting the wealth of American technology and military experience to a new and foreign environment. The evolutionary process in some cases has gone backward, as the people who first introduced helicopters now study ways of making better foot traps.

With varying degrees of success, America's armed forces are painfully adapting themselves to the new and often primitive face of war.

4

AMERICAN GADGETS

We Americans prefer to deal with things we can touch rather than with abstractions. Consequently, we seek solutions to our thornier problems through gadgets rather than ideas.

The matter of education is a case in point. When the Russians launched Sputnik I on October 4, 1957, many of our leaders went into a state of quiet panic. It seemed the Soviet Union had got ahead of us in the very field in which we believed ourselves to have been pre-eminent—technology. There seemed to be a gap between our level of technological education and that of the Russians.

A crash program was launched to overcome this gap, and the Congress passed the National Defense Education Act. American anxiety over the Sputniks pumped huge new funds into the American educational "plant," and concrete and glass institutions with the finest equipment sprang up everywhere. On a national scale, as well as locally, the feeling was that by buying ourselves fancier schools with more sophisticated gadgets we would have better educated children.

I question the truth of this assumption.

It seems to me the mere injection of funds into the realm of ideas does not necessarily spur thought. Albert Einstein began his greatest work as a clerk in a Swiss patent office, not as a $25,000-a-year research director in one of the great American "think tanks."

The very idea of creating "think tanks" is peculiarly American, and has played a big part in the Viet Nam war. In 1967 alone, the United States spent an estimated two billion dollars of public and private money on "think tanks."

A "think tank" is essentially an institution providing salaries, facilities and an organization for a group of men and women with special talents and intelligence. These men and women may be assigned to special projects in the fields of pure scientific research, technology, languages, and the social sciences. They may also be paid merely to explore ideas of their own not necessarily related to any immediate specific need.

Among the wealthiest and largest of the think tanks is the RAND Corporation of Santa Monica, California. At the end of World War II, various military and civilian leaders, notably Air Force General "Hap" Arnold, felt that it would be a national catastrophe to disband all the scientific minds that had been brought together to win the war.

To give these scientific leaders an organization to replace the defense establishment they had been serving, the Air Force advanced funds to create RAND, an acronym for "research and development."

RAND retained the full- or part-time services of leading university professors, scientists, anthropologists, linguists, psychologists and intelligence experts, among others.

Similar think tanks sprang up within the armed forces themselves, to create new weapons and counterweapons, and to evolve new systems of warfare. The first tactics of helicopter warfare were worked out in these institutions.

But the biggest challenge for the think tanks began some time after the Korean War when American military and civilian leaders began to realize that a new species of warfare was coming to the fore—insurgency. Actually, Mao Tse-tung and his party and army had carried off a spectacular success with the new type of war in 1949, when they swept an American-equipped Chinese Nationalist army into the sea. But it was not widely realized at the time that the communist enemy had used radically new tactics.

When French forces were smashed by the communist-led Viet Minh in Indochina in 1954, Washington was again made unpleasantly aware of the new type of warfare, by which an ill-equipped peasant army could defeat a modern, mechanized professional force.

But Washington's real consciousness of the new danger stalking the world did not begin until about 1960, when the pattern was perceived working once again in Laos and South Viet Nam. This time, President Kennedy and his team decided to do battle.

It was noticed by some that the communists in hungry Asia and elsewhere in the impoverished "Third World" were getting the best of the West, not by battalions and artillery, but by ideas, especially in the form of a highly developed propaganda.

Washington elected to fight this phenomenon of "insurgency" with the doctrine of "counterinsurgency," in which good ideas would be at a premium. True to Pentagon form, counterinsurgency became the acronym COIN, to be treated as a tangible thing.

And so it came to pass that we began "funding the think tanks" on an unprecedented scale, to beat the "Thought of Mao Tse-tung," the mystique of the other side.

For us, it was comforting to conceive of thought as something concrete, something that could be generated and stored in a tangible think tank. Not surprisingly, the vast bulk of thought that resulted had to do almost exclusively with tangible gadgets.

We lacked the depth of belief that stems from desperation. We lacked the tradition of humiliation that begets lasting hatred. We lacked the immediacy of widespread starvation in the face of corrupt plenty. We lacked the zeal of the patriot who sees his homeland invaded by an alien race. We lacked even interest in the war, much less any real, visceral urge to win.

War was all right as long as it could be carried out 30,000 feet over the battlefield, on a nine-to-five basis with air-conditioned PX stores and swimming pools at the headquarters compounds.

In short, American was flabby in mind and body when it went to war in Viet Nam.

And Washington's military leadership had to face and accept the infuriating fact that one Viet Cong guerrilla was worth, in military terms, between ten and twenty American GIs.

History will record that the gadgetmakers did everything in their power to even those odds, and they did a remarkable job, even if it all turns out to have been in vain.

Take the matter of insects. The Viet Cong, as noted in a previous chapter, used the nests of hornets and wasps as booby traps and projectiles. The United States sought to use the bedbug.

The bedbug exhibits certain reflexes when it smells human food, which it can do from a remarkably great distance, if the wind is right. It moves around rapidly and emits small noises. Amplified electronically, these noises can be used to operate meters showing the proximity of human beings.

One of the U.S. Army's think tanks devised a machine that could be carried by one soldier and operated by four or five bedbugs. The machine embodied a sniffing tube, a bellows, a special chamber for the bugs, and electronic gadgets. By pointing the sniffing tube at a suspected ambush site, a soldier supposedly could tell whether human beings were concealed there.

The bedbug machine failed the combat tests, although successful tests were conducted on a "people sniffer" employing chemical-physical apparatus instead of bugs. The mechanical people sniffer reportedly could detect the body odor of a concealed guerrilla from 200 yards away or more. Modifications were installed in low-flying observation planes to detect guerrillas under cover.

Ingenious though many of these inventions are, our American gadgeteers rarely seem to reckon on the propaganda side effects they may produce. Disclosure of the bedbug tests in Viet Nam resulted in a surprisingly negative wave of editorial comment in the Vietnamese press, including the anticommunist newspaper of Saigon.*

---

*The tone of these editorials is well reflected in these excerpts from an editorial signed by Ton That Thien (former director of South Viet Nam's official news agency) in the June 30, 1966, edition of the English-language Vietnam Guardian. Such remarks would not have got past the censor if they had not had at least the tacit approval of General Nguyen Cao Ky's government, which was, at least theoretically, America's ally. The editorial ran:

"Has it occurred to you that Vietnam may soon be rid of all its communists and be a free and happy country in which there will be no war, no foreign troops of any nationality, no terrorists, no outrageously high prices, no traffic jams, no road cuts, no this and no that?

"Do you know why? If you don't, you must really be indifferent to science and anticommunism. . . .

"The American scientists (they are American citizens now anyway), so it seems, are on the way to raising successfully a kind of bugs which can spot the communists! Just like that!. . .

"But the remarkable thing about the bugs raised by the above-mentioned scientists is that they can spot the VC in the jungles, and thus save the GIs a lot of slogging through the undergrowth and getting their clothes all torn to shreds. No more need for shepherd dogs, radar, air strikes and the like.

"The bugs will tell you exactly where to head for, and what to avoid. Guerrilla war will become such a pleasant thing: sunshine during the daytime, and an

It was quickly apparent that the toughest technical problem facing American forces in Viet Nam was the finding and identification of the enemy.

The Viet Cong and its North Vietnamese ally did not fight in regiments and divisions, as a rule, and they did not use mechanized equipment or roads. They moved as guerrillas. Concealed under the vast rain forests of the central highlands, they were invisible from the air. Dressed as farmers in the hamlets, they were indistinguishable from other citizens.

"What we need is some gimmick that'll tell us which side a man's on—maybe some kind of litmus paper that turns red when it's near a communist," a ranking U.S. Army officer said.

The think tanks (the U.S. Air Force alone has eight research and development laboratories employing 8,000) have yet to develop a political litmus paper.

But they have had somewhat greater success in ferreting out concealed human beings.

One of the means developed for Viet Nam is personnel radar, which comes in light enough packages that it can be carried by small infantry units. It is sensitive enough to detect moving human beings, and thus can alert a defense perimeter, in the dark, of an impending attack. Of course, the attacks happen anyway, but the radar may have helped to some extent.

Another very useful gadget is the Starlight Scope developed for use with the Army's M-16 rifle.

The faint glow of the night sky reflected from objets on the ground is amplified by the Starlight Scope so that the soldier can clearly see his surroundings, including human beings, who would otherwise be invisible. GIs have often scored kills firing into what appeared to the naked eye as inky blackness.

---

occasional swim in a cool stream, and the tender eyes and clasping hands of a hostess in the evening. . . .

"But I am sure that many Vietnamese, on hearing about those wonderful bugs, will wonder what would happen to their country when peace returns. . . .

"Our villages and our cities will then be swarming with bugs. And this, because, to the Americans the wonderful bugs (which will surely cost a great deal to raise), like much else needed for the war (guns, tanks, and Vietnamese darling girl friends), will be expendable, and will be left behind."

M-16 with Starlight Scope

Besides radar, odor and amplified light, sound has been used to detect concealed Viet Cong. The faint brushing of cloth against cloth emits sounds above 20,000 cycles per second, above the range of human hearing. This kind of sound can be detected by another army gadget aimed at cutting down enemy ambushes.

The techniques of aerial intelligence have moved at great speed in Viet Nam, and also are aimed mainly at finding the concealed enemy.

Infrared radiation detectors on airplanes can detect heat sources on the ground, such as campfires, even when concealed beneath the canopy of a tall forest.

Photo interpretation has been raised to a highly sophisticated art, as America was dramatically shown during the Cuban missile crisis of 1962, when high-flying U-2 spy planes spotted evidence of sites even before the missiles arrived. Photo reconnaissance planes used over North and South Viet Nam include, besides U-2s and Ryan "Firebee" pilotless drones, RF-101s, RB-57s, RF4s and other fast jets.

The craft of aerial intelligence depends in Viet Nam partly on special film emulsions. There is one that records normal, living foliage in a bright red hue. Foliage which has been cut down and is being used to camouflage men or equipment may still show to the naked eye as normal green, but is perceived by the film as purple-brown instead of red. Some Viet Cong camouflage schemes have been thwarted as a result.

One of the more spectacular schemes for depriving the enemy of concealment in Viet Nam goes under the code name "Operation Ranchhand."

As originally conceived in 1962 trials, Ranchhand aimed at defoliating the jungles and thickets adjoining roads, canals, power lines, railroads and other arteries, so as to spoil Viet Cong ambushes and to make patrols by air more effective.

The idea was not altogether new. French colonial forces in Indochina had tried the same thing against the Viet Minh, by chopping away or burning foliage from along certain key roads. (Often the French infuriated farmers by chopping into orchards into the bargain.) But the new gimmick was that the defoliation would be done by air. U.S. Air Force C-123 two-engined transport planes were modified to hold gigantic tanks and spraying apparatus, and the tanks were filled with a mixture of kerosene and weed killer.

Hugging mountain valleys and ground contours, the big planes dumped their loads of purple spray over the land. There were many crashes, especially in the mountains, where vicious downdrafts tugged pilots toward valley walls.

With characteristic lightheartedness, crews of Ranchhand

C-123s put up signs in their operations rooms reading: "Remember, only you can prevent forests."

The initial flights in 1962 were mostly unsuccessful. It was discovered that spraying must be during the time of the year when sap is running, to be successful. Gradually, however, wide swaths along canals and roads lost their cover of green leaves, as Ranchhand developed know-how.

Before long, Vietnamese Air Force crews began putting the spray to another use—killing rice crops. The reasoning was that while guerrillas can always find plenty to eat in the lush Mekong Delta, they have a much harder time feeding themselves in the mountains and bare upland prairies of South Viet Nam's central interior.

In the Haut Plateau, as this area is called, guerrillas and even North Vietnamese regulars are often compelled to grow their own rice, scratching paddies out of the rain forests and mountainsides. The region is very sparsely populated, so the Saigon government decided that anyone growing rice there was, prima facie, an enemy. Helicopter sprayers began killing rice in the Haut Plateau.

At first, the U.S. Air Force planes restricted themselves to defoliating ambush sites, but after several years, Ranchhand got into the crop-killing business also.

It must be noted here that rice has a status in Asia that few Westerners can ever really appreciate. Rice is not merely a food; it is a gift from heaven to be revered. Children are beaten by their parents for leaving so much as one grain of rice in their bowls at mealtime, and this habit persists even in wealthy families living abroad. To waste rice is a cardinal sin in Asia.

The psychological effect of seeing whole fields of rice destroyed by aerial spraying can easily be imagined. Killing crops no doubt achieves a useful tactical effect against a hungry enemy. But it creates a propaganda setback of the first magnitude. A poor man can witness the destruction of rice only with the bitterest of hatred in his heart for the destroyer. And his hatred helps drive him into the ideological fold of the Viet Cong, if only to get even with the American devils.

The Viet Cong naturally capitalizes on this. Outbreaks of food poisoning and epidemics in the countryside, which are always common, can conveniently be blamed on the American defoliating spray. Viet Cong agitators have little difficulty convincing peasants that America is engaging in ruthless chemical and germ warfare aimed at exterminating poor people.

Viet Cong leaflets are full of helpful advice. One says that produce contaminated by the spray should be buried at least six feet deep to avoid poisoning people. Children and nursing mothers are said to be especially harmed by the spray.

In fact, the Air Force says, the spray is harmless to humans and animals. At one time, Vietnamese officers toured the countryside eating bread soaked in defoliant spray to prove its nonpoisonousness. But the peasants remained skeptical.

Defoliation of ambush sites may or may not be useful. In sprayed areas, about 60 per cent of the foliage is killed. But it has yet to be demonstrated that ambushes have been significantly reduced as a result. It can be argued, for that matter, that defoliated roadsides give guerrillas a better field of fire for sweeping convoys with their guns.

In any case, Viet Cong guerrillas make their own cover— as often as not, a little stack of rice straw over a foxhole.

I think that defoliating sprays, on balance, have helped the Viet Cong more than they have helped Washington. They have been one more little defeat in the war of ideas, in which we seem consistently outmaneuvered.

Another case in point was America's use of tear gas as a military weapon.

The gases involved were compounded to cause tears, inflammation of mucous membranes and acute nausea and diarrhea, sometimes for several days. The idea behind their introduction into the Viet Nam war in 1965 was essentiallly humanitarian. It was reasoned that it is better to incapacitate occupants of caves, holes and tunnels with gas than to kill them with explosives and napalm. For one thing, tunnel occupants often turned out to be women and children trying to escape the fighting.

But, as usual, the Pentagon failed to reckon with the propaganda effect of its latest gadget. On March 22, 1965, an AP dispatch by Peter Arnett broke the story, saying: "U.S. and Vietnamese military forces are experimenting with non-lethal gas warfare in South Vietnam." As the AP's chief correspondent in Viet Nam, I had cleared every detail of the story after assuring myself of its accuracy.

International reaction to the story was as hostile as it was swift. North Viet Nam and China predictably redoubled their charges of atrocities against the United States. More surprisingly, the noncommunist nations of Europe reacted strongly. Censure of the United States was particularly harsh in Great Britain.

The fact that Britain had used exactly the same gases in controlling riots in Hong Kong, Aden and elsewhere did little to temper anti-American feeling in Britain.

An editorial in the British *New Statesman* said:

"The Americans, like Hitler and Mussolini in Spain, are treating the hapless inhabitants of Vietnam as a living laboratory in which to test their new weapons."

There were questions in Parliament about Whitehall's tacit support of American policies in Southeast Asia. And Foreign Secretary Michael Stewart, who was on a trip to the United States, called on Washington to "display what your Declaration of Independence called a 'decent respect for the opinions of mankind.'"

President Johnson at first denied knowledge that gas was being used in Viet Nam and then passed the buck to Secretary of State Dean Rusk, who said that the types of gas being used were not prohibited by the 1925 Geneva Protocol.

The use of gas was halted for about one year and then quietly resumed on a limited scale. But propaganda damage of a massive order had been sustained by Washington over a trivial aspect of the war.

Napalm is another case in point. While napalm is scarcely a new military gadget, it has acquired a peculiar new mystique in the Viet Nam war that stems entirely from its propaganda significance.

The very word napalm has become a rallying cry of American and foreign peace movements. Antiwar posters nearly always show Vietnamese children and women burned by napalm, and captions frequently carry only one word: Napalm. It is a word that engenders hatred and a will for revenge, be it even against one's own nationality.

I do not for a minute challenge the fact that napalm casualties are ghastly to behold. But what interests me is the fact that this is the first time any sizeable American group ever has worried about napalm this much.

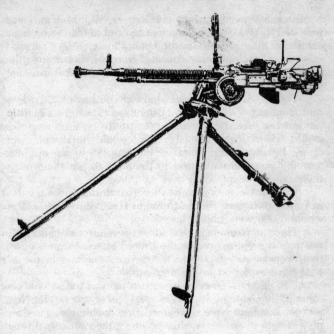

Chicom 12.7 mm. H.M.G. Type 54

Napalm, which is an acronym for the aluminum soap of naphthenic and palmitic acids, was invented by Harvard University scientists in 1942. It is a white powder which converts gasoline from a liquid to a jelly. The jellied gasoline burns more slowly than the liquid, and clings to anything it touches.

This horrible weapon, used both in flamethrowers and in bombs, was used very extensively in World War II and Korea. The massive firebomb raids on Tokyo just before the atomic bombs were used depended heavily on napalm. At the time, there certainly were no peace demonstrators picketing the chemical plants manufacturing napalm, even though women and children were being incinerated.

In the ten-day period that ended August 3, 1943, allied

bombers destroyed the city of Hamburg, and the bomb loads included 80,000 incendiary bombs and 5,000 phosphorus canisters. Like napalm, burning phosphorus clings to flesh. It can be extinguished by dousing in water, but it reignites when the water dries off. Besides that, phosphorus is extremely poisonous.

Thousands of phosphorus-burned German civilians leapt into Hamburg's central lake at the time of the great raids, to put out the fires. But, according to survivors, each time they would try to leave the lake, they would burst into flame again. Finally, brutal troops of the Nazi SS began machine-gunning phosphorus victims in the lake, to put them out of their agony.

Postwar German records show that during those ten days in July and August, the death toll in Hamburg was 40,000, of whom 5,000 were children.

Thus, it is obvious that killing women and children in wartime is nothing new for the United States. What is new is that propaganda effect, which America's enemies in the Far East have exploited to the maximum.

U.S. military officials argue that napalm (or, as it is now called, "Incendergel") is an essential tool of war in Viet Nam. Fighter-bombers have developed new techniques for dropping "nape" over forests, dive-bombing the canisters through the trees to make sure they will hit the ground and not splash harmlessly over the treetops.

Napalm's intense fire burns the oxygen out of air, and napalm splashed over the entrance of a cave or tunnel will cause an occupant to suffocate, even if the heat doesn't get him. Because the Viet Cong frequently fights from tunnels and foxholes, napalm is considered an ideal weapon against the enemy.

Napalm also is useful in splashing hillsides on which enemy troops are assaulting friendly positions. It can be used against snipes, mortar positions, troop concentrations, or any target that cannot be precisely fixed by artillery or mortars.

But on the negative side, napalm does kill and maim countless thousands of civilians along with the guerrillas. And in this war, there are usually photographers around to record the extremely unpleasant results.

The result has been a psychological link established in many minds around the world between "America" and "napalm." For many critics of the United States, mere mention of the word "America" results in a Pavlovian reflex in which "napalm" is suggested.

Despite napalm's unquestioned merits as a military gadget, I think its propaganda backlash in Viet Nam far outweighs its utility. Obviously, Washington does not concur in my view.

And Vietnamese children, who have grown used to the hellish fire from the skies, go on following it like little jackals. Many a time I have seen boys about ten years old dashing into the still smoking debris of a napalm burst, to recover the burned-out aluminum canisters in which it is dropped. These canisters can be recast into pots and pans and sold at a modest profit.

The American gadgets brought to bear on the Vietnamese war are practically limitless, and any attempt I might make here to catalogue them would be swiftly outdated. But these are some of the more significant ones:

• Basic infantry rifles have been undergoing major changes in Viet Nam. The Viet Nam war has seen a transition from the World War II M-1 Garand (still in service with many Vietnamese units) to the new M-16. The M-16, manufactured by Colt, is extremely light, and is made mostly from light

M-79 Grenade Thrower

alloys and Fiberglas. It can fire either semiautomatically, like a rifle, or fully automatically, like a machine gun.

The M-16 cartridge fires a tiny .223-caliber bullet at a speed roughly twice that of an ordinary rifle bullet. When an M-16 bullet strikes a man's shoulder it is apt to tear the whole shoulder off because of the crushing and tumbling effect of a projectile moving at enormous velocity.

Some peace groups have charged that the M-16 violates the Geneva Protocol banning dumdum or expanding bullets. A more serious immediate objection to the M-16 is a strong tendency in many models to jam when used in combat.

Despite that, the M-16 has become a very popular weapon. The Viet Cong always tries to capture them when they can.

• The art of grenade throwing has been refined into new gadgets in Viet Nam. Hand grenades themselves have been redesigned, and the old, segmented "pineapple" type used in both world wars and Korea is now scarcely seen. The new M-26 grenade has a smooth exterior, and is lined with a coiled strip of serrated spring steel.

This steel lining breaks up into shrapnel when the grenade explodes, and the killing effect is said to be much greater than in the old grenade. Needless to say, the Viet Cong jungle weapons factories rapidly began making copies of the M-26.

The infantry in Viet Nam now has a weapon designed to replace both old-fashioned rifle grenade launchers and the obsolete 60-millimeter trench mortar. The new gadget, which resembles a shotgun, is called the M-79.

The M-79 breaks open like a shotgun to receive an oversize cartridge. The projectile is a 40-millimeter explosive shell lined with the same steel coil as is used in the M-26 grenade. A foot soldier can fire this device several hundred yards with great accuracy, into bunkers, huts, or jungle. It is a very effective weapon.

Probably the M-79 will find its way into the hands of criminals in the United States, who will find it ideal for robbing banks or even blowing up police stations. Somehow guns like the M-79 always end up that way.

• Whole new families of mines have gone to war in Viet Nam. Some are seeded by air over jungles and areas where enemy guerrillas are expected to move.

One mine, the "Claymore," deserves special mention. The Claymore is curved like a horeshoe and contains a shaped charge. It fires a blast of ball shrapnel in a single direction, like a huge shotgun. The mine is aimed with a special sight, pointing at predetermined target spots, or down a trail at knee level. Detonated by a column of marching men, it can kill everyone in the column.

Claymores can be set up around a camp, and can be set off one at a time by a sentry with electric wires leading individually to each mine. This way, a sentry can pick off attackers as they come rather than waste an entire minefield in one blast.

Baby Claymores have been mounted on the sides, front and rear of trucks as protection against ambush attacks. The occupants of the truck are protected by steel plates mounted under the mines.

Viet Cong armorers were quick to apply the Claymore principle in their own mines. On June 25, 1965, Viet Cong terrorists demonstrated their command of Claymore weaponry by killing forty-three persons, including a number of Americans, and wounding eighty.

A small mine was set up on the waterfront of the Saigon River near the floating My Canh Restaurant, a favorite with Americans and wealthy Vietnamese. The small mine was set off. It caused few, if any, casualties. But it frightened diners at the restaurant so badly they began stampeding over the gangplank to land. A second mine of the powerful Claymore type was aimed along this gangplank, and when the terrorist saw his victims properly lined up, he cranked his magneto and fled.

The carnage was ghastly. I have never seen anything worse. It was never established whether the mine used by the Viet Cong was a captured Claymore or a skillful copy made of them, but it makes little difference.

"Minigun" machine guns and "Vulcan" cannon are innovations in Viet Nam. These weapons employ six barrels that fire cyclically, like the old Gatling gun. The 7.62-millimeter Minigun can spit out an incredible 6,000 bullets per minute (an ordinary machine gun fires about 600 bullets per minute), and the 20-millimeter Vulcan cannon fires explosive shells almost as fast.

Obviously, these weapons consume mountainous quan-

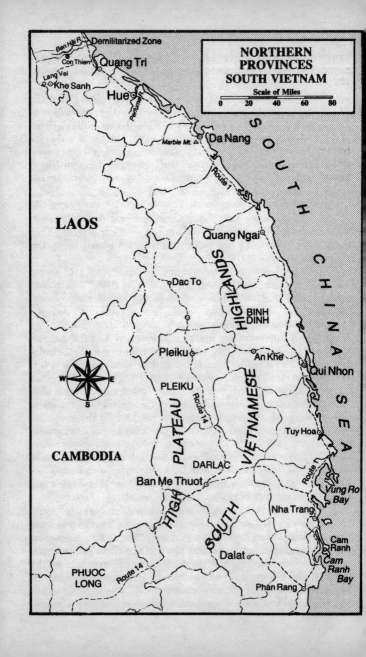

tities of ammunition—far too much for a small infantry unit to carry. Consequently, their use has been confined to airplanes.

"Puff the Magic Dragon" is such an airplane. Officially designated the AC-47, Puff is essentiallly the two-engined DC-3 airliner first manufactured in 1935. Oversize doors on its port side accommodate three Miniguns that will fire a withering total of 18,000 bullets per minute at the ground. Tracers fired from these guns at night make Puff seem to be emitting a giant tongue of flame that reaches all the way down to the ground.

The idea of the weapon is to spray huge areas of jungle in hopes of killing an enemy. Incidentally, each cartridge costs the United States more than a dime.

• The air war in Viet Nam will be discussed in a later chapter, but some of its gadgetry is noteworthy here.

Airplanes are used to spray aluminum dust on jungle trails. This dust appears on radar, so that other planes can attack trails in total darkness, hoping to hit the human target.

Airplanes and helicopters are guided over South Viet Nam by an ingenious navigation system that takes almost all the work out of navigating. On his instrument panel, the pilot has a gadget with a large-scale map and a mechanical pointer. Both map and pointer are moved by radio impulses automatically, and continuously show the pilot exactly where he is. The pointer leaves an inked tracing on the map to show where he has been and to indicate direction of flight.

Airplanes and helicopters are used extensively for communication and propaganda. Both are equipped with powerful loudspeakers capable of drowning out engine noise and beaming messages to the ground from 3,000 or more feet high. Loudspeaker planes often drop leaflets while talking. The messages call for Viet Cong to lay down their arms and rally to the government.

When television was introduced to Viet Nam in 1966, the combination antenna-station-studios were two four-engine Constellations that took off and flew circles around Saigon for about four hours each night. The "Blue Eagle" Constellations, as they were called, beamed two TV channels to the ground, one in English and the other in Vietnamese. The few hundred Vietnamese rich enough to buy TV sets could watch Vietnamese skits with heavy doses of government propaganda. American GIs in the field could turn on unit TV sets and watch the latest episode of *Combat*.*

A great range of weapons was used on aircraft in Viet Nam. The new "Snake-eye" low-drag bombs came into use, for instance. The Snake-eyes, which come in 500-, 750- and 1,000-pound sizes, have folding fins. Left folded, these fins allow the bomb to fall at high speed from a fast-moving jet. Triggered to unfold, the fins drag the bomb back, so that a low-flying plane will have time to clear a target before the bomb explodes. There also are bombs up to 2,000 pounds in weight with delay fuses to set them off days after a raid.

The "Lazy Dog" first came into use in Viet Nam. It is a canister of finned steel darts, each about an inch and a half long and weighing several ounces. Dropped at transonic speeds from a jet, these little darts fly nearly as fast as bullets, and tear into a jungle like shrapnel.

The Cluster Bomb Unit (CBU) is similarly used. Similar to Germany's World War II "Breadbasket Bomb," the CBU scatters small fragmentation bombs over a wide area, and can carpet an expanse of jungle. The fragmentation bombs contain ball shrapnel designed to cause heavy casualties.

Lazy Dogs and CBUs have become loaded propaganda symbols almost as potent as napalm. North Viet Nam and various peace groups have charged that these weapons have been frequently used over Hanoi and other populated centers, with the intention of causing heavy civilian casualties.

Missiles used in Viet Nam include the "Sidewinder," which homes on the jet exhaust of enemy planes, and the "Sparrow," which guides itself by radar and with which an American fighter can shoot down an enemy fighter from thirty miles or more away.

Other aerial weapons include the "Bullpup" missile, which fighter-bombers use against difficult ground targets such as bridges, and the big "Hawk" antiaircraft missile, used to protect such bases as Da Nang.

American mobile artillery in Viet Nam now includes

---

*By all indications, *Combat* was the most popular series with GIs at the time. Perhaps it was because *Combat* had to do with World War II, a much simpler war to understand, in which "good guys" and "bad guys" were clearly defined and arrayed against each other. It was a relief from the uncertainties and problems of Viet Nam.

M-50, "Onto"

huge 175-millimeter field guns and the Marine Corps tracked vehicle called "Ontos." Ontos is essentially a tank on which six 106-millimeter recoilless cannon are mounted. Heavy artillery support also comes from 7th Fleet cruisers and destroyers standing offshore. At least one battleship may join in.

GIs in Viet Nam have jungle boots (made largely of

canvas and vented with drain holes), new loose-fitting jungle jackets, new rifles and new body armor (made of Fiberglas plates). Military inventors have been experimenting with dyes that would make a uniform change color like a chameleon to match surrounding colors.

Close to the ultimate in American military gadgetry in Viet Nam is housed in a unmarked white house in the outskirts of Saigon. It is an IBM 1430 computer, programmed with tens of thousands of punched cards, so as "not to lose the enemy from view."

Some 1,100 persons work on this gadget. The basic idea is to digest all sources of intelligence about the enemy and predict the likeliest times and places for enemy attacks and ambushes.

Intelligence fed into the machine includes captured enemy letters and instructions, tips from villagers, results of prisoner interrogation, data on hundreds of thousands of suspected Viet Cong sympathizers, reports by local officials, reports from military patrols and secret agents, and aerial photographs.

The Viet Cong has always monopolized the intelligence field. By keeping open its channels of communication with local peasants, the Viet Cong almost always knows about American or government troop movements long in advance. While peasants rarely seem to tell Saigon forces anything about impending Viet Cong actions, Viet Cong commanders get all the information they need about Saigon's side.

Washington has, as a matter of course, sought to correct this situation with gadgets.

Lie detectors were applied to prisoner interrogation, but results were indifferent.

The computer was installed, and there were hopes that finally the Viet Cong intelligence system could be bested.

But the computer utterly failed to predict overwhelming enemy attacks such as one on June 25, 1967, at the Special Forces camp at Dak To. Dak To was overrun with disastrous losses in the surprise attack.

America has sought to fence off political ideology using physical gadgets. Fortified hamlets designed to keep noncommunist Vietnamese inside and Viet Cong out were tried. They were a woeful failure, by and large.

On September 7, 1967, Defense Secretary Robert S.

McNamara announced American plans to build a "barrier" between North and South Viet Nam to block infiltration of North Vietnamese forces and supplies. He said the barrier would consist of barbed wire, mines, and "sophisticated devices."

In the third century B.C., the first of the Ch'in emperors in China tried the same thing, completing a 1,500-mile wall across North China to protect the nation against Huns and other barbarians. It didn't work. The communists built a twenty-six-mile wall in Berlin in 1961, and that wall has been far from airtight. Century-old maps of Viet Nam show that a wall once stood between North and South Viet Nam, to block military incursions across Annam. It didn't work.

The French sought at one time to separate the secure parts of their Indochina colony from the Viet Minh with a *cordon sanitaire*—a barrier. It didn't work.

South Viet Nam has a 900-mile border with North Viet Nam, Laos and Cambodia, not counting its long sea coast. The land borders through which the guerrillas infiltrate are mostly in jungle-blanketed mountains. By comparison, the Demilitarized Zone separating North from South Korea is only a little over a hundred miles long, and is mostly denuded hillsides heavily fortified by bunkers. Despite that, North Korean agents cross the line with apparent ease nearly every night.

Perhaps the new American scheme for fencing off Vietnamese communism will bear some fruit. It seems to me, however, more like grasping at a straw, which can only result in more frustration and anger.

America has not lacked for imaginative mechanical ideas or military hardware in Viet Nam. But in this war, relations between human beings and abstract ideas have been decisive.

Our gadgets are superb, but they are not enough.

5

HELICOPTERS

It was early 1962, and few Americans had yet heard of Viet Nam or helicopter warfare.

The column of trucks had rumbled through the gate and was parked on the airport's concrete apron. The shadowy forms of troops were organizing themselves into groups of about a dozen each. It would be an hour until dawn, and there was shouting and confusion as Vietnamese NCOs shepherded their men from the trucks into columns in front of the dark forms of the helicopters.

Inside the ready room of the 57th Transportation Company (Helicopter), pilots in their gray-blue nylon coveralls were strapping on pistol belts, checking sector maps and reading notices on the operations board. Mostly young men they were, although a few were balding. Many sported handle-bar mustaches. They were warrant officers and lieutenants mostly, with a few captains. The enlisted gunners already were out at the helicopters checking fuel levels, instruments and controls.

The pilots yawned from time to time, but listened closely as a major briefed them on the landing zone, the suspected presence of several enemy heavy machine guns that must be skirted, a dangerous tree line, and the other little things that mean life or death for a helicopter pilot.

The thirty pilots pulled their navigation maps with plastic overlays from a big rack and chattered briefly about communications for the day, with frequent references to "Paris Control," Saigon's radar navigation center.

"With any luck we'll be back in time for martini hour," a pilot told his copilot.

"Yeah, if we keep our dog tags together this trip," the copilot said. "I hear Old Vic has two companies of hard hats two clicks from the LZ, and they have reckless rifles. We're

66

going to have to zap a few or they'll really spoil our day."

(Viet Nam, like all the wars in America's history, had produced military jargon. The preceding remarks mean: "Yes, if we live through this operation. I hear the Viet Cong has about two hundred hard-core regular guerrillas two kilometers from the landing zone who have recoilless cannons. We're going to have to shoot a few or they'll hit us badly, kill us.")

Pilots pulled on heavy flak vests lined with bullet-resistant Fiberglas plates and slogged along the muddy path to the dark flight line.

Inside the big banana-shaped H21s, dull blue cabin lights glowed. Pilots climbed up into their Plexiglas-surrounded cockpits and slipped on heavy white flight helmets. Switches were flicked, and red instrument lights glowed from dashboards.

At each helicopter, both gunners waited outside for the starting signal from the two pilots.

"We pull pitch [take off] in ten [minutes]," somebody yelled.

There was a tinkling of metal as resting troops stood up, rearranging their field packs. The packs were loaded with cooking utensils, and here and there a live duck hung by its feet from a soldier's pistol belt. The Vietnamese army, perhaps more than other armies, travels on its stomach.

It was time. Somewhere in the night, a pilot yelled to his gunner outside, "Clear?" "Clear, sir," the answer came back. The engine in the tail of the big machine churned as the starter cut in, a blast of smoke surged from the huge exhaust pipe, and a plume of blue flame shot into the night. All along the flight line, engines started with an ear-shattering roar.

Pilots adjusted themselves in their seats, changed their engine mixtures, and tuned up radios for communications checks. Forward gunners took their positions at the open doors on the right side of the H21s, just behind the cockpit. They fed belts of ammunition into their guns and swung the gun mounts around into firing position. Rear gunners gestured from their positions at open doors on the left side near the tail for the troops to come aboard. Each of the little Vietnamese soldiers got a helping hand up the high step from the door gunner.

Idling motors speeded up, transmission shafts along the ceiling of each craft began to whine, and the twin rotors began to turn. Red signal beacons on each helicopter were now blinking along the flight line.

Ferret Armored Car

The troops sat or squatted on the aluminum floor, since there were no seats. A few lighted cigarettes.

Pilots were tuned to several communications frequencies and listening to all of them simultaneously. To pass the remaining few minutes before take-off, some had tuned in the armed forces radio station in Saigon as well and were listening to an undertone of jazz along with the messages.

The helicopters were rolling forward now, out on a runway, one behind the other.

Pilots revved up their engines and pulled up gently on levers in the floor left of their seats, coarsening the pitch of their rotors just enough to "feel" whether the engine was putting out enough power to lift the machine. All the helicopters were up to par this morning.

The signal came, and the helicopters roared off down the runway, much like conventional airplanes taking off. Hovering or taking off vertically puts too much load on the engine of a loaded H21.

The predawn lights of Saigon sparkled below the wheeling fleet of helicopters as they maneuvered into formation, and the first tint of approaching sunrise gleamed in reflection from the curving Saigon River. The ungainly machines labored up to 3,000 feet, and the city was gone. The moon had come from behind clouds now, and sparkled brilliantly in the flat, flooded rice fields below. Through the oval portholes along the sides of the helicopters, the red of sunrise began to flood the cabins with light.

The operation was on its way now, flying at about eighty miles an hour southwest of Saigon to a target about a half hour away. There was time for cigarettes all around. Three thousand feet is a safe altitude where nothing much can go wrong.

The objective, a hamlet in the northern part of the Mekong River Delta, reportedly was currently occupied by about two companies of regular Viet Cong troops, that is from 200 to 400 well-armed professionals.

Like most hamlets in the delta, this one was strung for a half mile or so along a canal, hedged in by palm and pineapple trees and bamboo. A dense tree line separated the hamlet from the planned landing zone, an open rice field. Since the rear door through which the troops must unload is on the left side of helicopters, the whole formation would have to land with its left flank facing the tree line. The landing must not be so close to the tree line that enemy fire would cut the helicopters to pieces, nor must it be so far as to exhaust the troops running through the thick mud and water toward their objective. For this operation, a landing spot 200 yards from the tree line seemed appropriate. The pilots had their fingers crossed.

The watery green patchwork of rice fields, canals and stands of palm trees slid by below. The homes of farmers stood out as neat green squares dotted across the plain. Vietnamese peasants plant their fruit trees and pineapples in perfect rectangles surrounding their huts, affording both privacy and a pleasant break in the featureless flat rice terrain.

Ten minutes to go, and time to let down to contour flying. Helicopter pilots in Viet Nam have found that by far the most dangerous altitude from the standpoint of enemy ground fire is 700 feet. They like to pass through this particular height as fast as possible and as far away from enemy concentrations as possible.

The nose of the helicopter dipped down abruptly, and troops put their hands to their ears in pain from the sudden change in altitude air pressure. The ground leapt up until the entire formation had leveled out a scant ten feet high, charging at top speed across the paddies.

Herds of water buffalo swept into the pilots' field of vision, stampeding out of the way of the roaring H21s. Pilots squeezed their pitch control levers just enough to pull their machines over trees and huts, then back down "on the deck." Gunners no longer smoked, but crooked their fingers over the triggers of their .30-caliber machine guns, swinging the guns toward spots that might conceal snipers. At this altitude, the sound of an approaching helicopter does not travel far, and there were high hopes of catching the enemy by surprise.

Five miles away, four miles, three miles, and the tree line was now visible ahead. Suddenly, the whole formation banked steeply to the right, skimming along parallel to the tree line.

"We're drawing fire from those huts about ten o'clock from the flight," on of the lead helicopters radioed. The guns began to chatter, and orange tracers floated in toward the huts. Bushels of spent cartridges and machine-gun belt links spewed from the door guns over the tensely waiting troops inside.

Outside, the crackling of small arms fire was audible from the tree line, and an occasional puff of smoke marked the spot where one of the Viet Cong had fired.

It was time to land. The nose tilted up, and the big helicopter slowed and settled toward the ground like an ungainly bird. The troops were standing now, bunched near the rear door, close to the smoking hot machine gun.

The tall rice lashed in wild waves across the field and clouds of spray rose near the helicopters, as their beating rotors blasted a hurricane downward.

A noise like that of a sledge hammer against a kettle-drum sounded in the helicopter, and a few troops were speckled with blood spots where slivers of metal had hit them. The slug had left a silvery, jagged hole in the side of the machine and torn scores of flying fragments from an aluminum structural beam.

The helicopter jounced down into the paddy, water coming up nearly to the doorframe. The troops began leaping out, each getting a friendly whack on the shoulder from the American door gunner. As they jumped, they ran, hip deep in mud and water, holding their rifles high. The fifth soldier out of the helicopter took only ten steps before his face abruptly turned into a mass of red jelly, and he slumped to the ground. All twelve soldiers were out now, and the machine gun was back in firing position. The first few shots headed toward the tree line, and then the arc of fire swept aimlessly up into the sky. The gunner was hit.

Its rotors flapping wildly, the H21 heaved itself from its berth into the air, its dangling nose wheel skimming through the water. A few hundred yards away a column of orange flame and dense black smoke erupted from the field. One of the other H21s was down and out, perhaps hit by a recoilless cannon shell.

The rice field was dropping away now. Black-clad figures, some of them carrying rifles, were out in the open here, apparently caught by surprise by the helicopters. Now it was the turn of the right door gunner, who kept his finger locked on the trigger until the cabin was choking with the sweet-acid smell of burned powder.

One after another, the little black figures fell and lay still as geysers of mud and water flicked up around them.

The helicopter climbed painfully to 1,000 feet, and the right gunner dashed back to his wounded buddy. The round had gone through the soldier's chest near his shoulder, but he was alive and conscious.

Keeping his balance by holding metal beams, the right gunner moved back along the lurching helicopter, braced himself from slipping on the blood-slick floor, and hauled his wounded crewmate away from the door.

Flak jackets can stop spent bullets and shrapnel fragments, but they do not stop direct hits. The right gunner unzipped his buddy's pierced flak jacket and unbuttoned the bloody fatigue shirt underneath. Using the pressure dressings from both the wounded man's pistol belt and his own, the gunner pressed to stop the blood. The wounded man groaned, and his buddy lighted a cigarette and stuck it between his lips. It would be thirty minutes back to Saigon, with nothing else to do.

The latest American casualty would soon be on his way to the U.S. Army field hospital at Nha Trang, a coastal town northeast of Saigon once known as the finest ocean resort in South Viet Nam.

On the ground, the troops were pinned down and scarcely moving at all. For a half hour they had tried to inch forward, half swimming, half crawling toward the tree line. A number of soldiers had been hit, no one knew just how many. Another helicopter group would soon be bringing reinforcements, and meanwhile, four single-engine fighters were pouring cannon shells and rockets into the tree line.

Mortars were in action now, too, and the gray puffs of their shells could be seen behind the tress. From time to time, groups of a dozen or so troops would stand up, firing their automatic rifles and Tommy guns and running forward a few feet. The enemy fire slacked off, but progress still was agonizingly slow.

By noon, the first troops were trickling into the tree line and the huts behind. The fighting had stopped, the enemy was gone, and the huts were nearly deserted. Here and there a mother nursed her baby, or a child peered from behind a bamboo curtain. But there were no men or older boys.

Earthworks littered with spent ammunition attested to an enemy who had been around very recently. Smears of blood on some of the fortifications were still wet. But there were no bodies, no wounded men.

Beyond the hamlet was a wide canal that could be forded only by sampan, and beyond it more trees. Presumably the enemy was there somewhere.

But it was noon, the blazing sun stood high in the sky, and the troops were hungry. Many of the soldiers already were stretched out on the big polished tables in the huts, or under the shady palm-frond awnings in front. Some had whacked the tops from coconuts and were gulping down the sweet milk. A few had their pots boiling and were cooking rice. The order called for moving into this hamlet, and before anyone would go farther after the enemy, more orders from Saigon would be needed.

Some soldiers had found and raided a large supply of duck eggs in one hut and were laughing as they carried them over to their field mess, under the hard eyes of an old woman who lived in the hut. An intelligence officer with a

Sikorsky "Jolly Green Giant"

thin, scholarly face was making the rounds of the huts, asking how many Viet Cong there were and where they had gone. At each hut he was told, "I don't know, I didn't see them, I only heard a lot of shooting." Each time he would move on, sighing with resignation.

The operation would continue several days, covering more ground, exchanging a few shots with snipers, searching a few more huts. But for practical purposes, it was over already. If there were 200 Viet Cong around, they were gone now and had had ample time it break up into small, innocent-looking groups who could safely bide their time until the raiders had left.

In due course, the government would issue a communiqué: "Elements of the Seventh Division in helicopters of the U.S. Army's 57th Company attacked an estimated battalion of Viet Cong in AP —— hamlet of Dinh Tuong Province. After a two-hour clash, the enemy was routed and the objective seized. The Viet Cong suffered an estimated fifty killed, carried off by the enemy, and friendly troops seized fifteen pounds of documents, two grenades, a French MAS-36 rifle with six rounds of ammunition, and captured five Viet Cong suspects. Friendly forces suffered twelve killed including two Americans, and twenty-three wounded, including four Americans."

That was fairly typical of thousands of helicopter operations in South Viet Nam for the first few years. Many operations produced no enemy contact at all, and others resulted in major fights with heavy casualties. But the pattern was usually the same.

There were refinements in tactics on both sides as the war went along, of course.

The U.S Marine Corps, which had two companies (or rather, squadrons, as they call them) of troop-carrying helicopters almost from the beginning, worked along with the army groups. The marines use H34 helicopters, single-rotor aircraft that will carry the same number of troops or slightly more than the army H21. In 1964, some of the H34s were turned over to the Vietnamese Air Force, which began using them on helicopter operations of its own.

Helicopter warfare underwent a major innovation in late 1962 when the first of a new type of helicopter, the Bell UH1A, began arriving here. The UH1A, powered by a turbine engine, was much more powerful and faster than the obsolete H21s, although it would carry only seven or eight troops.

The first dozen or so of these machines, armed with four forward-firing machine guns and rocket pods, were organized into a unit called the Utility Tactical Transport Company. They were assigned the job of flying shotgun for the lumbering troop carriers, and in practice their mission was basically similar to fighter plane escorts.

This similarity led to an immediate controversy between the U.S. Army and the U.S. Air Force. The Air Force still objects to the Army's use of helicopters in close air support combat roles. The Air Force feels that fighter-bombers and any aircraft acting as fighter-bombers should be under its jurisdiction.

In any case, it became clear to the Army that something would have to be done to replace the old H21s, which had not been manufactured since the late 1950s and which were being rapidly worn out or shot to pieces in South Viet Nam. The last H21 flight in South Viet Nam was in the spring of 1964, and from that time on, all U.S. Army helicopter units in the country were equipped exclusively with the UH1A and UH1B, both for escort duty and for carrying troops.

After February 7, 1965, when the United States became an open combatant in the war, helicopters poured into the country, and among them were various new types.

The underpowered UH1A "Huey" was phased out. The

basic U.S. Army helicopter became the UH1B, and to this was added the UH1D, known familiarly as the "D Model Huey." The "D" has the same turboshaft engine as the earlier Huey, but is longer and can carry more troops, supplies or casualties.

Later, helicopter units acquired these other aircraft:

• The Sikorsky H-37, often called "The Jolly Green Giant" because of its large size and green paint. The H-37, powered by two 2,100-horsepower engines, can lift disabled Huey helicopters out of rice fields and carry them back to base. This helicopter also is widely used to rescue downed flyers from hostile territory, including North Viet Nam.

• The Sikorsky H-54 "Skycrane." This huge helicopter, powered by two 4,620-horsepower turboshaft engines, can pick up two disabled helicopters at a time, or carry a 15,000-pound cargo load, or carry a detachable compartment loaded with sixty troops. This compartment became known as a "people pod," and soldiers always had misgivings that helicopter pilots might accidentally jettison it. It was rumored that an important part of the pilot's body was always wired to the "people pod" as a reminder not to pull the wrong lever.

• The Bell H-13. This tiny, two-place helicopter remained in general use as a courier and for special observation missions.

• The Boeing-Vertol H-47 "Chinook." This turboshaft-powered helicopter can carry thirty-two troops or three tons of freight. It can fly two light howitzers to give helicopter assaults their own supporting artillery. The H-47 has a large rear loading ramp from which attacking troops can unload in a few seconds.

• The Kaman HH-43 "Huskie." This peculiar-looking but powerful little helicopter became the prime rescue and emergency craft of the U.S. Air Force in Viet Nam. Huskies have two intermeshed side-by-side rotors angled away from each other, and the blades flailing between each other truly look like an egg beater. The Huskie has a power winch and other equipment for hauling downed pilots up from jungle floors. It also is equipped with fire-fighting equipment and special rescue gear.

Huskie crews have performed some of the most heroic rescues of the war, snatching downed pilots from the very jaws of the enemy.

But the basic Army helicopter remained the Huey ("Huey"

is the closest pronounceable approximation of the initial model, the HU1A). As models and designations changed, the basic type was still called Huey.

Army development centers quickly added fillips to the Hueys to give them as much firepower as World War II fighters. Four M60 machine guns outside the helicopter above the landing skids were mounted in electrically controlled, movable turrets. The copilot, in his left-hand seat, was given a highly accurate electronic sight suspended from the cockpit ceiling. Grasping the handle of the sight, the copilot could aim it at any target in front of him or off to the sides. In aiming the sight, electric servomotors in the gun mounts automatically aim the guns.

Also mounted over the skids were rocket pods containing eight (or in later modifications, six) rockets each. Each of the 2.75-inch rockets carries an explosive nose large enough to blow a hut to pieces. On the ground, these rockets make a horrifying roar as they speed toward their targets, which no doubt has a psychological effect. They are not always reliable. On one firing pass, the writer was sitting next to a rocket pod when it was torn to pieces by the folding fins of one of the rockets. The fins had protruded prematurely, before the missile had left its rack. The helicopter was jolted to a near stop in mid-air. In common with all bombs and shells, rockets

Huey

can be set off if hit by tracer bullets, and, mounted as they are outside the helicopters, they are highly exposed.

This fact probably accounted for the destruction of one Huey, in Kien Hoa Province near the mouth of the Mekong River. While making a strafing run on a powerfully armed Viet Cong defense perimeter, the Huey blew up in mid-air, and its fragments scattered over hundreds of square yards. All four crew members were killed.

Like human beings, helicopters can be killed by single bullets. At the same time, a hail of bullets may pass through them without happening to hit anything vital. I have seen many an H21 limp back to base with as many as thirty hits. But on one operation, in the Ca Mau Peninsula at the southern tip of Viet Nam, I happened to be in an H21 that was brought down by just one small-caliber carbine bullet. The bullet entered the helicopter's side two feet from where I was sitting, near the rear door. It tore through a pressure line and four engine control cables.

The pilot reacted swiftly, saving my life and those of his three crewmates. All helicopters are equipped with clutches which can be disengaged, throwing the rotors into free-wheeling "autorotation." If the helicopter is traveling forward fast enough, the rotors will continue to whirl, keeping the aircraft up enough so that it can glide in for a landing. Obviously, forward speed is essential to this maneuver, and if a helicopter is not flying fast enough, the pilot must make it dive to get up speed. He cannot do this if he is too near the ground. For this reason, slow-speed flight at an altitude lower than about two hundred feet can be fatal in the event of engine failure.

Our pilot was just barely within the minimum specifications for crash-landing, and we settled into a thicket of brambles, machine guns from our doors blasting in all directions. It happened that the Viet Cong—in this case, perhaps just one lucky sniper—failed to follow up his advantage, and eventually another helicopter came to pull us out.

There is an evacuation drill that all helicopter crews must go through if they are downed in Viet Nam. Besides getting themselves out of their aircraft, they must remove all the guns—four mounted guns and at least two machine guns hand-held by the door gunners. They must also take as much of the ammunition as possible. If it looks as though the Viet

Cong is certain to capture the aircraft, it must be destroyed. The guerrillas love to capture guns and radios from downed helicopters.

The Viet Cong has never shown mercy to downed helicopter men, and has never taken one alive. In one downing, in mountains 250 miles north of Saigon, guerrillas moved in on the wreckage, where they found a wounded pilot strapped in his seat. Two other crew members were dead, and the fourth had escaped into the jungle without knowing there was another survivor. The wounded pilot was later found by rescue crews, shot through the head at point-blank range. The pilot, incidentally, was a colonel.

Communist North Viet Nam has issued a series of postage stamps in four colors, depicting the shooting down of helicopters by guerrillas.

Before regular American combat forces entered the war, helicopter crews suffered the lion's share of U.S. casualties. They continued to suffer heavy losses, even after helicopter warfare became highly developed.

The experts have tried to make them safer. In some models, armor plate has been installed around the pilots'

Piasecki H-21

seats and around important transmission and control lines. In most cases, helicopter companies have removed all but the pilot armor, because they don't like the extra weight and consequent loss of speed and power. But the whole crew wears flak vests, and gunners usually sit on extra flak vests or steel plates.

Frayed engine cables have been replaced and improved (usually after fatal accidental crashes), rotor cotter pins have been strengthened, and other safety measures adopted.

But helicopters have often flown on little more than sheer on-the-spot ingenuity. I once saw a helicopter crew, whose craft had been downed by a bullet through a pressure line, fashion a plug from a wood stake they found in the field, ram it into the hole, and take off again.

On another operation, an H21 had just unloaded its troops in an assault zone and was taking off when one of the two rear wheels hit a paddy dyke concealed under the water. The wheel broke off completely and the strut was rammed up into the fuselage, where it tore the main fuel tank. Viet Cong machine gunners were pouring fire at the helicopters, and an emergency landing was out of the question.

Under full power, the helicopter streaked for its base fifteen minutes away, a trail of high-octane gasoline gushing from its tail. The pilot signaled ahead for ground crews to quickly assemble sandbags into a cradle high enough for the H21 to land on without tipping over.

At the airstrip, the big H21 tried to settle down on the improvised cradle, only seconds of fuel remaining. A landing on flat ground would mean tipping over, and the rotors would break up, beating the helicopter to pieces and probably killing the crew. There were not enough sandbags, and the pilot had to think of something else fast. He spotted a water-filled ditch fifty yards away, picked up the helicopter, and slid it into the ditch at exactly the moment the engine quit. The crew got out without a scratch.

Others have not been so lucky. Helicopter crashes resulting purely from mechanical failures are common in Viet Nam, and have contributed heavily to the casualty rate.

Conditions for flying helicopters here are always terrible. For one thing, the war keeps them flying much longer hours than those for which they were designed, carrying staggering loads.

For another, it is usually hot in Viet Nam, and hot air lacks the density and lift of cooler air. This makes it harder for any flying machine to stay up, and engines must put out more power. The problem is more severe in the jungle-covered mountains of Central Viet Nam, where high altitudes make the air even thinner.

During Viet Nam's monsoon season, helicopters must fly in and out of rainstorms on most missions. Rain itself can be damaging to helicopter rotor blades, and they wear out often. The H21 had laminated wood rotors that were rapidly eroded by flailing against raindrops.

Viet Cong gunnery has improved markedly during the war, and with .50-caliber machine guns, the guerrillas can bring down helicopters easily, even when they are flying evasively at fairly high altitudes.

This philosophy behind the use of helicopters in Viet Nam is based on the idea of lightning assaults by large troop units in remote places.

In the early 1950s, when the U.S. Army began to experiment with helicopter tactics, the machines were used in much the same way landing craft are used against enemy beaches. Areas in which troops were landed by helicopter were called "airheads."

Vietnamese government troops and their American allies outnumber Viet Cong guerrillas, but despite the American escalation and continuing heavy Viet Cong casualties, the ratio continues to shift in favor of the enemy. This is partly the result of heavy local Viet Cong recruiting and partly of North Vietnamese infiltration. In any case, the allied superiority in numbers has never been even approximately sufficient. During the long British campaign in Malaya against communist guerrillas, the experts concluded that it takes ten or twelve regular soldiers to neutralize one enemy guerrilla.

At best, government forces in Viet Nam never have enjoyed an edge of more than six or seven to one over the guerrillas, and in certain key districts the guerrillas actually outnumber the troops.

To offset this disadvantage, Saigon and its American ally decided on helicopters. Troops cannot be moved rapidly on land because there is only one railroad line (which is sabotaged almost daily), very few roads (also constantly sabotaged) and relatively few canals that are not blocked, sabotaged, or ambushed by the Viet Cong. Even the job of clearing a road or canal is a major military operation, the fruits of which are generally undone wtihin a few days by the enemy.

So when helicopters began arriving in Viet Nam, they were put to work ferrying whole regiments into virgin territory.

Vietnamese commanders were delighted with the new toys. Generals like Huynh Van Cao, whose territory included the whole Mekong River Delta, spent days or weeks planning elaborate operations over huge areas. Plans always included huge sector maps with plastic overlays, grease pencils in at least six different colors, and teams of staff officers to post the position of blocking forces, artillery positions and so forth. Such maps always exactly showed the Viet Cong positions, too, with the estimated strength of the enemy in each place. They were nearly always wrong.

But the cumbersome planning was always the subject of much enthusiastic discussion. It was rare in those days that one could not go to any downtown Saigon bar and learn in detail the plans of an operation scheduled up to a week hence. The Viet Cong probably also patronized the bars.

Viet Cong intelligence in Saigon was demonstrated in late December 1961 just after the USNS Core had brought the first load of helicopters to Saigon. Within a few days, Radio Hanoi broadcast not only the numbers and types of aircraft that had been brought in, but their serial numbers as well.

For about a year and a half, the helicopters were used only for massive and usually unsuccessful raids. Troops brought into assault areas would move forward, rendezvous with other units, occupy hamlets, and do all the things called for on the master plan. Occasionally, by accident, government units stumbled into enemy units, and there were sometimes bloody clashes.

But usually, mopping up an area merely meant marching through it, picking up some suspects and raiding the henhouses, and then waiting for the helicopters to take the troops back to headquarters.

The master planners used to contend that these huge helicopter operations kept the Viet Cong off balance, frightened, constantly on the move, and tired. But the Army's tough Colonel "Coalbin Willie" Wilson, a senior U.S. advisor to Vietnamese forces, contemptuously described these operations as "rattle-assing around the country." He felt they did nothing to upset the enemy seriously, but merely exhausted friendly troops, helicopter crews and facilities.

Colonel Wilson, a tough disciplinarian, is said to have won the sobriquet "Coalbin Willie" in an incident while he was commanding a training unit in the United States. As punishment for a GI who got out of line, Colonel Wilson is said to have ordered the soldier to unload the coal from a coalbin, whitewash the coalbin, and then replace the coal. As all Army veterans know, this kind of punishment is common in stateside garrisons.

Coalbin Willie had a tendency even in Viet Nam to dress down his junior officers with too many outsiders present. Despite the unfavorable impression this made on many persons, I could not help but agree with his assessment of huge helicopter assaults. Colonel Wilson has since retired, by the way.

U.S. helicopter companies and American Army advisors generally had very little hand in the planning of these operations. The Vietnamese commanders looked on the pilots as little more than bus drivers. The only lever Americans could bring on the Vietnamese was a negative one—threatening to recommend removal of helicopters from a command to some other sector where they could be more effectively used.

But fairly early in the game, the two U.S. Marine helicopter squadrons which at the time were stationed in the delta began evolving a new helicopter tactic they called "eagle flights."

Eagle flights rarely comprised more than five helicopters loaded with tough troops, often Vietnamese rangers or marines. They were not given specific objectives, but were told general areas where intelligence indicated Viet Cong strong points.

The eagle flights would cruise around looking for trouble. Vietnamese observers went along to spot enemy guerrillas, and the helicopters (powerful H34s) flew at altitudes inviting enemy ground fire. The first sign of enemy resistance would be met by an assault on the spot.

Eagle flights produced some results. Helicopters were often hit, but troops got into bloody fights with the enemy much more frequently than in the big, planned operations. Often, the eagle troops racked up excellent successes against

H-34

enemy units, and brought back weapons and severed heads as trophies.

Some Vietnamese commanders objected strenuously, on grounds that the eagle flights were too dangerous and were piling up too many friendly casualties. It was reliably reported that Ngo Dinh Diem himself was unhappy with them.

After Diem's overthrow and death on November 2, 1963, the war in general almost stopped. Helicopter companies found themselves without missions day after day. Vietnamese commanders were shifted around or ousted, new tactics were discussed, confusion and apathy rose, and the Viet Cong politico-military war machine moved steadily ahead.

But emerging from the chaos was at least a government ready to work closely with American advisors, both in Saigon and in the field. As the war effort painfully got back into gear, the new emphasis was on small, fast-moving operations, leaving the big units on a semipermanent basis in the areas designated for "pacification."

Changes in helicopter tactics evolved. For one thing, all Army units in Viet Nam were equipped with Hueys by mid-1964, and Hueys are not mere flying trucks but have some of the characteristics of fighter planes as well.

The biggest innovation in helicopter warfare, however, was the introduction into Viet Nam of an entire helicopter-borne infantry division. This was the U.S. Army's 1st Cavalry Division (Air Mobile), which began moving into its permanent base near An Khe in the central highlands in late 1965.

The division still was called the "First Cav," and its men still wore the huge yellow and black horsehead shoulder patch used as the unit's emblem since frontier days a century ago. But the horsehead was all that remained of the unit's historic tradition. This was an entirely new concept in warfare, built around the helicopter.

Unlike conventional infantry divisions, the First Cav was issued very few trucks or other heavy equipment. Mobility was to depend on helicopters, not roads. The entire division could be lifted in its own huge fleet of helicopters, most of them Hueys. The division also had ample Chinooks to carry light artillery and supplies into battle.

Operations by the First Cav were generally massive, especially in the early days when both its officers and its troops were green.

Typically, eight-engine B-52 bombers flown by the Strategic Air Command from Guam or Thailand would roar over an objective and plaster it with bombs. Then the First Cav would blacken the sky with its helicopters, and drop into the zone where the B-52s had just finished. The whole thing was very noisy and impressive.

But the results were often extremely meager. I had the impression many times that the Big American helicopter operations of 1965, 1966 and 1967 were merely replays of the old Vietnamese "rattle-assing around," from which we had apparently learned nothing. Instead of concentrating on small, quickly executed "eagle" operations, our operations became larger and more ponderous.

The arguments favoring helicopter warfare are obvious. Helicopters provide unprecedented mobility, and do, in fact, help even the odds against fast-moving guerrillas.

But helicopters have a negative aspect often overlooked. In a way, they make war too easy. In common with airpower, they create a military reliance, both real and psychological, on gadgets. The unit that has helicopters is not likely to conduct operations on foot that may involve weeks of slogging through jungles. It prefers to get to the ultimate objective in ten minutes.

Viet Nam is not a war of objectives. A road or a hill or a ridge line or a town can be seized or lost with little or no effect on the ultimate outcome of things.

It is a war with no front or rear, and it flickers like heat lightning over an otherwise peaceful countryside. Most of all, it is a war for people, not real estate.

And under the circumstances, the trip to an objective is generally much more important than the objective itself. It is useful that, for instance, the First Cav is able to keep the strategic road from Qui Nhon, on the sea, to Pleiku, in the mountains, open for supply convoys.

But the Viet Cong is generally not to be found along this road. The Viet Cong *is* to be found by small infantry outfits filtering for weeks or even months through the vast rain forests and mountains of the region.

Unfortunately for its cause, America much prefers air war to jungle war.

"After all," a U.S. Army infantry adviser told me once, "the Viet Cong have no helicopters or airplanes. They didn't have any during the Indochina War either, but they still won. Helicopters are a partial substitute for infantry discipline, dedication and energy. They are useful in emergencies, but they are no substitute for first-class infantrymen willing to fight.

"After all, when you come to think of it, the use of helicopters is a tacit admission that we don't control the ground. And in the long run, it's control of the ground that wins or loses wars."

Of course, helicopters are used for many things besides carrying troops into assaults. One of their more important functions is ferrying Vietnamese provincial officials out to hamlets and district capitals to collect taxes, count noses and administer. In many areas, the only link between isolated islands of government control and the central government is the helicopter.

Helicopters are used constantly to bring ammunition, supplies and even food to beleaguered outposts. It has been effectively argued that there should be no isolated outposts in the first place, since they are too easy for the Viet Cong to overrun and sack for weapons. But the outposts still exist, and probably will continue to do so.

A detachment of helicopter ambulances (known by the code word "dustoff") also flies almost continuous missions, often under extremely hazardous conditions. At least one flight surgeon with the unit has been nominated for the Silver Star for his gallantry in picking up and treating wounded troops under heavy fire at night.

Night helicopter operations have become routine and are primarily directed against Viet Cong onslaughts against outposts. The helicopters are guided to the outposts by "Paris Control," a radar navigation network operated from Saigon. Over the targets, post defenders mark the enemy with flares, lighted signals and their own tracer fire. Sometimes helicopter pilots can see the enemy's muzzle blasts. It is always a dangerous kind of mission, because the enemy is always very close to friendly troops.

Helicopter crews and the mechanics who keep the machines flying generally get home to soft beds, good meals and a beer or two at the local service club every night. But they lead lives that could scarcely be envied by infantrymen.

Casualty rates are very high, and crews must keep flying day after day on increasingly dangerous missions. Those who live at Saigon airport sleep in shacks little better than Quonset huts, sweltering hot at night. They have good field messes, a PX, several service clubs, and get to see movies every night. But they rarely have time or energy to get downtown to Saigon.

At other helicopter bases, conditions are even less attractive. At Soc Trang in the Mekong River Delta, the monsoon season invariably inundates everything but the airstrip and hangars themselves, and the town of Soc Trang is usually off-limits to American servicemen. Up the coast in Central Viet Nam, the city of Da Nang has a good ocean beach and the most attractive night life outside Saigon. But there, again, helicopter crewmen are normally restricted to their base because of the pressure of their work. Very few of them are ever sorry to leave Viet Nam.

Pilots of the helicopters seem to keep getting younger each year, as the schools at Fort Rucker and other helicopter centers in the States churn out replacements for Viet Nam. There are eighteen- and nineteen-year-old warrant officers flying here at this writing, some of them already sporting the handle-bar mustaches that are almost traditional with helicopter men.

The critical shortage of trained commercial airline pilots in the United States has proved a boon to veterans who flew choppers in Viet Nam. Many American lines are hiring former GI helicopter pilots for training on Boeing 707s.

Helicopter traditions and even unit historians have begun to flourish. I once wrote a feature story on the 57th Helicopter Company, one of the first two companies to arrive in Viet Nam, in which I referred to the unit's men as "the deans of helicopter warfare." The name stuck, and men of the 57th and its successor company, the 120th, now wear the word "deans" on their uniforms. Among them are veterans of several wars, and beardless privates. There are outspoken publicity hunters, and there are modest, quiet men who just work. There are helicopter men who earned the title "soldier of the month" in army competitions, and there are helicopter men continually in trouble with the MPs.

But as a subjective judgment, it seems to me that the American helicopter men in Viet Nam are as efficient, hardworking, dedicated and courageous a group of U.S servicemen as I have ever run across. Like all Americans, some of them are brilliant, some of them are stupid, and most are somewhere in between. Their missions are often frustrating and unsuccessful, and when they are shot up day after day by enemy forces, their morale is sometimes low.

Many helicopter men, in common with Americans in Viet Nam in general, are puzzled and worried about the political implications of this strange war.

It strikes me as a testament to American fighting efficiency that helicopter men go on doing as good a job as ever in the face of potential sudden death, despite all the uncertainties. They are good soldiers.

6

FEBRUARY 7, 1965, AND ESCALATION

Wars generally begin at specific times and places, which is a convenience for the writers of history books.

World War I began, for example, at a few minutes past noon on June 28, 1914, when a student shot and killed Austria-Hungary's Archduke Francis Ferdinand and his wife in the town of Sarajevo.

World War II began at 4:45 A.M., September 1, 1939, when the German army rolled across the frontier into Poland.

For America, that war began at 6 A.M., December 7, 1941, when Japanese carrier pilots roared away from Admiral Nagumo's fleet toward Pearl Harbor.

At about 6 A.M., June 25, 1950, a North Korean army under the command of Marshal Choe Yong Gun crossed the 38th Parallel into the South, beginning the Korean War.

The beginning of the war in Viet Nam is not so easy to pin down. But from America's standpoint, I think the war must be dated from 2 A.M., February 7, 1965, at the windswept prairie town of Pleiku in South Viet Nam's central highlands. It was here that the spark occurred that changed the whole scope and scale of the war.

Perhaps history books will skim over that date, as, in fact, most Americans did at the time.

Normally, the second day of a war is a time of fiery speeches, expectancy and excitement.

But on February 8, 1965, the day after America joined the Viet Nam war as a belligerent, President Johnson called for a program to beautify the nation's cities, and he created the White House Conference on Natural Beauty. There was no "day of infamy" speech, no call to the Congress, no martial music on the radio.

The President, of course, was aware of the significance

and danger of the events of the preceding day. But it is a characteristic of the Viet Nam War that America's leaders attempt to make it seem as peaceful as possible, except when asking for higher draft calls or more taxes.*

At any rate, the United States did not declare war on North Viet Nam or the Viet Cong, even as late as the close of 1967. President Johnson and his cabinet said repeatedly that the overthrow of North Viet Nam's leaders was not an object of the fighting, and that the United States did not wish to fight on North Vietnamese soil.

On the enemy side there was no declaration of war either. But in July 1966, Hanoi's ambassador to East Germany, Bui Lam, said in an interview that his nation was at war with the United States. That at least made Viet Nam a war of record.

Aside from quibbling over the proper definition of war, big changes really did occur after February 7, 1965.

A day before, on February 6, America had 23,500 servicemen in Viet Nam, none of whom technically was a combatant. They were there as advisors, pilots and support troops who could shoot at the other side only if shot at or directly menaced. In fact, there were many ambiguities in those days as to exactly when a U.S. serviceman could get into a firefight.

---

*Mr. Johnson faced most of his escalation decisions alone. One of his favorite party anecdotes was the famous "little monk" story, which involved his younger daughter, Luci (Mrs. Patrick Nugent).

On the night of June 29, 1966, Luci is said to have found her father looking tired and worried, having just ordered out planes to bomb close to the hearts of Hanoi and Haiphong. The big worry was that by accidentally bombing Russian ships docked at Haiphong, the raid might provoke the USSR into a direct confrontation with the United States, which could quickly lead to a nuclear war.

Luci is supposed to have said: "Whenever I feel blue or worried I visit my little monks." She had converted to Roman Catholicism in 1965, so as to be of the same faith as Mr. Nugent.

She then suggested that the President join her in a midnight visit to St. Dominic's Roman Catholic Church in southwest Washington, and Mr. Johnson agreed. Later, after the President and his daughter returned from their prayers, he was informed that all but one of the American planes had returned from the raids, and World War III had not begun. When the President told this to Luci the following morning, she is said to have replied:

"I'm not surprised, because my little monks usually come through."

There is at least one Vietnamese who considers this anecdote in the same class as the one about Marie Antoinette's suggestion that the starving masses eat cake.

But from February 7 onward, Americans could start firefights on their own, hunt for the enemy, and act as if Viet Nam were an American war, which, of course, it was.

American combat pilots dropped the pretense that they were flying only as advisors, and began bombing and strafing openly.

American combat units poured in for the first time, and by the end of 1965 there were 181,000 servicemen in South Viet Nam alone, not to mention the 7th Fleet fighting offshore, or the Air Force units supporting operations from Thailand, the Philippines, and so on. By the end of 1967, there were close to half a million Americans in Viet Nam.

Perhaps most significant, U.S. aircraft began systematic daily bombing of North Viet Nam that never let up except for brief lulls. The officially announced reason for this bombing was the need to destroy North Vietnamese supply lines to the Viet Cong in the South. In fact, the bombing went far beyond this limited objective, which, indeed, was never achieved to any important degree.

In short, America moved rapidly toward a major war that could at any time explode into World War III.

American casualties rose rapidly, too. During America's four years advising and transporting Vietnamese forces, it had lost fewer than 250 men killed. But in 1965 and the following years, casualties soared into the many thousands of killed.

I was at Pleiku on February 7, 1965, and will describe here what I saw and heard. While this is not a history book, so much nonsense has been written about Pleiku since then, I feel an obligation to record my observations.

Obviously, no war is ever started by one trivial incident. There is always a background of hostility that builds to the point of war, requiring only one crisis to start things going. So it was in Viet Nam. This was how things stood at the time:

South Viet Nam never enjoyed much real political stability at any time after its founding as a nation in 1954. President Ngo Dinh Diem had managed to suppress many of the organizations seeking to bring him down, but the suppression never was wholly successful. In 1959, open armed rebellion began again, this time under the Viet Cong flag, but with the assistance of many of the groups (for instance, the Cao Dai, the Hoa Hao and various political parties) that Diem supposedly had crushed.

In 1963, the leaders of South Viet Nam's Buddhist faith also revolted against Diem, and the flames of insurrection eventually spread through the armed forces. On November 1, 1963, Diem was overthrown, and on the following day, insurgent officers murdered the President and his powerful and sinister brother, Ngo Dinh Nhu.

The nation was free of the Diem dictatorship, but in political turmoil. Technically, the nation was ruled by a mixed civilian-military government, but in fact there was no government at all. Needless to say, the war against the Viet Cong was all but forgotten in the uproar.

After three months of chaos, Major General Nguyen Khanh staged a swift, bloodless coup and established a military directorate for the nation of which he was boss.

But even the military was unable to keep things going. Khanh, a South Vietnamese, was immediately opposed by the powerful North Vietnamese refugee groups, which included many of the top military officers. Among them was the commander of the Air Force, Air Commodore Nguyen Cao Ky, who later became premier himself.

Khanh was opposed by Catholics, since he was a Buddhist. But he also was opposed by Buddhists, because he had not granted power enough to Buddhist leaders to please them. Khanh was cordially disliked by many Americans (especially Ambassador Maxwell D. Taylor) partly because of his blunt South Vietnamese way of expressing things* and partly because of the devious tricks he often used to maintain power.

In common with all the military governments that followed the fall of Diem, Khanh's was under heavy American pressure to hand power to a civilian democracy. On August 29, Khanh briefly (for five days) ceded power to civilian Nguyen Xuan Oanh, but did so only to halt bloody street rioting in Saigon. When the rioting stopped, Khanh stepped back into his offfice.

On September 22, a general strike paralyzed Saigon.

On October 26, Khanh, under pressure, agreed to the appointment of Phan Khac Suu, a civilian, as chief of state.

---

*Khanh, whose friend and occasional confidant I became, frequently was infuriated by Taylor. He told me once: "When [Ambassador Henry Cabot] Lodge quit, I asked Washington to send me another Lodge. Instead, they sent me this 'uncertain trumpet.'" (Taylor is the author of *The Uncertain Trumpet*, a book attacking the "massive retaliation" strategy of the Eisenhower administration.)

But the political storms continued to drain the war effort. On October 30, one year after Diem's death, Ambassador Taylor said: "There has been deterioration and loss of momentum in the recent weeks and months."

On November 4, a South Vietnamese civilian, Tran Van Huong, was installed as Prime Minister and promised the nation a tough crackdown on corruption, general belt-tightening and all-out war against the Viet Cong. (On the same day, incidentally, Johnson was elected to his first full term as President.)

But Khanh had no intention of ceding any real power to either Suu or Huong, and he let it be known that anti-Huong rioting by North Vietnamese refugees and Catholic extremists would be tolerated.

On November 25, more than 100 were injured in street battles in Saigon as government forces stood by doing nothing. On December 18, Khanh named a new ruling junta of officers, and on December 20, he carried out a purge of the civilians, leaving Prime Minister Huong in office but with less authority than ever.

On January 20, 1965, Huong was forced to back down again in the face of more rioting encouraged by Khanh. Huong reshuffled his cabinet in favor of North Vietnamese and Catholics.

Two days later, a large group of Buddhist monks staged a noisy anti-American demonstration in front of the U.S. Embassy in Saigon, and the following day in Hue, 400 miles to the north, Buddhist rioters sacked and burned the U.S. Information Service library.

On January 27, Khanh fired Huong as Prime Minister, which marked Khanh's final break with Ambassador Taylor and Washington.

Perhaps to assert his authority, Khanh had the first fully public firing-squad execution carried out in Saigon's central market, in front of the National Railways Building. On January 29, Viet Cong terrorist Le Van Khuyen was shot, but a largely apathetic public paid little attention to the gruesome spectacle.

On February 6, the day before America entered the war, South Viet Nam was coming apart at the seams politically. Its freshly ousted Prime Minister, Mr. Huong, had sought refuge at the British Embassy, where he was granted protection.

Riots were ripping the nation, and the overwhelming political strength of the Viet Cong was apparent everywhere.

The war was going disastrously. On December 19, 1964, the Chairman of the Viet Cong's Central Committee, Nguyen Huu Tho, had delivered a radio address, claiming that three quarters of South Viet Nam's land area was under Viet Cong control, as well as more than half of the people. This claim seemed approximately correct.

Roads, railroads and canals throughout the country were controlled by the Viet Cong. Terrorism was reaching even into supposedly secure areas. On Christmas Eve, 1964, two Viet Cong agents disguised as Saigon army officers blew up one wing of the Brink Hotel, a U.S. officers' billet in downtown Saigon.

On December 28, Viet Cong forces sucked government troops into the battle of Binh Gia, which was by far the costliest fight of the war up to that date. Partly as the result of government corruption, three of Saigon's best battalions were mauled in this action. Total friendly casualties were about 500, including about 300 killed or missing. Five Americans were killed.

Shortly after New Year's Day, 1965, the Viet Cong launched offensives nearly everywhere.

On January 29, 107 government troops were wiped out in a valley in Binh Dinh Province, for example.

At the time, there seemed a real possiblity that the Viet Cong could win a quick military victory, rosy official Washington statements notwithstanding.

In the face of all this, American air and naval activity in the Indochina area had been quietly but drastically picking up for some months.

Following a Viet Cong mortar attack on Bien Hoa Air Base fifteen miles from Saigon on November 1, 1964, U.S. forces began strengthening defenses at all camps and bases. The Bien Hoa barrage had resulted in twenty-seven aircraft damaged or destroyed, and American casualties were four killed and seventy-two wounded.

Around December 15, the first contingent of U.S. Air Force F105 Thunderchief fighter-bombers arrived in Viet Nam and Thailand, and bombing of jungle infiltration routes in Laos was started. Bombers from the 7th Fleet also began flying missions over Laos.

All this was secret at the time, of course. American military action in Laos never was officially confirmed for the first two years it was going on, since the United States had signed the 1962 Geneva Accords by which Laos was neutralized.

Another open secret was the fact that the United States was flying combat missions from Thailand. The Thai government would be embarrassed by an open admission that its territory was being used by U.S. combatants, Washington officials told reporters.

On January 13, 1965, two U.S. Air Force combat planes—an F100 and an F105—were downed over Laos. There was no official comment.

On January 15, the Air Force finally confirmed that F105s were flying missions from Da Nang in South Viet Nam. A week later, Vietnamese Air Force planes carried out the heaviest raid on their own country to date, dropping 353 tons of bombs on Boi Loi Forest near Saigon, trying to destroy Viet Cong bases. Results were very meager.

The stage for really big escalation was set by the two Gulf of Tonkin incidents, which have been regarded by some as trial balloons by the Johnson administration to test American and international public opinion on the subject of war with North Viet Nam.

On August 2, 1964, the destroyer *Maddox*, cruising off the coast of North Viet Nam in the Gulf of Tonkin, said it was

Convair F-102 "Delta Dagger"

attacked about thirty miles from land by three PT boats. The destroyer captain said he opened fire, sinking one PT boat and damaging two others.

On August 5, the *Maddox* and another U.S. Navy destroyer, the *C. Turner Joy*, reported a new attack by North Vietnamese PT boats sixty-five miles off the coast. This time, 7th Fleet planes sank two of the boats.

But the 7th Fleet took another giant step later in the day, on orders from President Johnson. Planes from its carriers made the first raid of the war against North Vietnamese territory.

The 7th Fleet claimed its planes destroyed twenty-five PT boats at their bases as well as major facilities at the bases themselves, including an oil depot at Vinh, a provincial capital in North Viet Nam. Two Navy planes were lost in the raid as the result of heavy North Vietnamese ground fire.

On the night of August 5, the United States tried to sneak some jet bombers into South Viet Nam without the outside world finding out about it. One reason for the secrecy was that such a build-up was a clear violation of the 1954 Geneva Accords on Viet Nam.

Thirty U.S. Air Force B-57 light bombers took off from the Philippines for Viet Nam, but in the darkness and confusion, four of them crashed or were damaged on landing at Bien Hoa. The disasters immediately called attention to the new arrivals.

A contingent of Air Force F102 Delta Dagger jet interceptors also arrived in Viet Nam on August 5 to provide security for Saigon against air attack in case North Viet Nam felt like retaliating for the raid on its bases. Hanoi's air force was known to have a half dozen IL-28 light jet bombers capable of reaching Saigon.

But nothing happened. On August 13, the "crisis" was declared over.

The next incident, which still is cloaked in mystery, occurred September 18, when the destroyers *Richard F. Edwards* and *Morton* reported having been "menaced" by four unidentified vessels in the Gulf of Tonkin. The destroyers opened fire and reported sinking at least one "vessel," although the whole incident might have involved nothing more menacing than an aberration on a radarscope.

The stage was set on an international scale, in a way

reminiscent of the Spanish Civil War, in which Germany and Russia fought each other by proxy.

On February 6, Aleksei N. Kosygin, the Soviet premier, arrived in Hanoi for a four-day good-will visit to North Viet Nam. He undoubtedly talked with Hanoi's leaders about their military needs, including missile defenses.

Also on February 6, McGeorge Bundy arrived in Saigon at the head of a special fact-finding mission sent to South Viet Nam by President Johnson. Bundy, who served both Presidents Kennedy and Johnson as coordinator of national security functions, had enormous power. Both the State Department and the CIA were under his influence. On arriving in Saigon he warned that "foreigners must stop their aggression against South Viet Nam."

February 6 was the last day of the truce that always goes into effect in Viet Nam during the lunar New Year holidays. Without any meetings or documents, fighting on both sides just stops.

The ceasefire ended at midnight, and four hours later I was awakened by the jangling of the phone in my Saigon apartment. It seemed that radio messages were arriving from Pleiku 250 miles to the north, where a full-scale Viet Cong attack was in progress.

I made ready to fly to Pleiku on a military transport, while trying to piece together what details I could in Saigon.

I learned later that the Viet Cong had destroyed a large fuel depot by mortar fire at Tuy Hoa on the central coast on February 6, and early in the morning of February 7 simultaneously attacked Pleiku, the air base at Soc Trang in the Mekong River Delta, and an outpost at Viet An about 400 miles north of Saigon.

The Soc Trang shelling was minor, but the Viet An attack cost Vietnamese government forces thirty-nine killed, thirty-nine wounded (including five Americans) and twenty-six captured by the enemy. The Viet Cong also destroyed two 105-millimeter howitzers at the post, and captured two mortars and a recoilless cannon.

But Pleiku was the worst. In commando attacks about two miles apart, the Viet Cong destroyed part of a U.S. Army officers' billet and smashed the U.S. air base called Camp Hollaway.

I arrived at Pleiku at about dawn, as a red sun was

sending its first streaks of light across the desolate landscape. Pleiku is on a barren highlands plateau, and the vast, open prairies of the region somehow suggest Wyoming. There are scarcely any trees, and few thing grow well in the leached red earth. Native tribesmen try to enrich the terrible soil by burning off its grass and brush each year, but the technique doesn't work very well.

One can see for miles in all directions in the Pleiku region, and it would be hard for a large body of men to move around undetected. From the air base, visibility is unobstructed by vegetation.

As our plane touched down, fires were still blazing and smoke was rising all over the field. The remains of shattered aircraft were everywhere. Incidentally, when a Huey helicopter burns, it all burns, except for the steel rotor blades and engine turbine. The rest, being light metal, burns up like flash powder.

Few of the one-story shacks around the field were untouched, and many were spattered with fresh blood and in ruins. Most of the dead had been gathered up, but there still were many casualties everywhere.

Among the Americans helping with the casualties was Bill Mauldin, creator of the great "Willie and Joe" GI cartoons of World War II. Mauldin happned to be at the base at the time of the attack, partly to make cartoon sketches but mainly to visit his son, Warrant Officer Bruce Mauldin, a helicopter pilot stationed there. Neither father nor son was wounded in the attack.

At 2 A.M., a concentrated barrage of mortar shells began falling on the tents and shacks in which hundreds of Americans were sleeping.

Simultaneously, firing broke out on the airstrip and around the barbed wire perimeter of the field. Parked aircraft began blowing up.

At almost exactly the same time* a series of heavy explosions rocked the stucco villa where U.S. Army advisors were living, about two miles from the air base. The rattle of machine-gun fire followed.

*One of the U.S. Army think tanks made a statistical analysis of Viet Cong night attacks on bases and posts. It was discovered that 2 A.M. is the most probable time for these attacks to begin. Unfortunately, this information doesn't seem to have reduced night attacks much.

Two armed helicopters took off seven minutes after the firing began and pumped machine-gun fire and rockets into suspected Viet Cong positions around the base. There is no evidence that they hit anything.

In the darkness and confusion, wounded and screaming GIs were running around, banging into each other. Bill Mauldin at first sought to calm some of the wounded GIs and later helped teams of medics.

It was many hours after the attack ended that stock could be taken.

Many buildings had been destroyed, including part of the advisors' villa. One of the Americans killed was a sentry at that villa who spotted the Viet Cong moving in and gave warning by opening fire on them. He was killed in the blast of one of their pole charges.

Eight Americans were killed and 126 were wounded. Nine helicopters and one two-engine transport plane were destroyed and eight other aircraft were damaged.

It was a remarkable feat for the Viet Cong. The commando squad that carried out the raid probably numbered only a few dozen men, and it is probable that they got off without suffering a single casualty.

Considering the magnitude of the train of events they started, it's perhaps unfortunate that history probably will never record the names of those Viet Cong raiders.

At least three groups of Viet Cong were involved.

One small group attacked the officers' villa with pole charges and submachine guns. The Vietnamese outposts supposedly guarding the Pleiku area were only at half-strength, since many soldiers had not yet returned from lunar New Year's passes. The few Vietnamese sentries in the vicinity heard nothing.

The pole charges killed the American sentry and smashed several walls. Several mortar shells crashed through the roof.

The air base was attacked by two groups. One had carried six American-made 81-millimeter mortars into a hamlet 1,000 yards outside the barbed wire ringing the post. The residents of that hamlet never gave the slightest hint to Saigon or American forces about the Viet Cong mortars being moved in.

One of the Americans at Pleiku that gruesome morning was Colonel Theodore Metaxis, a senior U.S. Army advisor to

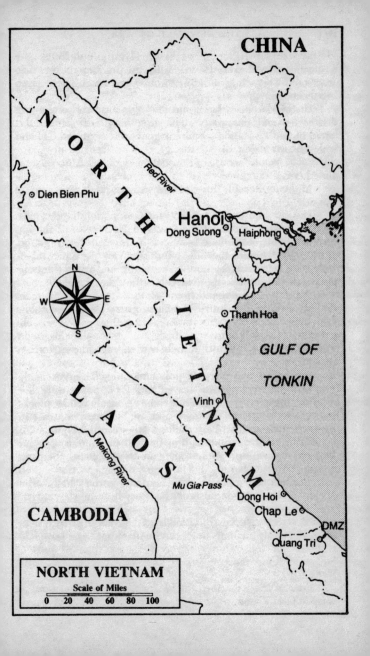

Vietnamese forces and a veteran of many upheavals and battles. Colonel Metaxis was with the military forces that attacked on horseback in 1937 to put down rioting strikers in San Francisco.

He said the Viet Cong mortar crews probably smuggled their guns and the many shells used in the attack on the backs of half-naked mountain tribesmen. The guns and shells had probably been disguised to look like firewood or something that would arouse no suspicion. Colonel Metaxis surmised the smuggling operation had probably been going on for some considerable time before the attack—days, or even weeks.

The six mortars were set up *inside* the huts of the hamlet, since the hamlet itself was in clear view of the air base. Imprints of the base plates of these mortars were found in the mud floors of the huts later. The Viet Cong had taken their time setting everything up carefully, and when the time came for the attack, they merely lifted the thatched roofs from the huts and opened fire.

Afterwards, the entire Viet Cong group got away without casualties and with its mortars.

The second group was made up of commandos, who entered the base by cutting their way through the surrounding barbed wire.*

The squad was carrying pole and satchel charges made from bamboo sticks, palm leaves and TNT. Some were left behind, unexploded. The TNT came in small yellow blocks that looked like cakes of soap, and might have been cast in the jungle from dud artillery shells or other captured ordnance.

Firing their weapons as they moved, the commandos put their charges on one aircraft after another, blowing them up in order. These charges did far more damage to the parked aircraft than the more or less random mortar shells. The mortar shells caused most of the casualties in the billets, however.

The highly successful Pleiku raid became a pattern of other Viet Cong air base attacks. A similar attack was launched

---

*Great numbers of wire cutters and other simple tools are used by the Viet Cong. Some 20,000 wire cutters were confiscated from one Viet Cong sampan alone, being floated down the Bassac River from Cambodia. Such tools often are of communist Chinese origin.

at the Marble Mountain facility near Da Nang some months later, with the assistance of a small boy who had worked for the Americans but actually was a Viet Cong spy.

It has been written that Pleiku was the work of large North Vietnamese regular army units equipped with "highly sophisticated weapons infiltrated from the North." The enemy squad might have been made up of North Vietnamese (although I doubt it, in this case; Southerners are much better guerrillas than Northerners).

But Pleiku was scarcely the work of "sophisticated weapons."

Pleiku resulted from the rock-bottom morale of the Vietnamese forces supposed to be protecting the base, American laxity, the political skill of the Viet Cong in getting the local population to help them, and the sheer guts of the guerrillas themselves.

Pleiku base officers quickly put together blackboard displays and charts with which to brief the high-level team expected.

As I recall it, General Khanh, the Vietnamese premier, was the first to arrive, aboard his converted C-47.

The next arrival was a U.S. Air Force two-engine C-123 transport which had originally been sent as a present by General Curtis LeMay to his friend General Paul D. Harkins, former commander of U.S. forces in Viet Nam. I had flown with General Harkins in this plane several times, and had been impressed with its inner luxury. The plane, called the *White Whale*, had a comfortable command post, a compartment for staff officers, and even a galley staffed by an airman who was reputed to be a good cook.

The *White Whale* brought General William C. Westmoreland (Harkins's successor as commander of U.S. forces), Ambassador Taylor, McGeorge Bundy and some others.

General Westmoreland remarked to General Khanh, "This is bad. Very bad."

The American high command was angry that the Vietnamese forces had failed to protect the base.

Bundy was wearing a white shirt, open at the collar, and slacks. The strong wind blew his sandy hair over his face as he grimly strode through the debris and listened to briefings. Army officers nervously warned him away from the hundreds of unexploded bombs, shells and rockets lying everywhere, marked off by white engineer tape and awaiting demolition squads.

Back in the United States it was the evening of February 6. At about the time the official party was examining the rubble of Pleiku, President Johnson was making the final decision to enter America into the war. He is said to have made the decision some time between 7:45 and 9 P.M. (EST) on Saturday evening, February 6.

The word from President Johnson traveled fast.

At about noon, General Westmoreland asked the entire official party to step into the parked *White Whale* so as to get away from prying ears. During the twenty-minute conference, the various Vietnamese and American officials were informed about the decision.

I didn't know what the conference was about, of course, but I remember that General Khanh looked rather pleased as he stepped down from the *White Whale*.

For months, Khanh and his top officers had been beating the drum for "Bac Tien" ("Forward to the North")—meaning, a land invasion of North Viet Nam. Most of South Viet Nam's military leaders, including all of Khanh's successors, have advocated war against both North Viet Nam and China as the only solution for South Viet Nam, even if it means World War III.

Khanh saw the Johnson decision as a new lease on the life of his regime.

At about 1 P.M., the steam catapults on the decks of 7th Fleet carriers hurled forty-nine planes into the air toward North Viet Nam. The attacking force swept in low to strafe, bomb and rocket barracks and other military installations near the provincial capital of Dong Hoi, some fifty miles north of the South Vietnamese frontier, and about 260 miles south of Hanoi. Several South Vietnamese Air Force planes also bombed targets in the North for the first time.

Visibility was poor, and results were indifferent.

One U.S. plane was shot down.

In comparison with what was to come in the months and years ahead, it wasn't much of a raid, but it was a start.

A few minutes after the last Navy plane slammed to a stop against the arrester cable on its carrier deck, the world was told. A White House statement said the U.S. air raid had been conducted "in response to provocations ordered and directed by the Hanoi regime."

Later in the day, Ambassador Taylor directed that the 1,800 dependent women and children of U.S. officials and officers in Viet Nam be evacuated, to "clear the decks." That brought an end to lush American villa life and smart cocktail parties in Saigon.

On the second day, February 8, a battery of U.S. Marine Corps Hawk missiles arrived at the strategic Da Nang Air Base, which was about to begin mounting heavy raids against the North. When the entire Marine unit arrived it consisted of seventy-two missiles and about five hundred officers and men. The Hawk can down aircraft flying from 60,000 feet high all the way down almost to treetop level.

On February 9, Air Commodore Ky, the future premier of South Viet Nam, personally led a strike by South Vietnamese propeller-driven A1H Skyraiders over the North. The formation encountered ground fire, and Ky's plane was hit, a bullet grazing his black flight suit. He returned to Saigon to receive an accolade from young female admirers.

But the initial raids did nothing to deter Viet Cong activity.

On February 10, Viet Cong assault squads attacked a U.S. Army enlisted men's hotel in the picturesque coastal town of Qui Nhon 280 miles northeast of Saigon. Several of the guerrillas shot their way into the lobby of the three-story concrete building and left suitcases filled with explosives on the floor.

The gigantic blast that followed leveled the building. After three days of digging and tunneling in the pile of masonry, rescue squads managed to get the survivors out. It was a heroic and desperate piece of work, and twenty-one wounded men were saved. But twenty-three other Americans died, and rescuers at one point had to watch rats gnawing on parts of the bodies that could not be reached immediately.

On the following day, American pilots, with fire in their eyes, returned to North Viet Nam. A force of 100 U.S. Navy planes was joined by twenty-eight U.S. Air Force planes and twenty-eight Vietnamese Air Force planes in attacks at Thanh Hoa, 160 miles north of the frontier, and at Chap Le, forty miles from the frontier. The attack on the Qui Nhon hotel was given by Washington as one of the reasons for the raid.

Three Navy planes were downed.

On February 24, U.S. Air Force jets began strikes in

South Viet Nam. Until then, all strikes were flown by Vietnamese planes, although Americans were at the controls more often than not.

On February 25, Khanh, ousted in a coup, left Viet Nam for exile abroad. By then, Ky had emerged as the dominant military figure, and soon afterward he became premier.

But the war still looked very discouraging. February was the bloodiest month of the war for Vietnamese ground forces fighting the Viet Cong. They suffered 4,140 casualties that month, including 870 killed and 1,450 missing. The Saigon government lost a staggering 2,590 weapons captured by the Viet Cong that month.

And on March 8, the first U.S. combat troops to arrive in Viet Nam piled ashore at "Red Beach II" near Da Nang. The initial force was 3,500 marines of the 9th Expeditionary Brigade, supported by their own tanks, artillery and helicopters. The leathernecks were assigned to defending the Da Nang base in depth—that is, going out to look for the enemy. Four days later they fought their first minor skirmish.

American troops arriving in Viet Nam, however good their training may have been, immediately ran into difficulties.

The first marine casualties were inflicted by other marines with jitters and tight trigger fingers. In the darkness, anything that moved was a suspected enemy, and there were tragic mistakes.

But a far more serious problem was heat prostration. With characteristic "gung ho," many green marine commanders pushed their green troops too far and too fast in those days. In one early operation, some fifty marines became casualties of the hostile sun, and required evacuation. The Viet Cong stayed out of the way, sizing up the new enemy quietly.

Water consumption was a big problem. American servicemen were not yet seasoned to tropical warfare, and most found it necessary to carry three canteens of water—a heavy load to drag around in combat. In time, a soldier gets used to the climate and can get by with one or two canteens on a normal day.

This problem continues, by the way, since very few U.S. servicemen stay in Viet Nam longer than one year. As replacements and new units arrive, the seasoning process must begin all over.

On March 22, a new kind of raid on North Viet Nam was started. It was called "armed route reconnaissance," and its object was to shoot up anything moving on roads, canals or anywhere else. The idea was to paralyze communications in the North—a new strategic objective, clearly no longer a mere retaliation for Viet Cong action in the South. Soon, raids included bridges, rail lines, ferries and power lines.

Three days later, communist China made the ominous announcement that it would "not stand in the face of U.S. aggression against North Viet Nam," but Peking did nothing.

On March 30 the Viet Cong carried out one of their most spectacular terror bombings. Agents drove a car loaded with explosive right up to the U.S. Embassy building, got out, and tried to escape on a waiting motor scooter. Police shot one Viet Cong and captured another. But the car exploded with a crash that knocked me out of a chair ten blocks away.

The heavy concrete walls of the five-story embassy were not damaged, but all the windows were blown in, and neighboring buildings were heavily damaged. Many cars were crushed.

In all, twenty-two were killed and 190 wounded, but miraculously, only two Americans were among the dead. One was a young secretary—the first American woman killed by Viet Cong terrorism.

Besides American troops that had begun to pour in, Korean troops (paid by the United States but officered entirely by Koreans) started arriving. By late 1967, there were about 45,000 Korean soldiers in South Viet Nam. Some 6,000 Australian troops also joined the fighting.

As the weeks wore on, Vietnamese government officers began reporting that North Vietnamese regular units were fighting as units in the South. The American command categorically denied this, saying that although North Vietnamese troops were fighting, they were doing so as replacements in South Vietnamese Viet Cong outfits.

On April 26, the Washington line changed radically. Intelligence officials announced that they were convinced the 2nd Battalion of the 101st Regiment of the 325th Division of the North Vietnamese Army was fighting in South Viet Nam.

Nine days after this American announcement, as if in response to the threat posed by the North Vietnamese unit, the first U.S. Army combat unit in Viet Nam—the 173rd Airborne Brigade—began unloading from transport planes at Bien Hoa and Vung Tau. The paratroopers fought their first skirmish May 27, suffering two wounded by snipers. Cursing GIs sweated in the sun, setting up tents, preparing field messes and digging in. They especially missed plumbing.

Interestingly, Washington has always announced upward revisions of its estimates of enemy strength just before escalating. These intelligence announcements seem carefully timed to coincide with responses.

For instance, on June 5, American officials let it be known that they believed enemy strength in South Viet Nam had risen by 25,000 men in the preceding four months. The new estimate of the enemy's order of battle was sixty-four battalions (one of which was the North Vietnamese unit mentioned above), totaling as many as 138,000 guerrillas.*

Four days later, 2,500 U.S. Army engineers landed at Cam Ranh Bay 190 miles up the coast from Saigon, to begin building the biggest port facility on the Indochina peninsula, complete with its own roads and airport.

It is interesting to note here that at least some of the escalation of 1965 and later years was for professional rather than purely military reasons.

Viet Nam had begun by June 1965 to look like a proper war, and any American military outfit worth its salt obviously should be in it, the reasoning went.

For example, friends of mine with high Air Force ranks have told me that officers of the Strategic Air Command were worried not to be getting any of the Viet Nam pie at first. Strikes in both North and South Viet Nam were the exclusive domain of tactical aircraft—F105s, F4s, A4s, and other ground support planes, mostly single-seaters. SAC wanted to get in with its eight-engine intercontinental B52 "Stratofortress" bombers, designed originally to carry atomic bombs from Colorado to Moscow.

---

*Estimates by Saigon and Washington always have been highly questionable. In 1961, for instance, Lieutenant General Lionel C. McGarr, then commander of the U.S. military mission in Viet Nam, told me he doubted that there were as many as 18,000 guerrillas in South Viet Nam. But in the following six months, Washington and Saigon estimated that very nearly 18,000 of the enemy had become casualties. Far from being wiped out, the Viet Cong at the end of 1962 was far stronger than at the beginning.

Republic F-105 "Thunderchief"

On June 18, 1965, the B52s flew their first raid over Viet Nam. They have been carpeting Viet Nam with bombs ever since.

Similarly, the Navy wanted capital ships in addition to carriers in on the war, if only for the sake of tradition.

On June 8, the cruiser U.S.S. *Canberra* shelled the coast of South Viet Nam with its eight-inch and five-inch guns—the first coastal shelling by a U.S. Navy cruiser since the Korean War. Shelling by cruisers and destroyers was escalated in both North and South Viet Nam, and plans were even made to take a battleship out of mothballs to add to the war.*

Ashore, a small U.S. Navy detachment had for several years advised Saigon's tiny navy, coastal patrol fleet and amphibious river forces. But when the American commander of this detachment was promoted from captain to rear admiral, it was obvious that he would have to have more Americans under his command, as befitted his new rank. He got them.

Vietnamese commanders were unhappy about letting the American combat units go to war right away. Most of Saigon's general staff at the time wanted to see American troops used to defend American bases and certain towns and installations, leaving the Vietnamese to do most of the fighting. American commanders, on the other hand, were eager to get their forces into the fray.

Any professional man wants to practice his profession, and for career officers, war is a profession.

Consequently, when General Cao Van Vien's troops got into desperate trouble in the battle of Dong Xoai July 10–14, Vien was under immediate and almost irresistible pressure from U.S. leaders to let American troops into the fight.

Dong Xoai is a hamlet in wooded, rolling terrain about sixty miles north of Saigon (a later chapter discusses an ambush sprung by the Viet Cong at this point early in the war). On July 10, the Viet Cong overran the town, and then waited for government forces, with the intention of grinding them to pieces.

Vien, a tough and courageous man, probably blundered at Dong Xoai by committing his troops too few at a time, in

---

*In 1967 North Vietnamese shore batteries began shooting back, and the first hits were scored on U.S. Navy destroyers and a cruiser, but with only light damage.

the face of powerful and entrenched enemy forces. In the end, he lost 600 of his men killed. A roughly equal number of Viet Cong were killed, and about 150 civilians were killed in the fighting, which made it the bloodiest up to that date.

Vien's 52nd Ranger Battalion finally retook Dong Xoai, but only after suffering terrible casualties. Two other Vietnamese battalions, the 7th Airborne and the 1st Battalion of the 7th Infantry regiment, were virtually wiped out in earlier fighting.

All the while, the U.S. Army's 173rd Airborne Brigade was standing by within close helicopter distance at Phuoc Vinh, its commanders pawing the ground with the smell of Dong Xoai in their nostrils.

I was with General Vien during part of the battle. An ardent nationalist, he wanted no part of the American forces, despite the beating he was taking.

"I'm a Vietnamese, and I would rather die a Vietnamese than live in debt to the Americans," he said. "I'm taking a terrible gamble, and if it fails, I'm finished. But would you do otherwise?"

Vien succeeded, both in dislodging the Viet Cong from the hamlet and keeping the Americans out. But America's absence from the big battles was about to end. In 1967, U.S. forces were fighting even in the Mekong Delta, an area from which Vietnamese commanders had long tried to exclude them.

On June 28, forces of three nations teamed up for the first international operation of the war. Some 4,000 troops, consisting of two U.S. Army airborne battalions, one Australian battalion and two Vietnamese battalions, roared into the jungle thirty miles north of Saigon for a three-day sweep.

American and Australian officers, sure they would find a major battle, went into the fight eagerly. The more seasoned Vietnamese commanders took the operation with a grain of salt. At the end of the sweep the total result was one Viet Cong guerrilla killed.

On July 1, a small Viet Cong assault squad goaded U.S. forces once again by sneaking into the Da Nang base, despite all the Hawk missiles, tanks and marines guarding it.

The score or so of guerrillas managed to destroy three planes and damage three others, killing one American. Later that day, the U.S. Marine Corps landed an emergency force of 900 more leathernecks to meet the threat. And one week later, 8,000 more marines began coming ashore at Da Nang and Qui Nhon. The escalation was on in earnest.

On July 9, American and Vietnamese officials made an extremely ominous announcement. They said that Washington was about to send 50,000 tons of rice to South Viet Nam to reduce the disastrously inflated price of rice and help the economy.

In normal times, the idea of sending rice to Viet Nam is truly like carrying coals to Newcastle. Viet Nam and Cambodia comprise the rice bowl of Southeast Asia, normally exporting huge quantities of the vital grain to other Asian countries.

Vietnamese farmers were still growing rice, although military operations had cut down production to some extent. The problem was that the Viet Cong was by now able to cut roads and other communications routes at will, and had decided to try starving Saigon and other key cities.

The same day as the rice announcement, Washington announced that Ambassador Taylor had resigned and would be replaced by the same man he had succeeded—Henry Cabot Lodge. Lodge had decided to have a second go at the frustrating but fascinating war.

On July 9, President Johnson grimly told the world that the war "will get worse before it gets better." The push for escalation was becoming stronger.

On July 11, Secretary of State Dean Rusk said in Washington that "the idea of sanctuary is dead," meaning that the North Vietnamese Air Force could not use China as a base for its operations against the United States, as the North Korean Air Force did during the Korean War.

As if in response to all this, Hanoi announced on July 11 that North Vietnamese volunteer troops were departing for South Viet Nam. This was the first open declaration by Hanoi of its participation in the war.

The following day, July 12, the U.S. Army's 1st Infantry Division, the "Big Red One," began landing at the new facility at Cam Ranh Bay. Marines and allied troops continued pouring in, and on July 20 the U.S. Coast Guard joined the war with eight of its eighty-two-foot cutters to patrol the South Vietnamese coast against infiltration.

Subsequent arrivals included the U.S. Army's 101st Airborne Division, which began disembarking on July 29, and the Army's 25th and 9th Divisions. The build-up raced on.

As men poured into Viet Nam it became evident that supply lines were not keeping pace. Part of the reason was the usual confusion and lack of organization that goes with any rapid military build-up.

For instance, almost all the new troops, and especially those of the 1st Division, lacked the new jungle boots. The GIs had regular leather combat boots, of course, but in tropical jungles these boots did not stand up, and after several weeks were literally rotting off their wearers' feet.

There were shortages of replacement fatigue uniforms as thorns and other jungle wear-and-tear took their toll. Actually, the army had a new type of jungle uniform which Special Forces men had been wearing for years. The new uniform was made of lighter, stronger material than the old fatigues, and the top was a loose jacket instead of the old shirt style. Both jacket and trousers of the new uniform were baggy and loose fitting, and had many huge pockets to carry the things needed by soldiers.

These highly practical new uniforms were in tremendous demand, but the only place soldiers could get them was at the Saigon black market from sweet old ladies who could also sell them new jungle boots, helmets or even weapons.

Even "church keys"—the cheap metal openers used on beer cans—were in very short supply in those days. You could buy one only on the black market, and it cost up to fifty cents.

But a more serious cause of shortages was the joyful faith of officials in Washington that the war now would be won quickly, and it would therefore be better not to gear the American national economy too strongly to defense production. Contracts let for war materiel were therefore tightly limited. An especially serious case in point was the production of aerial bombs, which came to be a very sore point with the Air Force.

From the beginning, the tonnage of bombs of all sizes dropped by American planes on Viet Nam was vast. The B52 raids alone consumed up to 65,000 pounds of bombs per plane per raid, and about thirty B52s were bombing Viet Nam nearly every day.

Even by World War II standards, this scale of bombing was huge.

The Defense Department was unprepared. The thinking

had been that "iron bombs"—bombs filled with chemical explosive as opposed to atomic or hydrogen bombs—were obsolete. The B52 itself was designed and built to carry hydrogen bombs, not TNT bombs.

World War II left the United States with large quantities of surplus bombs, many of which were eventually sold to other nations, including even Germany. Germany wanted them to convert the explosives to fertilizer.* Later the United States bought many of them back at a staggering loss to itself (or, rather, to the American taxpayer).

At any rate, by early 1966, a year after the United States came into the war, the bomb shortage had begun to become acute.

On April 11, 1966, Arthur Sylvester, the Defense Department spokesman, conceded that "a problem in distribution of bombs" had resulted in a temorary reduction of air strikes in Viet Nam. He said the distribution problem was the result of civilian rioting and disturbances in Da Nang (including a strike of Vietnamese dock workers), so that bombs could not be unloaded.

But Washington quickly saw that it was stuck with a politically hot potato. The government that fails to pass the ammunition to its troops in wartime invites public censure or worse. Washington chose to dispose of this public relations problem as it has many other times during the Viet Nam war—by lying.

House Minority Leader Gerald R. Ford of Michigan accused the Johnson administration of "shocking mismanagement" of the Viet Nam war effort. Secretary McNamara said on April 14 that, by June, production of bombs would be keeping pace with the Viet Nam raids. This rate, he said, was about 50,000 tons dropped on Viet Nam every month. In any case, there was no real bomb shortage, he said.

Two days later, April 16, the story was out about the United States buying bombs back from Germany. And on

---

*In January and April 1964, for example, the U.S. Defense Department sold 7,562 surplus 750-pound bombs to Kaus and Steinhausen Company, Schweinge, Germany. The Pentagon said this represented about 2 per cent of its total supply of 750-pound bombs. These bombs had cost the Pentagon $330 each originally (that is, $2.5 million for the lot), and by 1966 their cost had risen to $440 each. The German company bought the lot of them for $12,736. In the spring of 1966, the Defense Department was forced to buy back 5,570 bombs from this lot, paying $114,500!

April 19, highly placed Air Force sources said that the shortage had forced reduction of bombing sorties to only 43 per cent of their former level.

Secretary McNamara, who was almost always at odds with his Air Force generals, said on April 20 that reports of a bomb shortage hampering the war effort were "baloney," adding that "No nation has been as well prepared for military operations as this nation today."

The following day, April 21, the Pentagon, realizing it had got caught in a political meat grinder, said it was dropping plans to buy back some half a million bombs and shells it had sold to Germany.

Spokesman Sylvester bluntly announced, "We don't need them."

Two days later, though, the Pentagon acknowledged under intense questioning by reporters that it had already bought back or reacquired some 18,000 bombs it had earlier distributed in six countries. Sources in the Pentagon said these "reacquired" bombs would go immediately to Viet Nam. Some had been sent to allied nations as aid and were merely repossessed by the USA; others were bought back.

On June 2, the Pentagon, under heavy criticism for not having ordered enough bombs for Viet Nam, said the United States would produce about one million bombs during the final third of 1966, amounting to some 300,000 tons. By comparison, the United States dropped about 480,000 tons on Viet Nam in 1965.

The British munitions industry quickly smelled the chance to trade pounds of explosive for pounds sterling. On June 23, a British source acknowledged that Britain and the United States were discussing the sale of bombs and rockets to the Defense Department for Viet Nam. Such sales would "come under the category of things that we might sell to them," the source said. "As is well known, Britain has had a fairly long shopping list to offer the Americans for a long time."

On June 24, a heavily censored version was released of Air Force testimony in March to the Senate Preparedness Subcommittee headed by Senator John Stennis. It was revealed that Air Force Secretary Harold Brown and Lieutenant General T. P. Gerrity, Deputy Chief of Staff of the Air Force, had told of a shortage of 750-pound bombs and 2.75-inch rockets.

Production of bombs increased, but as late as the fall of

McDonnell F-4C "Phantom"

1966, friends of mine serving as pilots in the Air Force, Marine Corps and Navy still were complaining bitterly about the shortage of certain types of bombs (notably 750- and 1,000-pound bombs) and of 20-millimeter aircraft cannon ammunition.

One Air Force F4 Phantom pilot I knew sent an anonymous letter to the editor of *Aviation Week & Space Technology* which was printed in the September 19, 1966, issue. He spoke of the demoralizing effect the shortage was still having on combat pilots, and he was one of many pilots who told me they planned to get out of the service as soon as possible.*

More to the point, they complained that when dive-

---

*The following excerpts from the pilot's published letter indicate the flavor of pilot feeling in those days:

"We receive equal amounts of 81s and 82s (Mk.81 250-pound and Mk.82 500-pound, low-drag bombs), but there are no 750s available in Vietnam. They must be well hidden, for I have heard Mr. McNamara state time and again that there is no shortage. This must be one of the 'isolated exceptions' he mentions....

"Policy dictates... that pilots will be briefed on the shortage of 20-mm. (cannon) ammunition, and will use it only when deemed absolutely necessary by the flight leader or the FAC (forward air controller). This places somewhat of a handicap on the weapons systems' use....

"There is nothing more demoralizing than the sight of an F-4 taxiing out with nothing but a pair of 81s or 82s nestled among its ejector racks.

"However, it looks much better for the commander and the service concerned to show 200 sorties on paper, even when 40 or 50 would do the same job. It also helps Congress when the services are fighting for their appropriations, for the one with the highest number of sorties obviously needs more money."

bombing enemy antiaircraft sites, they could knock ground defenses out with big bombs, but not with the smaller ones they had. In practical terms, they said, this meant that the bomb shortage was costing the lives of many pilots who never pulled out of their bombing runs.

The scandal slipped back into obscurity, but the hatred stirred within the administration and the armed services was far from forgotten. The weapons of censorship and reprisal were still sharp.

In December 1966, Major General Jerry D. Page, commandant of the Air War College, gave a private talk at a secret seminar of senior Air Force Reserve officers at Montgomery, Alabama. He is said to have discussed the bomb shortage in Viet Nam and its effects on the war.

Among the reserve officers at the session was Colonel Samuel P. Goddard, a Democrat, a friend of the Johnson administration, and, at the time, Governor of Arizona. (He was defeated for reelection the following November.)

Two months after General Page's briefing, he was reassigned without official explanation to a relatively obscure post on Okinawa.

Another reserve Air Force officer, Barry Goldwater, former Arizona senator, charged that Goddard had complained to the Defense Department about Page's bomb-shortage briefing. Goldwater's accusation was forwarded by Senator Margaret Chase Smith of Maine to the Defense Department. The Pentagon's reply to the charge was labeled a "classified document," and there the matter apparently ended.

I have written at some length about the bomb shortage case, because I think it well illustrates the political approach Washington has taken toward the Viet Nam War. Indeed, it has often seemed to me that the administration is really far more concerned with the public relations aspects of the war than the war itself.

This public relations orientation has been prominent in the escalation, from the start.

The administration sought to create the public impression from 1965 onward and that U.S. escalation was being carefully throttled as a limited response to enemy actions. The idea, in short, was that planning was carried out on a day-to-day basis, according to which the war might easily end next week, if the Viet Cong would just fall in line.

In fact, the evidence was that the administration was doing its escalation planning as much as a half-year or more in advance, and that nothing the enemy might do short of unconditional and immediate surrender would change things.

A highly illustrative case in point was the visit Secretary McNamara made to Viet Nam in July 1965. These trips have always seemed to many reporters more in the nature of public relations junkets than real fact-finding missions.

McNamara (and, for that matter, any other ranking official) can receive the same briefings in Washington that he gets in Viet Nam, and by the same people. McNamara and other officials could no more do any independent fact-finding research in Viet Nam than they could on the moon. The days are long past when kings went forth incognito into their lands to see how their people fared.

The July 1965 visit was fouled up in advance by a July 15 AP report from Washington that the Pentagon had recommended an increase in U.S. strength in Viet Nam from 72,000 to 179,000 by the end of the year. This report infuriated administration officials, because it indicated not day-to-day planning but an escalation plan nearly six months in advance.

McNamara and his team, which included spokesman Sylvester, arrived in Saigon on July 16. The Secretary testily denied that there was any substance to the Washington story. Unfortunately, he then let the stage directions get into the wrong hands.

The following day, McNamara advised the director of Saigon's national bank, Dr. Nguyen Xuan Oanh, to take anti-inflationary measures, since American strength in Viet Nam by the end of the year would be around 190,000.

Dr. Oanh, who had received his doctorate in economics at Harvard University and had been a professor of economics in the United States for many years, counted many American reporters as his personal friends. And Secretary McNamara's advice was quickly known to the press.

But the show went on. The day the team arrived, U.S. military briefers dramatically announced that all of North Viet Nam's 325th Division was now fighting in South Viet Nam.

Vietnamese officers had been saying this for months, but American spokesmen had denied it. On July 16, the timing was finally right for the American announcement, since it all fitted in with plans that already had been made to escalate another notch.

That night, Sylvester was asked again about the Washington escalation story and said, "I can't answer because I don't know. I don't think any of the figures I've heard are any good. We'll just have to see what's needed."

On the following day, Sylvester took the play a step further by conceding that American officers in Viet Nam had presented Secretary McNamara with a "staff study" calling for more troops.

The Saigon government conveniently asked at that point for more American troops (the announcement of this was made first by U.S. military briefers).

To the surprise of no one, Washington announced a few days after the McNamara trip that it had been decided to send more U.S. troops to Viet Nam, although the number had still not been decided.

Recalling that the first AP tip story had mentioned a figure of 179,000 U.S. servicemen in Viet Nam by the end of 1965, the actual number in Viet Nam on January 31, 1966, was 181,392—a figure remarkably close to the AP figure that had been denied by all top administration figures.

Escalation in Viet Nam has been attacked by some Americans, including Senator Mike Mansfield of Montana, as "open-ended," meaning that it seems to go on without any predetermined cutoff limit.

This may well be. One thing is certain: the American strategy is basically as simple as can be. The whole war, in President Johnson's eyes, is a matter of increasing military pressure on the enemy by steps until he is finally destroyed or forced to give up.

On the enemy side, the strategy is equally simple: to match each American escalation with a countermove, outwaiting and outfighting Washington, until America's campaign finally collapses as the result of political and moral decay.

Both sides, at this writing, seem equally sure of eventual success, although President Johnson is under pressure to conclude things before the November 1968 election.

It seems to me that neither side has any real understanding of the weapons, strengths and weaknesses of the other, even at this very late date.

Some day it would be amusing to bring President Johnson together for a chat with North Viet Nam's Defense Minister, General Vo Nguyen Giap. I have a feeling both would be stunned by the blindness of the escalation of the past years.

But there never will be such a chat. The escalation is far from finished, and it becomes more fatal each month.

7

AIR WAR

In World War I, hundred-plane dogfights churned over the trenches. In World War II, great battles were decided in the air over Britain, the Coral Sea and throughout the world.

In Viet Nam, despite the dangers, the air war is more often dull routine than high drama, and nothing decisive seems to come of it, despite the great hopes America has pinned to it.

One of the dullest but most typical missions I watched from the back seat of a jet fighter-bomber was on October 15, 1965. On that date, the flight of five F100 fighter-bombers of the 481st Tactical Squadron wrecked a hamlet.

The sortie was flown from Bien Hoa Air Base about fifteen miles from Saigon.

There was no hustle or scramble involved; in fact, scrambles in Viet Nam in which pilots actually run out to their aircraft are very rare. This mission had been "fragged" (ordered) several hours in advance.

Twenty minutes or so were spent being briefed in the operations room about weather, enemy ground fire and the target, which was a hamlet in the Mekong River Delta forty-three miles southwest of Saigon. Intelligence reports said 200 Viet Cong were concentrated there.

We strolled to the shack next door to pick up our flight gear, which hung from racks. On each rack there hung a white helmet, a "G suit," a parachute and some other odds and ends. The G suit is a kind of tightly fitting combination corset and leggings, and compressed air is ducted into it when the plane is in a tight bank or pulling out.

Its purpose is to keep the pilot from blacking out when high centrifugal force drains blood from the brain. Without it, high-angle dive bombing and steep turns would be impossible in jet fighters.

T-28 "Trojan"

Our flight was made up of four regular single-seat F100s and one two-seat F100F, in which I was to ride. Its name was *Lillian*. Each of the fighters was parked in a concrete revetment all by itself, enclosed on three sides. On November 1, 1964, the Viet Cong had attacked this base with mortars, and many parked planes were destroyed because there were no concrete walls around them at the time.

The pilots carefully checked each plane, including tire pressure. The whole thing seemed like a civilian preflight inspection for a regular commercial flight. All five of the fighters were in order, and we slipped into our chutes, which are very heavy. With difficulty, each man climbed the ladder hooked into the side of his plane and swung his legs over into the cockpit. The idea is to stand on the seat first and then slide in.

Buckling in takes some time. Besides the usual seat belt, there is a shoulder harness, straps around each calf (to yank the legs back in case of an emergency ejection), and various fastenings to the ejection seat. There also is a compressed air coupling for the G suit to hook up to, a communications cable to hook into the helmet for earphones and microphone, and the oxygen tube for the face mask.

When properly strapped in, the pilot feels about as free and comfortable as a condemned man in the electric chair. Besides the discomfort of confinement, the heat in the cockpit of a fighter waiting to take off from a Vietnamese airfield is nearly unbearable. A T28 pilot tole me he regularly lost two pounds every flight as the result of profuse sweating.

F100s are equipped with air conditioners, but the genial young pilot with whom I was flying that day, First Lieutenant Rod Dorr, was reluctant to turn his on any more than necessary. The air conditioners in jet fighters are so powerful they pour artificial snow into the cockpit, which can obscure vision at bad moments.

Once the helmet is on with the earphones in place, outside sound is blotted out, especially once the canopy is lowered and locked.

A few feet outside, the air may be rent by the shattering hypersonic blast of an after-burning jet engine; bombs may be exploding underneath the plane; 20-millimeter cannon inside the plane may be roaring out shells. But the pilot (and his passenger) hears none of this. In the earphones there is almost constant technical chatter between planes, ground control and forward air observers. Besides that, there is an eerie moaning sound in the earphones, produced by the complicated electric gear in the plane.

To hear only that moaning sound, like the sighing of wind around the corner of a house, whem bomb blasts are erupting and huts disintegrating just below, or when napalm splashes so close below as to scorch the plane's paint, is a phenomenon pilots call "cockpit isolation." Outside there is the din and horror of jet-age war; inside there is the calm and quiet of a computer room. The pilots are glad to be spared the sounds they create. I have sometimes wondered whether it might not be better for some Air Force officers to be better acquainted with the ugly cacophony of warfare.

We taxied in line to the waiting area, our canopies still open to get what little cool air we could. The Super Sabre, which is not a bad-looking little plane, is not at its most attractive when taxiing.

The nose landing gear is long, so the fighter's nose rides high. The bottom of the Super Sabre is almost flat and the top curves; with its flattened nose air intake, it looks like a fish. Our flight of five was carrying 250-pound bombs and plenty of cannon ammunition.

As at any other big airport, we had to wait about ten minutes to take off. A long line of transport planes and other aircraft was ahead of us. Off to one side of the strip Air Force mechanics were working over two jet-black U-2 spy planes, in preparation for a mission. The U-2 carries no national markings, and looks more like a glider than a plane. It rests on one undercarriage wheel, with two outrigger wheels at the ends of the very long wings. The wing wheels drop off when the plane takes off. Most of the other aircraft at the field already were camouflaged with the new three-color Air Force scheme of dark green, medium green and earth brown. Our F100s were still bare metal.

At length, our turn came and the pilots lowered and locked the canopies. We all pulled a set of safety pins, to which little red flags were attached, from the ejection apparatus of our seats. Ejection seats fire their occupants upward by means of 37-millimeter cannon shells, and it is highly undesirable to fire an ejection seat other than in an emergency. (A pull on a striped black and yellow handle attached to the seat fires it.)

Incidentally, jet pilots regard their ejection seats with a mixture of gratitude and fear. Being shot upward out of a disabled jet may save one's life, but it may also break one's back, or at least result in permanent injury as the result of severe spinal compression.

The black throttles on the left side of the cockpits slid forward, and we sailed down the runway into the air, climbing gently over rice fields, huts and water buffalo grazing at the end of the runway.

Airborne, the five of us grouped into a loose formation, pilots constantly working throttles and flight controls to keep us at the right intervals. The sky was crystal blue except for great masses of fleecy clouds, and the sun blazed through the plastic canopies over us. In a few moments, the whole of the great Delta was spread out below us, flat and drab from the air at that season, apart from the brown, winding branches of the Mekong and the silvery slashes made by the countless canals across the countryside.

We were at 15,000 feet now, and talking by radio with "Beaver 79," a little L19 light plane putting along far below us, looking for the target. At length, we spotted him coasting along above a line of trees growing next to a canal.

The pilots of those forward air controller planes are brave men. Most are jet fighter pilots assigned to duty as FACs, and they take at least as much pride in their work as the jet pilots. They make fine targets for enemy gunners, flying, as they do, slowly and at very low altitude. They also have to be careful to get out of the way quickly when the fighters drop down for their strikes. Some of the FACs sported great mustaches, World War I-style leather helmets, goggles and long silk scarves, until some commander told them to stop it.

Beaver 79 had found our hamlet and told us he would indicate it with a smoke rocket, one of several he had on racks under his wings. We broke into a wide circle and watched Beaver 79 sail along a canal, firing a puff of smoke into a cluster of thatched huts. From where I was sitting I could see no sign of life. Pilots tell me they rarely see people on the ground.

As a matter of fact, from 15,000 feet, one is hard put to see any small detail on the ground.

The silver fish continued circling for a moment, the circle growing tigher and the centrifugal force building up. As the banks grew tighter, one could hear labored breathing in the earphones, as pilots strained under the pressure. Conversation almost stopped, and there was only moaning.

The first fighter broke from the circle and headed down. "I bomb," its pilot announced. We watched the silver speck of his plane almost touch the target before pulling up, leaving a swirling gray smudge under him where his bombs had hit.

One after another, we went in. The dive down seems vertical, and at one point the ground actually seems to rotate over one's head. The hamlet leapt up to meet us, and now I could see flames coming from some of the tiny objects on the ground. "I strafe," Lieutenant Dorr said. Simple declarative sentences are used for communicating at times like this, partly for brevity and partly because the G pressures on pilots are too great for them to say much.

While we still were what seemed to me a long distance above the ground, our cannon began to fire. Actually, I heard very little but the moaning in the earphones, but the whole plane vibrated from the firing, like an electric massager. Streams of shells ripped into the houses below us, and I could see flashes of light where the shells were exploding. Abruptly, Lieutenant Dorr pulled back the stick and we pulled out just above the hamlet, zipping through a column of black smoke.

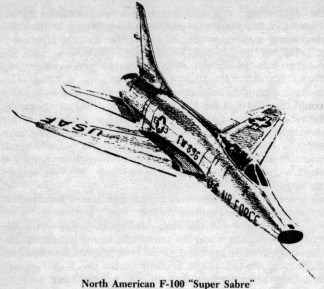

North American F-100 "Super Sabre"

The pressure of the pull-out was, as usual, absolutely crushing. In fact, a human being is strained close to his physical limits by dive bombing.

First, the speed is so great that everything happens in the space of a few seconds. Timing must be perfect. Second, a dive from 15,000 feet almost to sea level in the space of a few seconds produces excruciating pain in the eardrums as the result of the terrific air pressure change. This pain persists throughout the rest of the mission. Third, the downward crush of the pull-out almost paralyzes the lungs, pulls the flesh on the face downward, and makes arms and legs weigh six or seven times what they normally would. Hands on sticks and throttles and feet on rudder pedals become monstrous weights, and it is all a pilot can do to hold them in place, much less keep them under control in the delicate movements required in a pull-out.

We repeated our firing passes several times and our objective looked properly battered. At length, Beaver 79 radioed: "That'll do it nicely, I believe. Thank you, gentlemen, and I look forward to seeing you again." In his official report, Beaver 79 said we had destroyed eight structures, damaged six others, and obliterated 30 percent of the target area.

On the way home, Lieutenant Dorr let me take the controls for a while, and I was surprised at the lightness and responsiveness of the stick. Lighting the engine's afterburner in level flight produced an exhilarating thrust forward, and I could imagine that the F100 must be very pleasant to fly, or, rather, "drive," as its pilots insist on saying.

Before we landed one of the pilots noticed that his air speed indicator and altimeter were not working—instruments without which landings are extremely dangerous in a jet fighter. Dorr helped him land by flying at his wingtip, keeping him advised constantly on speed and height as we dropped down on Bien Hoa. As we hit the runway, tail parachutes snapped open to slow us, and the sortie was over.

We taxied up to the flight line and climbed out of the cockpits, all of us drenched with sweat. The man who had had trouble with his instruments was visibly unnerved and talking rapidly. As yellow tractors hauled the F100s off to a hangar for refueling, rearming and servicing, the pilots walked back to unload their gear, get debriefed and hit the showers back in the billeting area. In the evening after chow at the officers' mess there would be time for a movie, a few beers and perhaps a letter home.

Somewhere, miles to the south of us, the embers of a community were still smoldering and the blood was still fresh from the death that had struck from the sky that afternoon. But pilots rarely think or talk much about the results of their work, except in terms of military targets hit.

Sometimes these raids kill enemy guerrillas. Sometimes they merely kill women and children cringing in improvised shelters. Pilots have no way of telling which, and they are at the mercy of forward observers and men sitting at desks who take coffee breaks and make human mistakes.

One of the worst kinds of mistake that can happen has to do with map coordinates. On military maps, square sections of real estate are designated by two letters (such as WR). A mention of the two designator letters roughly locates an area. Following these two letters are six numbers, three each for coordinates reading across and vertically. A complete coordinate, consisting of two letters and six numbers (i.e., WR825439) locates any spot in the world to within a few hundred feet.

When a pilot is told to bomb one of these coordinates he follows orders, assuming that his orders are correct. Unfortunately, however, the same slovenly work attitudes that prevail in the United States extend to the American military, even in war theaters. And if care is not taken, two or more numbers in a map coordinate may accidentally be transposed. If the transposition is gross enough, the pilot will notice immediately that something is wrong. But if only two final digits are transposed, the result may be off by only a few miles, which is not a great enough distance to warn a pilot.

Because of exactly such a transposition, U.S. planes swooped down on the village of Lang Vei on the night of March 2, 1967. Lang Vei, about 400 miles north of Saigon, was a hard-working little community considered friendly to the Saigon government.

When relief workers moved in after the raid, they found eighty civilians dead and 120 wounded. America promptly apologized to the South Vietnamese government, and sent blankets and rice for the survivors of Lang Vei.

About two months later, it happened again under ironic circumstances. Washington and Saigon for years had sought to persuade Viet Cong to defect and start new lives on the government side. Inducements of cash and amnesty are offered.

Some Viet Cong do come over under the "Chieu Hoi" ("appeal to return") program, and they are grouped in camps for "reeducation." Unfortunately, many of these camps are little more than concentration camps, where prisoners are without adequate facilities or food.

In the spring of 1967, a flight of U.S. Air Force jets which had been given transposed coordinate numbers attacked the provincial capital of Ben Tre in the Mekong Delta.

Fortunately, the bombs did not fall in the populated center of the city, where they would have killed hundreds. Instead, they landed in the outskirts—right in the middle of a camp for Viet Cong defectors, a number of whom were killed and wounded. Hanoi radio lost no time in crowing about this error.

Still another transposition error had occurred earlier, on August 9, 1966, in what U.S. officials at the time called "one

Boeing Vertol CH-47 "Chinook"

of the worst cases of mistaken identity of the war." Two F100s swept down on the Mekong Delta village of Truong Thanh and sprayed it with 20-millimeter cannon fire. The civilian toll was fifteen killed and 180 wounded.

The ever helpful U.S. AID Mission rushed in bandages and blood donors.

Some of the almost daily accidents are the result of pilot error in the split-second timing of the jet age.

The town of Tan Uyen, population about 3,000, has the misfortune to lie less than ten miles north of Bien Hoa Air Base and close to a Viet Cong stronghold. Tan Uyen is a district capital and considered under Saigon control. But because of its location it gets accidentally bombed from time to time.

On July 1, 1966, for instance, tragedy struck at 9 A.M. It was a Friday morning, and classes at the Tan Uyen two-room elementary school were in session. It was customary for fighter-bombers returning to Bien Hoa Air Base from missions to dump their empty or party empty ordnance canisters into the Dong Nai River as they swept over it. That river is presumably full of sunken explosives by now, which future generations of Vietnamese fishermen will presumably come across.

But on that tragic Friday morning, as three F100s were returning to base and dumping their unused rockets and bombs into the river, one pilot pushed his jettison button a second too late.

All but one of the canisters fell into the river one mile from Tan Uyen. But one fell into Tan Uyen's schoolhouse. Of the eight persons killed and fifty-two wounded, most were children.

The U.S. command was very sorry, and sent medical supplies of the latest type to Tan Uyen. The F100 pilots had not the slightest idea what had happened and simply returned to base. The F100 unit later volunteered to help Tan Uyen. But the accidents continue, and the victims often are American troops.

There has been great praise in Washington about the "surgical precision" with which the Air Force, Navy and Marine Corps carry out their bombing and strafing attacks in North and South Viet Nam. From what I have seen of the air war there, these claims are grossly exaggerated.

For one thing, attacking pilots actually see very little, and they must react to impressions of what they have seen in split seconds.

Thus it was, on August 11, 1966, that a flight of two U.S. Air Force F4C Phantom fighter-bombers and one B57 twin-jet bomber was flying along the Central Vietnamese coast at night, dropping flares and looking for targets. Just offshore, in the South China Sea, they found something. It looked like one of the steel vessels North Viet Nam was thought to be using for the coastal infiltration of weapons and supplies to the Viet Cong.

The three jets raced in, hammering the target with cannon shells and rockets. The planes made three passes at the ship, under the light of flares.

The target turned out to be the U.S. Coast Guard cutter *Point Welcome*, a 125-foot vessel with a crew of thirteen. The *Point Welcome* had tried frantically to signal the jets, but without success. Two crewmen were killed and four others were wounded. Another wounded man was Tim Page, a British freelance newsman who happened to be aboard.

Countless sampans thought to be carrying Viet Cong but later found to be loaded with civilians have been destroyed by U.S. planes on the waterways of South Viet Nam.

In 1966, U.S. jets attacked the small bridge spanning the Ben Hai River separating North from South Viet Nam. The raid was an accident, since at that time the Demilitarized Zone was still off-limits to American raids. Pilots had thought they were hitting a bridge ten miles farther north, in North Vietnamese territory.

In the process, a friendly village on the southern shore of the river was demolished, killing about a score of civilians and wounding nearly 100 others.

It is pointless to try to detail all the accidental attacks by U.S. aircraft in North and South Viet Nam, but the death toll is obviously very high. In many a crushed hamlet, even I have been tempted to shake my fist at the silvery specks passing through distant blue skies.

On March 18, 1966, Representative Clement J. Zablocki, a Wisconsin Democrat normally friendly to President Johnson's policies, commented on the problem. Zablocki, who was chairman of the House Far Eastern Affairs Subcommittee, said he understood that allied forces were killing or wounding at least two civilians for every Viet Cong slain.

This, Zablocki contended, was a major reason for the very high desertion rate from the Vietnamese army.

"Unfortunately," he said, "no reliable statistics are avail-

Viet Cong 37 mm. A.A.

able. In an effort to determine the actual ratio of civilian to Viet Cong casualties, a close study should be pursued."

Such a study was, of course, impossible. Many of the casualties occur in areas controlled by the Viet Cong, and cannot be checked by outsiders.

At any rate, the air war accelerated fast. In bombing North Viet Nam, Air Force F105s (officially "Thunderchiefs," but known to their pilots as "Thuds," because of their great weight and the noise they supposedly make when they crash) and Navy A4 Skyhawks assumed the brunt of the load.

This was a departure from the classical bombing tactics of World War II, in which fleets of big multiengine bombers, streamed over objectives at high altitude. The F105s and A4s, single-seaters, did most of their work as dive bombers, often flying right toward the mouths of antiaircraft cannon.

Often, attacks were as simple and uneventful as the one I have just described, on a hamlet in the Mekong River Delta. The Red River Delta in North Viet Nam is similar terrain and conditions are generally similar. "Operating over the Red River Delta is no harder than operating over your own home town," one Air Force Phantom pilot told me.

But much more often, pilots over North Viet Nam are in mortal danger.

Soviet aid to North Viet Nam has equipped that country with the most formidable antiaircraft defenses the United States has ever had to face. The effectiveness of the enemy system is reflected in the mounting American loss rate. By the end of 1967, the United States had lost around 700 aircraft in North Viet Nam alone, to say nothing of the many aircraft shot down over South Viet Nam and Laos.

Probably as many as 20,000 Russian technicians and advisors worked in North Viet Nam setting up the system. There also were, almost undoubtedly, pilots from North Korea, communist China and Russia flying as advisors in the North.

Enemy hardware included about 10,000 fast-firing cannon in 37-, 57- and 85-millimeter sizes, all aimed by radar. There also were hundreds of SA-2 surface-to-air antiaircraft missiles and a fleet of about 100 planes.

North Vietnamese defenses are designed in layers. The top layer is the missile defense. When American planes come over at high altitude, the 20-foot-long SAMs come roaring up.

Although these missiles have been obsolescent for years (the Soviet SA-3 missile is far more effective, but at this writing, none has yet been supplied to Hanoi), they still bring down planes.

In fact, for every fifteen SAMs fired, one U.S. plane is brought down. By comparison with the best rate Germany was able to achieve against the United States in World War II, this is excellent. It took the Germans 8,500 88-millimeter shells to down each American plane.

The SA-2 is easy to see on the ground (even though its factory silver finish was eventually camouflaged with paint), especially during its blast-off. The missile rises slowly at first, and U.S. planes are equipped with detectors to tell pilots when missiles are being fired, even when they are not visually spotted.

The SA-2 is guided by ground radar, and it can chase planes to some extent. But if target planes turn too tightly or dive, they can usually shake the pursuing SAMs, since SAMs travel much faster than jet planes, and are not very maneuverable. For this reason, pilots are not in constant terror of missiles. But they do have to remain constantly alert, and must react immediately when a SAM is spotted coming up.

Normally, the pilot "jinxes"—turns violently, and dives. This evasion gets him clear of the SAM, but brings him down to the effective range of enemy radar-controlled flak. This flak is extremely dangerous. Besides, jinxing also spoils the bombing run, which must be started all over.

A pilot may try to drop below the effective range of explosive flak, but then he is liable to run into withering small-arms fire. Typically, North Vietnamese militiamen and militiawomen are armed with rifles and ordered to aim at a preset spot in the sky. Instead of aiming at an airplane, the militia, often several hundred strong, fire on command. The wall of bullets that flies up simultaneously very often hits attackers.

North Vietnamese propaganda describes missile launch crews in competition with each other for high kill scores. Hanoi's Missile Unit 61 is frequently praised; it supposedly once brought down five U.S. planes in the space of a week. (Similarly, 7th Fleet carrier plane units compete for the most sorties flown in a week.)

Hanoi's small air force has done little more than harass

American sorties. While the North Vietnamese initially had only a few Soviet-built Mach 2 MiG-21 jets, more MiG-21s kept trickling in to bring the total to 100 or so. Vietnamese pilots were being trained at Soviet bases somewhere east of Moscow.*

Even fledgling air forces have their share of heroes. North Viet Nam's air force consisted mostly of subsonic MiG-17s, built only a few years after the Korean War. These tiny and very maneuverable MiGs were affectionately dubbed "Silver Swallows" by their Vietnamese pilots. Hanoi propaganda often represents Captain Nguyen Van Bay, pilot of Silver Swallow No. 2019, as one of its greatest heroes. He wears a leather jacket and helmet with goggles, just like a World War I ace, and by mid-1967 was supposed to have shot down seven American planes. Washington doubts the claim.

Certainly, communist pilots have just as much pride in their profession as Western ones. I talked to Captain Lee Hsien-ping, a Chinese communist pilot, shortly after he defected and flew his two-engine IL-28 jet bomber to Taiwan on November 11, 1965.

Captain Lee was paid off in gold for his defection and was quickly given captain's rank in the Nationalist Air Force, where he expected soon to be flying American-made jets. Dressed in air force blue, he was genial, self-confident, in superb physical condition, and a believer that airpower can accomplish miracles. He had liked his Russian-built IL-28, "but I think 'our' B57s are probably better for most missions."

Generally, North Vietnamese MiG pilots try to stay away from the numerically superior and far better armed Americans. America's F4 Phantom, after all, is probably the most deadly combat plane in the history of aviation. The North Vietnamese find it better to make hit-and-run attacks, but

---

*Some of the training the Vietnamese MiG pilots reportedly receive is highly unorthodox, by Western standards. On January 21, 1967, the Soviet news agency Tass reported that Vietnamese pilots in Moscow were using "purely Vietnamese training methods" in their spare time, which consisted of watching birds, butterflies and the "finer movements of embroiderers." The idea supposedly was to accustom the pilots to the rapid, precise movements a fighter pilot must make. Two weeks earlier, American pilots had downed nine MiG-21s over North Viet Nam in the space of four days—a not very favorable reflection on Vietnamese air force training standards.

even so, they have been losing about five MiGs for every
U.S. plane the MiGs shoot down.

American planes and Silver Swallows met on April 3,
1965, during a U.S. Navy raid on Dong Phuong, North Viet
Nam. The MiG-17s made a few firing passes but missed and
fled.

The following day, April 4, Silver Swallows drew the first
blood of the air war over North Viet Nam, however.

Just as commercial airliners often must circle over busy
airports waiting their turn to land, U.S. bombers sometimes
must circle over targets in North Viet Nam waiting their turn
to attack. On April 4, five F105 Thuds were thus circling in
haze, high over a bridge at Thanh Hoa in the southern
panhandle of North Viet Nam.

The F105 is one of the fastest jets in the world, but when
it is carrying a heavy bomb load it is relatively slow and
unmaneuverable. To fight it must quickly dump its load and
light its afterburner. This takes time.

From out of the sunny haze, four Silver Swallows pounced
on the circling F105s. Cannons blazing, the MiGs made only
one pass, but it was enough to down two of the F105s. The
MiG-17s dashed off into the haze and escaped.

From then on, fighters were assigned to fly top cover on
all bombing missions.

But the guerrilla attack by the flight of Silver Swallows
on a far superior American force had shown U.S. Air Force
officials something else—that sometimes obsolete weapons
can outfight modern ones. The basic fighter the United States
was using in Viet Nam was the superb Phantom, which was
armed with radar-guided Sparrow missiles and heat-seeking
Sidewinder missiles. The designers of the Phantom had assumed
that the dogfighting air wars of the past would not recur, and,
accordingly, the Phantom carried no guns.

Unfortunately, it turned out that while the MiG-17 was
much slower and more lightly armed than the Phantom, it
could turn much more tightly. When a Silver Swallow could
maneuver in close, it could use its cannon at ranges too short
for American missiles to be effective.

There was an urgent need for fighters with old-fashioned
guns in them, and the U.S. Air Force had to order some
F104s to Viet Nam. The F104 carries cannons as well as

Lockheed F-104 "Starfighter"

Sidewinder missiles. Subsequently, modified Phantoms went into production with cannons built into them.

More than one year after the first American encounter with MiGs, the fearsome MiG-21 made its first appearance over the North. The first brief clash involving MiG-21s occurred on April 23, 1966. Neither side scored a kill. But on April 26, three days later, a MiG-21 was downed in combat for the first time.

This historic kill was scored by Major Paul J. Gilmore, a thirty-three-year-old Phantom pilot of the 480th Squadron stationed at Da Nang, and his copilot, First Lieutenant William T. Smith, twenty-seven. It happened about sixty-five miles northwest of Hanoi.

Phantoms have generally outfought MiG-21s ever since then.

The big danger remains flak. On July 18, 1966, a Phantom flown by Captain Dave Moruzzi and his copilot, First Lieutenant John F. Preston, was shot down over North Viet Nam. Both pilots made it out unhurt, and Preston, a twenty-four-year-old father of two, told me what it had been like:

"Dave and I had talked it over many times, and we'd

decided we'd rather take the chance of blowing up than eating rice and fishheads for the next fifteen years. We'd been road-reccying [flying armed road reconnaissance, looking for targets of opportunity] southward along the road that runs north-south in North Viet Nam.

"We started a left turn toward the sea to the east. But there was real heavy 57-millimeter flak, bursting in big black smudges all over. We were jinxing [flying evasively] and everything, but we took a hit, and we could sure feel it. Both engines went dead instantly, and Dave radioed to the flight leader, "Spider Lead, I'm hit, both engines afire." He tried to say a few more things, but the radio went dead.

"We looked in the mirrors behind us, and man, we were just one big ball of flame. The flight leader said later that we looked like a comet.

"We were about ten miles from water when we were hit, and knew we'd have to glide all the way with no power, if we were going to make it.

"It seemed like an eternity, with the flame getting closer. The flight leader said it had reached the rear cockpit where I was sitting, although I couldn't feel a thing. I kept my eyes glued on the air speed indicator and altimeter. Then we crossed the beach and Dave said, 'Sorry, Jack, this is as far as I can take you. Good luck.'

"The altimeter was just going through 1,000 feet and we were doing about 240 knots when I punched out [ejected]. The plane was about 600 feet when Dave left it. And then the plane hit. But it all happened much faster than I'm telling it—I punched out, Dave punched out, and the plane hit and exploded in a fireball, boom, boom, boom.

"The ejection stunned me, of course, but it wasn't as bad as I thought it would be, from all the stories about people breaking their backs. When I went out, the seat started tumbling, and I remember seeing the airplane moving away. I was conscious, but I just dimly remember feeling the terrific deceleration when the chute opened.

"We were in the water about thirty minutes, under fire from the North Vietnamese on the shore the whole time. They were mostly firing machine guns, and the fire was very accurate. I'd duck under water over the side of my raft [ejection seats are equipped with rafts that inflate automatically] every time a burst came close. One time I came up, and the raft had been hit and sunk.

"Sampans had headed out toward us from shore to capture or kill us, and Dave and I were swimming as fast as we could toward the Philippines. The rescue chopper arrived just in time."

Preston and Moruzzi were issued a new Phantom and were back flying missions over the North the following day.

By mid-1967, U.S. planes were flying more than 800 strikes each day—100 in Laos, 300 in North Viet Nam and 400 in South Viet Nam.

From early in the game, there have been incidents and even occasional clashes with Chinese communist planes. On April 9, 1965, U.S. Navy Phantoms on a raid over North Viet Nam strayed over nearby Hainan Island, which belongs to China and has several fighter bases. Chinese MiG-17s roared up and shot down one Phantom. One MiG was probably downed.

But excepting for incidents like that, China has largely avoided the air war, despite fears that American escalation might provoke Peking to join in.

At the same time, China has cooperated with Russia up to a point in keeping North Viet Nam supplied with antiaircraft defenses. For a while, China halted rail deliveries across its territory from the Soviet Union to North Viet Nam, but in late 1967 a face-saving arrangement was worked out by which North Vietnamese officials would receive technical delivery of munitions at the Chinese-Soviet frontier. That way, the goods were in the hands of Vietnamese, not the hated Russians, as they moved across China.

The question of military supplies, especially flak and missiles, has troubled the Pentagon all along. There has been heavy U.S. military pressure to bomb all North Vietnamese ports, especially Haiphong, and to cut overland links from Moscow to Hanoi, even if it meant bombing China.

Escalation of the air war was at first geographic. The first raids in February 1965 were in the southern panhandle of North Viet Nam.

As the weeks passed, the raids crept farther north, by-passing Hanoi and extending almost to the Chinese border. The raids also extended northwest into the mountains

near Laos and the region around Dien Bien Phu—the place
where France was finally smashed by the Viet Minh eleven
years earlier.

On June 17, the first two MiGs of the war were shot
down in an American raid a scant forty miles south of Hanoi.

On June 18, thirty eight-engine B52 Stratofortress bombers flew all the way from Guam for their first raid on Viet
Nam. Two crashed in mid-air and a third turned back for
mechanical reasons, but the twenty-seven that got through
dumped 500 tons of bombs on a three-square-mile patch of
jungle twenty-five miles northeast of Saigon. This was the
beginning of pattern bombing in the country, designed to
wreck hidden Viet Cong base camps.

Ground forces that moved into the jungle following that
raid found gigantic craters everywhere, but no evidence that
even one Viet Cong had been killed.

Despite the initially indifferent results, B52s flew more
and more high altitude raids, guided to their targets by radar.
The U Taphao Air Base near Sattahip, Thailand, was built
especially for these huge planes so they wouldn't have to fly
halfway across the Pacific from Guam for each raid.

In mid-April 1966 the B52s were sent on several raids to
attack Mu Gia Pass in North Viet Nam, which is near the
Laotian border and considered a prime route for sending
supplies through the jungles into South Viet Nam.

In two raids, the B52s managed to start landslides that
buried sections of the road through Mu Gia Pass. The Air
Force assumed that the route would remain cut and North
Vietnamese supplies along it would stop. But each time, the
road was open within a few days after the raids. Armies of
laborers had repaired the roads. The Strategic Air Command
gave up on Mu Gia Pass.

While B52s continued to carry out occasional raids short
distances into North Viet Nam, they kept away from the
coastal cities, the Hanoi-Haiphong area and the Red River
Delta. The risk was just too great that SA-2 missiles would
drop the big bombers like flies.

Meanwhile, the B52s had incurred the contempt and
fury of tactical fighter-bomber pilots, who were doing most of
the work.

The greatest respect in the working ranks of the Air

Force was always reserved for the pilots of the F105 Thuds*
who flew at suicidal altitudes and who were shot down in
huge numbers. Running a close second for prestige were the
crews of evacuation helicopters who often landed on North
Vietnamese soil in the midst of enemy army units to pick up
downed fighter pilots. Also close to the top were the Navy A4
pilots and all the F4 pilots of all services.

To all of them, however, the B52s seemed unforgivably
wasteful of precious bombs. It also seemed to the men who
risked death or capture every day that the B52 crews had no
right to the security they enjoyed at high altitude over
essentially defenseless territory. Hostility between B52 crews
and the others flared into many a barroom fist fight in
Okinawa and elsewhere.

On July 24, 1965, the SA-2 missile claimed its first
wartime victim. The raids had been moving farther and
farther north, and on that day Air Force Phantoms were
flying cover for F105s attacking the explosives factory at Lang
Chi, fifty-five miles northwest of Hanoi.

All of a sudden, pilots noticed things zipping up and past
them that "looked like flying telephone poles." One of the
Phantoms was destroyed.

Three days later, American planes began bombing every
missile-launching site they could find, but it was a hopeless
game. Many missiles and missile facilities were knocked out,
but there were always many more. The launching units were
mobile and never in the same place for long.

Raids at first aimed mainly at communications, but after
more than two years of bombing, North Vietnamese communications continued to function.

North Vietnamese roads were kept open by armies of
laborers. Piles of gravel and dirt were prepared at intervals
along all roads, to fill in craters. Concrete and steel bridges
were blasted out, but replaced with pontoon bridges or cable
bridges that could be sunk out of sight during the day.
Daytime traffic on all routes in North Viet Nam virtually
ended, but trucks, troops, supplies and everything else moved

---

*For a firsthand, man-in-the-cockpit account of the air war against North Vietnam,
read *Thud Ridge* by Colonel Jack Broughton USAF (Ret). Another authentic
Bantam War Book.

at night. Mountain passes were kept open with muscles and determination.

Then the raids began blasting steel factories, power plants and such light industries as bicycle plants. By New Year's Day, 1967, raids were striking so close to Hanoi, the capital, that bombs frequently fell in the city itself.

Still, the docks and ships tied up at the ports of the North were spared.

Tass had announced some Russian casualties in various raids. But U.S. State Department Kremlinologists felt that actually bombing a Russian ship in port could provoke major Russian escalation. Among the things that might happen would be shipments by Russia of SA-3 missiles to replace the SA-2s. Some Air Force leaders believe the SA-3 would make American raids too costly to continue. The Russians might also start sending Hanoi surface-to-surface missiles of the type they once installed in Cuba.

Such missiles could be used against the 7th Fleet and nearly every city and base in South Viet Nam. If nuclear warheards were supplied with them, the world would be brought very close to the final holocaust.

Despite these dangers, U.S. planes increased their probing harassment of North Vietnamese ports, and the Russians began grumbling increasingly loudly.

Then on June 2, 1967, American planes attacked at the port of Cam Pha, where the Soviet freighter *Turkestan* was tied up. Within twenty-four hours, the Russians had fired off a protest, charging that the *Turkestan* had been hit, with one crew member killed and two others wounded.

The United States at first denied the charge, but conceded on June 18 that planes might have accidentally hit the *Turkestan* while shooting at antiaircraft defenses. But the American note sourly added: "The Soviet government knows that shipping operations in these waters under present circumstances entail risks of such accidents."

The war seemed to be going nowhere, despite the escalated air raids.

In the United States, there were insistent calls from "doves" to end the bombing of the North, which apparently was accomplishing nothing but steady bloodletting. There was still heavier pressure from Air Force generals, right-wing groups and such congressmen as Senator Stennis to "win now." The formula for quick victory was seen by most of these people in terms of an obliteration bombing campaign against North Viet Nam.

Observers closer to the scene felt that the bombing war had become an exercise in futility.

On August 11, 1967, General Cao Van Vien, the South Vietnamese chief of staff, said he was convinced that bombing could never halt enemy infiltration from North Viet Nam into the South, which was the original stated purpose of the raids.

A few days later Secretary McNamara said that the war would never be won by bombing alone.

But, as usual, the Johnson administration moved with the hawks.

American jets as early as April 21, 1967, had attacked inside the city of Haiphong, destroying a power plant.

On August 8, President Johnson authorized the bombing of a number of previously off-limits targets. The American commander in the Pacific, Admiral U. S. Grant Sharp, told the Stennis subcommittee on August 12 that these included transportation and industrial facilities in Hanoi and Haiphong and rail links to China.

And on September 10, U.S. planes attacked the actual docks and other port facilities at Cam Pha.

As 1967 moved to a close, the United States was fast using up the possible escalation notches it could apply to the air war in Viet Nam.

Still, North Viet Nam showed not the slightes sign of yielding.

A decade after World War II, Adolph Galland, commander of Nazi Germany's fighter plane forces, wrote of the gigantic American and British air raids on German cities:

"It seemed as though the conflagrations in the cities had welded the people together, as though the misused phrase, 'community spirit,' had become reality for them in a common will to encounter the threatening extermination with all their strength."*

Similarly, the evidence was strong that the North Vietnamese people had decided to take the raids in stride and

---

*Adolph Galland, *The First and the Last*, Henry Holt and Co., Inc.

fight on. Women and children were evacuated from the larger cities.

It must be remembered that North Viet Nam, unlike Germany, is an agricultural country whose small industry is by no means essential to the survival of the nation. Hanoi's army, unlike the Wehrmacht, is still essentially a guerrilla militia, and it does not depend on tanks, airplanes or even roads. It supplies itself by foraging in the field and it moves by stealth, even when moving in great numbers.

Hanoi itself has only a little more than half a million inhabitants in normal times, and has none of the importance of a Western capital.

President Ho Chi Minh, Premier Pham Van Dong and the rest of the government could presumably move, bag and baggage, from Hanoi into the jungle, if the going got too bad.

They were forced to do that once before, when the French returned to their Vietnamese colony in 1945 to find Ho Chi Minh in office in Hanoi. Ho stayed away from Hanoi until his triumphal reentry in 1954, after the French flag was hauled down for good.

It is probably possible to conduct a successful war of annihilation in Viet Nam with nuclear weapons. The U.S. Air Force or Navy could easily kill nearly all North Viet Nam's sixteen million inhabitants, and as many in South Viet Nam as necessary.

There are some who contend that the present war is aimed at annihilation. They cite the alleged dropping of Cluster Bomb Unit (CBU) antipersonnel bombs over North Vietnamese towns as evidence that the objectives are not essentially military.

Be that as it may, the escalation in the air war seems to me a tacit American admission that the United States has lost the war on the ground.

Infantry warfare is exhausting, bloody work. As applied to a guerrilla situation it is even worse, because the enemy is usually unseen and may strike from any direction. To fight the guerrilla, an army must stick to the jungle, miles from roads, towns, mess halls and service clubs. Worst of all, it may take many years.

In other words, infantry warfare is essentially incompatible with the American character of the 1960s. The only alternative, therefore, is air warfare, which is relatively tidy and comfortable, despite its dangers.

I can't help wondering whether we may not someday see the Air Force called upon to put down riots in our own cities. It would certainly save the National Guard a lot of effort.

8

AMBUSH

Ambushes continue to take place. When you analyze an ambush you can always tell in retrospect what was done wrong. Many of them take place at the end of the day when people are tired and they assume the day's work has been done, and they're simply returning home.

Everybody, I'm sure, from [South Vietnamese Premier] General Khanh on down on that side, and General [William C.] Westmoreland [commander of U.S. forces in Viet Nam] down on our side, is unhappy about ambushes. Genreal Westmoreland has spent a lot of time thinking about this and consulting with his advisors, studying the ambushes, recommending the use of aircraft overhead, asking advisors to recommend [to the Vietnamese] improved tactical security—people out front, people on the flanks, people in plain clothes. Whether or not this has had any effect at the present moment, I just don't know. . . .

Ambushes are placed where no American soldier would expect one. For example, we've been trained to expect an ambush where the road goes through a tree line or through a defile—in other words, where we would put an ambush. And yet, we have all seen ambushes that have been put along roads right out in the open, against all the tactical principles that one has ever been taught. As a matter of fact, if I were commanding a rifle company and I were moving across a wide-open space with a road entering a woods, in accordance with my training I would be concerned about an ambush at the wood line. But I wouldn't, until I came over here

143

[Viet Nam], have been concerned about an ambush out in the middle of an open field. And yet, we're finding them. . . .

Our fervent hope is that they'll [the Viet Cong will] stick their neck out with about six battalions around here some day and try to hold something, because as of that time, they've had it. We can move more battalions to any point in Viet Nam faster than they can and keep feeding them in, and the Vietnamese Army can beat the Viet Cong in a stand-up fight any day of the week, and the best thing that could happen to defeat the VC would be to have them come out in the open and fight. . . .

In due course, this [ambush] challenge has got to be met, and it can't be met by putting troops up and down the highway in a defensive position. It eventually has to be met by offensive operations against the VC units that are operating in the general area.

You can't defend a road effectively against ambush. The road's too long, unless you put twenty battalions along the road, which aren't available. But if you strung out six or seven battalions along the road, even then, at night, at any one point on the road, the density of troops would be less than what you could bring in against it, so that is a forlorn strategy, to try to hold the road defensively. The only way to keep the road open is to attack the VC units, which in turn have been attacking the road. . . .

The VC are excellent at ambushes, but that's kind of a coward's way of fighting the war, and almost anybody, if you can open fire with an overwhelming volume of fire at the beginning and get the psychological advantage, anybody's army would have a hard time withstanding it, and anybody else's army would have a good chance of success.

But if you catch them out in the open, where they've got to maneuver and move and react to new situations, I don't think the VC are ten feet high.*

---

*Excerpts from the transcript of a press conference given October 6, 1964, in Saigon by Brigadier General William E. DePuy, operations officer of the U.S. Military Assistance Command for Viet Nam, following a month of particularly bloody Viet Cong ambushes against Saigon units.

A few days before Christmas, 1961, a young American soldier, Sp4 James T. Davis of Livingston, Tennessee, was riding with ten Vietnamese soldiers in a big "deuce and a half" truck a dozen or so miles from Saigon. It was to have been Davis's first Christmas away from home, and his thoughts may have been straying back to Tennessee. The road was good, and there was no reason to worry about anything in particular.

Without warning, a huge blast erupted from a mound of earth at the side of the road, smashing the truck like a toy and spewing bloody troops in all directions.

Davis was alive and mad, and his carbine had been loaded. He managed to empty two magazines of cartridges at the attackers. But the men in the bushes had machine guns. And so, on December 22, 1961, Specialist Davis became the first American serviceman to die in combat with the Viet Cong. It is in keeping with the character of this war that Davis died in an ambush.

Since then, many thousands of other Americans have died in Viet Nam.*

Despite elaborate efforts by the U.S. command to reduce the terrible effectiveness of Viet Cong ambushes, the enemy continued to spring his bloody traps. These traps snapped closed nearly as often on battle-hardened veteran GIs as they did on green recruits.

At one point, General Westmorland issued wallet-size cards to all American serviceman in Viet Nam outlining the precautions that can be taken against getting ambushed. But in 1967, after two years in Viet Nam, U.S. paratroopers still were being caught.

Long before America came into the war in force, the Viet Cong was sharpening its ambush techniques in meat-grinder operations against Saigon government forces. Ambushes of all shapes and sizes were developed and refined by the enemy. Some were applied against single vehicles (including my little Volkswagen). Some were applied against columns of tanks.

Ambushes were sprung at high noon and at midnight. They were mounted in the jungles, where a man cannot see more than ten feet in any direction, and they were mounted

---

*The casualty rate roughly doubled in each year of war. By the end of 1967, concluding six years of war, more than 14,000 Americans had died in Viet Nam.

on straight roads where visibility on all sides extends for miles. They happen in Viet Cong base areas, and in suburbs of Saigon itself, assumed to have been completely secure.

There is one thing most Viet Cong ambushes have in common. The guerrillas nearly always see to it that the advantages of surprise, superiority of firepower and local superiority in numbers are on their side. Throughout the nation, government forces may outnumber the Viet Cong ten to one, but in the battles themselves, the Viet Cong always tries to get the odds on its side.

I once visited Dong Xoai on National Route 14 a few hours after one of the typical big ambushes. It happened this way:

The rich, alluvial flatlands of the Mekong River Delta extend north to Saigon. But north of Saigon, the verdant rice fields trail off into uncultivated jungle dotted here and there with enormous rubber plantations. The rubber trees and scrub growth of the jungle look from the air like a continuous green canopy, slashed in places by narrow roads. For more than fifty miles north of Saigon, this flat jungle extends to the foothills of the forbidding and remote Central Vietnamese mountains, where the real forest begins.

From Saigon, there are three main roads heading north.

The first is National Route 1, which goes fifteen miles north of Saigon to Bien Hoa, then cuts due east across the great flat jungle to the South China Sea coast, and then 400 miles north, right along the coastline, to the border of communist North Viet Nam. South Viet Nam's only railroad line runs parallel to this road.

The second road, National Route 14, slices north-northeast of Saigon, up through the flat jungle, to the highlands capital of Ban Me Thuot 160 miles away.

The third road, National Route 13, goes due north of Saigon, through the flat jungle and many rubber plantations, to a place called Loc Ninh which is almost on the Cambodian border. The road ends at Loc Ninh, sixty miles north of the capital. There used to be a railroad spur paralleling this road, but the Viet Cong mutilated it so badly it has not been used in years.

Along all of these roads are hamlets and towns, with military posts and headquaters. Hamlets are concentrated along these three main roads because the rest of the country-

side is so isolated from communication with the outer world.
Hamlets mean tax collection and administration, and therefore are guarded by military post. These posts, in turn, have
to be supplied with ammunition and equipment, and their
troops must be paid.

Resupplying posts on any of these three roads is a risky
business. The things carried by truck to military posts are the
very things the Viet Cong needs most and will try to get at all
cost. For this reason, supply runs are always escorted by
troops and sometimes with armor.

This convoy was a routine monthly supply run from the
province capital, along Route 14 about thirty miles northeast,
to a post a few miles beyond the hamlet of Dong Xoai. Troops
along the way would receive drums of gasoline for their
vehicles, rice and other provisions, replacement weapons
and fresh stocks of ammunition, some new field radios, and a
payroll of two million piastres (about $20,000).

The guerrillas had been active lately, and it would be
better not to take chances. So the province chief made up the
convoy this way:

The first vehicle and the last vehicle would be "Ferret"
armored cars, with 37-millimeter cannons in their turrets.
The second and third vehicles would be jeeps for use by the
convoy commander and his aides. The next seven vehicles
would be two-and-a-half-ton trucks loaded with the supplies
and escort troops.

Each truck was open, giving troops riding in the back
clear fields of fire. Behind the cab of each truck a ring-
mounted heavy machine gun would add more firepower.

In short, this was to be a "heavy" convoy, protected by
armor, two antitank cannons, seven heavy machine guns and
about fifty soldiers, many of them carrying Tommy guns or
other automatic weapons.

The convoy commander, a major named La, had a lei-
surely breakfast at an open-air coffee shop in town near
province headquarters. He told officers with him he hoped
to finish the day (a Friday) early, because he was planning to
go down to Saigon over the weekend to see his family.

The officers, all in battle gear and carrying weapons,
were relaxed and cheerful as they sipped glasses of coffee
made sticky sweet with condensed milk. This resupply job
had been planned many days in advance, right down to the

last detail, and nothing could go wrong. Some civilians drinking coffee at other tables listened quietly as the officers talked.

An hour later, at about 9 A.M., the convoy rolled boisterously out of the barbed wire barricades of the province headquarters compound, dogs yapping at the wheels of the armored cars. It was a sunny, cool morning, and the soldiers were looking forward to the ride.

The cars and trucks roared through the market place, taking street corners so sharply that bicycles and pedestrians ran up on the sidewalks for cover.

The main street narrowed to a smooth blacktop road, and the houses, shops and junk yards gave way to jungle. This was Route 14 proper.

The jungle was dense, but not quite so dense as in parts of the delta, where trees and vines grew right at the edge of the pavement, hiding anything more than ten feet from the road. Here, the trees were taller and the scrub growth more spread out. The flanks of the road had been cleared fifty yards or so on each side of the pavement. The road itself was level and ran straight as an arrow for miles, with only slight curves at a few points. The pavement was in good condition, and the convoy sped along at fifty miles an hour, the vehicles spaced about fifty yards apart.

Here and there the road passed mountain tribesmen's small settlements surrounded by sharpened picket fences.

The huge tribal "long houses," on stilts and with towering eaves, contrasted sharply with the small ground-level Vietnamese huts.

Major La, sitting in the front of his jeep next to his driver, yawned with boredom and peeled a banana he had brought along. It would be only a matter of four miles before the first stop, where the hardest part of the trip would be over.

Hidden in camouflaged foxholes and under bushes on the right side of the road 100 yards ahead were more than 1,000 Viet Cong guerrillas, but nothing showed.

The first thing Major La saw was a geyser of orange flame and debris crunching against the armored car just ahead. The next thing was the blast of a recoilless cannon somewhere off in the bushes, and the almost instantaneous impact of an armor-piercing shell on the armored car. The third and last thing was the simultaneous roar of twenty-five mines exploding all along the convoy, the shattering crack of more recoilless cannon fire, and the roar of such concentrated machine-gun fire that the sound of one shot could not be distinguished from another.

The entire convoy was stopped, burning and bleeding, in the space of ten seconds. A huge fireball had burst from one of the trucks loaded with gasoline drums. The leading armored car was burning fiercely, its ammunition exploding inside the red-hot hull. The stricken machine heaved with each blast in its innards, like a dying beetle.

Most but not all of the troops were dead or dying. Some were still fighting.

The entire convoy was stopped, and burning vehicles blocked the road, both fore and aft. The only hope of survival was to fight. Three of the heavy machine guns were in action, firing continuously into the bushes.

But after the first volleys of mines, recoilless cannon and machine guns, the Viet Cong had left their holes and were now swarming over the convoy. They were sturdy young men dressed in baggy black trousers and blouses and armed to the teeth. They moved like lightning, darting in and out of exposed areas and up on the trucks themselves. From time to time, one of the convoy machine guns would catch a cluster of them in the open and cut them to pieces.

Major La's jeep had rolled over on its side after swerving off the road. He was wounded but still alive when they found him. A guerrilla yanked La's pistol from his hand, laughed, and shot the officer through the eye. In the back of the jeep, the intruder found a cloth sack containing the payroll. He grabbed it and ran back to the bushes.

The guerrillas clawed their way up even on the burning vehicles, shooting and knifing the defenders, and stripping off radios and machine guns with the speed of skilled mechanics. Hordes of unarmed guerrilla bearers had now joined the assault force, carrying and dragging bags and crates off into the jungle. Some of them were picking up the bodies of guerrillas killed in the fighting, and lugging them off, too.

Fifteen minutes after the first explosion, some of the convoy guns were still firing, but it was all over. One of the guerrillas blew a few shrill blasts from a police whistle, and the whole mass of black-clad men fell back as fast as it had attacked.

One of the radios in the convoy had had time to send out a distress signal before the end came, and a relief column was being slapped together. The relief column, which consisted of four truckloads of troops and four more armored cars, arrived two hours later, at about noon. I came along with it.

The ambush site was eerie. Jungle life had nearly returned to normal, and all was deadly quiet except for the chirping of a few birds and the hissing crackle of brush fires and burning vehicle tires. Every few minutes a shot would ring out and troops would jump for cover. But each time it was only a cartridge exploding from the heat of flames.

The trucks and armored cars were slewed around at odd angles, one of them turned completely around. For a half mile around, the jungle stank of cordite smoke, gasoline fumes and roasted flesh. The pavement was bloody, and the moaning wounded lay jumbled together with the dead.

All but two of the heavy machine guns had been carried off by the guerrillas, along with about forty rifles and submachine guns, five field radios, ammunition, two heavy mortars and a lot of other things. Nearly every dead soldier had been stripped of his watch and his wallet. Out of the whole convoy, fewer than one third of the men were still alive, and only a half dozen who had taken cover in bushes on the other side of the road were without wounds.

But the right side of the road showed that the guerrillas had not emerged unscathed. Shreds of black clothing and odds and ends of field gear clung to the bushes, all of which were spattered with blood. Twenty-seven guerrilla bodies were strewn around in the bush, some of them curled up like embryos in the holes where they died.

Some had been literally chopped to pieces by .50-caliber machine-gun fire. At one spot, I found an arm and shoulder around which still hung a canteen made from a bamboo log and filled with coconut milk. The rest of the body was nearly ten feet away. There was mute evidence that many of the dead guerrillas had been carried off by their comrades. Under a bush about fifty yards from the road I found a human brain so completely intact that it looked like the result of a surgical dissection. Next to it was a chunk of skull about five

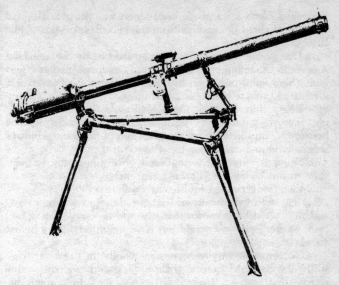

57-mm. Chicom Recoiless Rifle Type 36

inches square, with fragments of scalp and hair still attached. But there was no body within thirty yards of the place, only a trail of blood on the bushes leading back into the high jungle.

The guerrillas plainly had taken losses, although it was impossible to estimate how many. But by their own standards, the ambush had been a brilliant success. Enough arms and ammunition had been looted from the convoy to equip an entire guerrilla heavy weapons company, along with a payroll that would make the political commissars back in the jungle happy for weeks.

The backbone of the ambush had been mines and recoilless cannon. We found later that forty mines had been planted along the road, only twenty-five of which had exploded. Demolition crews dug up the others, and found that they all had been made from captured American 105-millimeter howitzer shells. The nose fuse had been unscrewed from each shell and an electric primer cap inserted into the well instead. Wires from each mine led back to a place about a hundred yards from the road where the guerrillas apparently had used some kind of electric generator. We also found a number of cartridge casings from the recoilless cannon shells they had used.

The perforated brass cases appeared to be the standard American 57-millimeter variety, but weapons experts said later there were marks on the bases of these shell cases that identified them as Chinese communist.

I have described the Dong Xoai ambush in some detail, not because there is anything extraordinary about it, but because it was so typical of hundreds and perhaps thousands of similar minor disasters for the Free World.

The guerrillas outmaneuvered government forces from start to finish, for the following reasons:

Viet Cong tactical intelligence was excellent. The guerrillas knew exactly when and where the convoy was to go, and they must have known that it would be carrying supplies they wanted, or they would not have mounted such a heavy attack.

Government intelligence was wholly inoperative. Despite the fact that more than a thousand guerrillas and bearers had moved through fairly populous areas near the road, had dug up road shoulders for a half mile to place their mines, and had lain in wait for several hours at least, no word of warning ever reached government authorities. Many peasants and children must have wandered right through the ambush and must have known what was planned, but nothing was said.

There is a standing rule with the Viet Cong that battle must never be given unless guerrilla forces outnumber the enemy in men and weapons by overwhelming odds. Therefore, the guerrillas had to know in advance fairly exactly how strong convoy defenses would be, and they did know.

Finally, the guerrillas had psychology on their side. They picked a harmless-looking spot for their ambush, nowhere near a turn in the road or a hill or a tree line or any other obvious route, knowing that the troops would be relaxed and off guard as they neared their destination.

As the convoy moved through the fatal spot, it had fairly dense foliage on its left but fairly open scrub growth on its right. A West Point-trained officer would expect, if there was an ambush at this point, that the guerrillas would hide themselves in the cover offered by the left side of the road,

which would give them a clear field of fire through the
convoy and into the open side. Instead, the guerrillas did
exactly the reverse. Furthermore, they had studded the
bushes and reeds on the left side of the road with barbed
steel nails and sharpened bamboo foot traps on which a few of
the convoy soldiers who had tried to fall back were wounded.

According to later intelligence, only about two hundred
of the guerrillas were armed, regular Viet Cong troops. The
rest were peasant youths living in the area, pressed into
service by the fighters to serve as coolies in digging foxholes
and mine emplacements and to carry off equipment and
bodies. But none of these "extras" turned traitor to their
bosses, and all of them worked with the same courage and
discipline as the regulars.

No matter how you look at it, this kind of thing is
depressing. A really successful ambush is always a morale
booster for the Viet Cong. Normally, the guerrillas pull out
fast when they have completed the job. But sometimes they
stick around long enough for their field photographers to do
some work.

Many a captured or dead Viet Cong is found carrying
war photographs pasted into his field manual. Such pictures
most often show a guerrilla holding a Tommy gun or rifle, his
bush hat cocked at a rakish angle, standing with one foot on
the neck of a government soldier, with a burning truck or
jeep in the background. Sometimes the guerrillas ham it up
for the photographers, and even carry bugles hung with Viet
Cong pennants. One of their proudest pictures showed a trio
of guerrillas standing atop the wreckage of a U.S. Army H21
helicopter, grinning and with their arms akimbo.

Not all ambushes are successful, of course. Sometimes
an ambush may consist only of one mine in the road and ten
or twelve guerrillas ready to open fire on the hapless vehicle
it disables. My own life has been saved more than once by
drivers with quick reflexes who stamp on the gas when the
mine goes off. The mines nearly always are planted at the
side of the road, not directly under the vehicle, and there is
usually a fair chance of getting away, even if it means driving
at seventy miles an hour on flat tires.

It is possible to drive through even Viet Cong base areas
without incident if you are lucky and you don't look military.
Because of an emergency (an attempted coup in Saigon and

the consequent grounding of all airplanes), I once had to drive all the way from Ca Mau at the southern tip of Viet Nam to Saigon, through 160 miles of the most dangerous terrain in the country. I rented a rusty and badly dented 1938 Chevrolet sedan for the drive, and the local province chief insisted on assigning me a troop escort for the first ten miles out of his headquarters. There were sixty soldiers concealed in two gaily painted produce trucks which followed me at a very discreet distance.

Soon after the trucks turned back, in a desolate stretch of woodland, two men in black on bicycles darted from the foliage into the middle of the road, forcing me to stop short. They pedaled slowly past the car window, looking me over closely, and then past the car and back into the forest. Apparently I passed inspection, and nothing further happened.

Single vehicles often are checked at Viet Cong road-blocks. On the highway leading fifty miles from Saigon to the picturesque seaside resort of Cap St. Jacques, thirty or forty cars and buses sometimes are halted at a time by a Viet Cong agitprop (agitation and propaganda) block. Traffic on the highways is especially heavy on weekends, and a good share of it is diplomatic—especially French and English officials off for a day of sunshine and lobster dinners. In keeping with the social caliber of this traffic, the Viet Cong who man the blocks along this road generally are polite and avoid violence.

Typically, the Viet Cong guard, dressed in a crisp khaki uniform without insignia, walks up to the car driver, salutes, and says (in French): "Good afternoon sir, I hope you have a pleasant day at the beach. The National Liberation Front would appreciate it if you would take these brochures along to read at your convenience. You may proceed, but I would advise you to return to Saigon before dark, or else stay over at Cap St. Jacques until tomorrow. Thank you."

The brochures, neatly mimeographed leaflets in French, always begin "Dear foreign friend," and are signed "The Phuoc Tuy Provincial Central Committee of the Front for the Liberation of South Viet Nam."

A few miles farther down the road, the driver comes to a government check point, where police salute smartly, wish the driver a pleasant day at the beach, and collect a ten-cent tourist toll, if the car happens not to have diplomatic license plates. The whole thing is very correct and proper. Even

Americans normally go through the check points with no trouble, since identification papers and nationalities are not checked, this being a Viet Cong "showcase road." French drivers take no chances, and their cars always have little tricolor flag decals stuck to their windshields and rear bumpers.

Only an occasional eyesore mars the road. In a few places, the holiday driver can see the burned-out wreckage of military trucks. At one point, a simple concrete monument erected by Madame Ngo Dinh Nhu, former Vietnamese first lady, marks the place where two girls from Madame Nhu's paramilitary women's corps were butchered by the Viet Cong.

On other roads, the Viet Cong is a little rougher on passersby. Buses are often stopped and searched. If any passengers turn out to be soldiers, in or out of uniform, they invariably are taken off in the woods. The rest of the passengers normally pay a tax (whatever jewelry they have, and most of their money) to the Liberation Front men, and then attend a mandatory lecture in the woods. After a few hours' delay, the buses generally are allowed to pass.

This is not to imply, of course, that American servicemen are let off by Viet Cong ambushes. A GI caught in an ambush is very lucky to be taken prisoner; most are killed on the spot. Even being captured is no assurance that a life is permanently spared.

American military and civilian captives of the Viet Cong are killed from time to time, especially as hostages, in retaliation for execution by the Saigon government of captured Viet Cong.

Gustav Hertz, the senior administrative officer at the U.S. AID Mission in Saigon, was captured while riding his motorcycle near Saigon, and after many months of captivity eventually was put to death.

Theoretically, trucks used in road convoys in Viet Nam are supposed to have been modified so that their seats for the soldiers are removed from the sides—in which position the soldiers must sit facing in—and replaced by seats in the middle, on which the soldiers face out. Actually, there are almost none of these modified trucks, and troops still ride along with their backs exposed to the sides of roads. A few trucks also are supposed to have been fitted with armor around the troops, but I have yet to see one.

Somehow, the monotonous horror of convoy ambushes

never abates, and increasing numbers of Americans are dying in these slaughters. The death toll along Route 13 in particular has earned that awful road the name "Bloody Route 13."

The particular aspect of both Routes 13 and 14 is that they very nearly bisect the huge, flat jungle zone owned by the Viet Cong just north of Saigon. To the north and northeast of Saigon is a 2,000-square-mile stretch of jungle known as "D Zone."

Since French colonial days, D Zone has been a primary base area for the guerrillas, and they still operate in enormous strength under its protective green shroud. Because of the huge trees that blanket the whole area, helicopter landing pads must be blasted out of the jungle, and parachute drops are extremely risky. D Zone is a bad place for a paratrooper to get hung up in a 200-foot tree. There are virtually no roads in the area, and movement of ground troops over this vast pocket of wilderness is agonizingly slow. From the air, only an occasional rivulet or stream bed breaks the terrain, and fighter planes practice their strafing and rocket runs here. The trees are so high the tracers and rockets just disappear into the green carpet below, with no sign of explosions or impacts.

To the west of D Zone and more or less contiguous with it is another vast wilderness sometimes called "C Zone," which stretches all the way to the unmarked frontier between Tay Ninh Province and Cambodia. The same jungle extends many miles over into the Cambodian side, and it is impossible to tell without maps where the border lies. The supreme headquarters of the National Liberation Front operates somewhere within this huge C Zone. So does a powerful Viet Cong propaganda transmitter which Saigon and American forces never have managed to silence permanently.

Despite increasingly frequent American forays into C Zone, the guerrillas continue to have a fairly free hand both there and in D Zone. C Zone can be reached easily from Cambodia, which extends up through increasingly high and remote mountains to the Laos frontier. The part of Laos where the South Vietnamese and Cambodia borders meet, incidentally, has been controlled for years by the communist-led Pathet Lao, the Viet Cong's sister organization.

Combined Pathet Lao and Viet Cong territory from there on runs all the way up through North Viet Nam to the frontier of communist China. Travel through this rain-soaked jungle-choked part of the world, where food is always scarce and tigers are plentiful, is arduous and unpleasant. But the Viet Cong has had decades to learn how to do it.

To return to my subject, Routes 13 and 14 lie crimped between C Zone and D Zone, and their strategic importance is obvious. For the Saigon government, they are the sole overland communications link to the north central highlands and the various hamlets and posts along the way. They also serve some very large French-owned rubber plantations that continue somehow to operate profitably right in the Viet Cong's back yard.

For the Viet Cong, neither of these two roads provides any difficulty in communication between C Zone and D Zone, since neither road can be guarded adequately without deploying every soldier in South Viet Nam along it. But they are useful arteries from which to suck government blood and materiel. The government is forced to continue using them, if only for the reason that to abandon these two deathtraps would mean virtually surrendering a sizable hunk of Viet Nam to the enemy altogether. Posts can always be resupplied by air, but this does nothing to solve the ultimate problem of regaining control of the countryside.

On the other hand, no measures aimed at securing Routes 13 and 14 ever can be effective until Viet Cong strength is broken in the huge zones flanking them. These two roads thus pose a dilemma to the Saigon government that has all the marks of a vicious circle.

American forces, including the 173rd Airborne Brigade, the 1st Infantry Division, the 25th Infantry Division and other outfits, have fought many frustrating clashes in this region. Place names like "Iron Triangle," "Ho Bo Woods," and "Boi Loi Forest" all are in the area and all recall many bloody American fights.

The kind of terrain I have been describing is next to useless for fighting big battles. Air cover is extremely handicapped. Artillery must fire blindly. Ground troops get lost in the maze of trees. The enemy has the advantage of prepared positions and mastery of the terrain. A division of regular troops can get mired in such a maze without finding anything more than a few snipers. But this is ideal country for ambushes.

The Dong Xoai ambush was a fairly simple, straightforward operation compared with many the Viet Cong has mounted.

In February 1964, for instance, the Vietnamese decided to jump three battalions of paratroopers on a field operation—a venture requiring extremes of courage and tactical shrewdness. This particular operation (near the edge of C Zone) was under the command of Colonel Cao Van Vien himself, the top government paratroop officer, and was supported by M113 amphibious armored personnel carriers.

As usual, Viet Cong intelligence was excellent and their planning nearly perfect. Fifteen hundred crack government troops with armor comprises too much of a bite for most Viet Cong units to chew, so the Viet Cong decided to try to knock off just the headquarters company and Vien himself.

Vien's force had been moving eastward along the Cambodian frontier in fairly open country. His battalions were strung out more or less in column, although the troops were not moving by road. With them were several American advisors. Vien's headquarters company was toward the rear of the line of march at the time. This company was just passing about a hundred yards south of a deserted-looking hamlet when the Viet Cong in the hamlet opened up. With Vien were fewer than 200 men, all out in an open field and right under the guns of the concealed Viet Cong emplacements. The guerrillas had many 57-millimeter recoilless cannon and a solid wall of machine guns, all dug in at ground level to produce grazing fire, the most dangerous kind.

Vien's men were dying like flies all around him. Several of the armored personnel carriers had been disabled or forced back by cannon shells. A Vietnamese brigadier general who happened to have accompanied the operation was driving one of the M113s, desperately trying to rally the other vehicles.

Vien saw only one chance: An old-fashioned frontal charge right into the Viet Cong lines. He yelled to his men, and got up and ran. Many of the little unit were cut down, and Vien was shot through the shoulder. An American advisor with Vien found himself at one point staring into the muzzle of a Viet Cong recoilless cannon, and felt sure he was about to be blown to fragments.

The enemy gunner tried to fire, but the cartridge was a dud, and the American shot him as he started to run.

From there on, it was a bitter trench fight. Vien's unit

found that it had fought its way only into the first of five lines of Viet Cong fortifications concealed in the hamlet. But by now, relief forces had got themselves turned around and were moving in to help Vien. Eventually, the bulk of the Viet Cong forces slipped out of the rear of the hamlet into the marshy fields beyond and escaped.

Vien's forces had suffered heavy casualties, but at least this time the enemy had left behind a satisfactory pile of bodies. Vien was shipped to a hospital in Saigon. A few days later, the Premier himself, Major General Nguyen Khanh, stopped around to pin the Cross of Gallantry and brigadier general's stars on Vien's pajamas.

Increasingly, the Viet Cong have been learning how to set up decoys in planning their ambushes. The usual way is to send a company or two of guerrillas to attack some government post which can normally be approached along only one route. The guerrillas lob mortar and cannon shells into the post and cut it up with machine guns, but make no effort to overrun it. This normally at least frightens the post defenders enough that they call for help by radio. The Viet Cong, incidentally, also have radios tuned to the same frequencies as the post defenders, and eavesdrop with interest on such conversations.

Meanwhile, a much larger Viet Cong force sets itself up in ambush a few miles away from the post and waits for its inevitable quarry.

This technique has been sophisticated to such a degree that sometimes the primary ambush is not the main objective, but itself becomes the bait for a second and much larger ambush as a relief force is sent to relieve the relief force. When the Viet Cong feels it has hooked a fish of regulation size, it then chews fast and moves out before the thing starts turning into a conventional battle.

Anything that channels a Vietnamese government or American force into a predetermined line of march can be used to set up an ambush. Roads, canals, trails, mountain passes and railroads are some examples. On June 22, 1967, the enemy used a ridge line to set up an ambush in which seventy-six American paratroopers were killed and another twenty-five wounded.

The enemy outfit, believed to be a battalion (about 400 men) of the North Vietnamese Army's 24th Regiment, pre-

Sikorsky CH-54 "Skycrane"

pared about seventy-five bunkers along the ridge line, which extends two miles southwest of Dak To. Dak To is an isolated fort about 280 miles north of Saigon, in mountains densely covered by jungle.

Brigadier General John R. Deane, who commanded the 173rd Airborne Brigade, planned to sweep the hills and ridges near Dak To completely clean of enemy. Before sending his forces into Operation Greeley, he talked confidently to reporters at his Dak To command post:

"What we're doing up here is trying to find the enemy. If there's any here, we'll destroy them," he said. "General Westmoreland has never mentioned it to me, but I think he considers this brigade the one to send when there's trouble. Many people refer to it as Westmoreland's Fire Brigade."

One company of the 173rd moved out of Dak To at 7:30 A.M. on June 22, inching its way along the northern slope of a ridge line. Two other companies of the 173rd were in the same area, but separated by several hundred yards.

The Viet Cong was armed with machine guns, carbines, recoilless cannon and grenades. In the course of the day, they cut all three companies to pieces, and air strikes were unable to blunt the VC assault.

Later, after the Viet Cong had left, American forces found about ten enemy bodies, along with the seventy-six slain paratroopers.

That ambush was no particular reflection on U.S. paratroopers; no American units have been spared.

One week prior to the ambush just described, units of the U.S. Army's 1st Infantry Division walked into a Viet Cong ambush a scant forty miles north of Saigon. In two hours of fighting, thirty-one GIs were killed and 113 wounded.

And the U.S. Marine Corps is continually ambushed, often with terrible results.

In the latter half of 1967, enemy units did all they could to harass marine units operating just south of the border between North and South Viet Nam. Almost continuous duels broke out between North Vietnamese mortar and artillery units and marines based at or near Con Thien, two miles south of the frontier. Marine artillery and Air Force bombers blasted the enemy positions in the "Demilitarized Zone" between the two Viet Nams and in North Viet Nam proper, but the enemy went on fighting.

On July 31, 1967, a battalion of marines of the 9th Regiment was returning to Con Thien from an operation in the Demilitarized Zone (DMZ) when North Vietnamese mortar fire roared in. The marines were strung out for nearly a mile, and the mortar shells drove them even farther apart.

At that point, the hitherto concealed enemy began blowing whistles and yelling, and attacked. As usual, fighting was at such close quarters that neither U.S. air strikes nor artillery could do much to help the leathernecks.

The North Vietnamese were badly mauled in the fight, and U.S. officers said forty enemy bodies were found later.

But during the action, twelve tanks, two of which were equipped with flamethrowers, were pinned down by the enemy and were unable to support the troops. One marine helicopter was shot down. And twenty-three marines were killed and 191 were wounded.

Fewer marines than Vietnamese had been killed, but the fight was not the kind the marines like to see happen often.

While the conventional military ambush makes use of existing cover and terrain features, the Viet Cong uses some fiendish tactics that have something in common with judo. There is, for example, an oblique crossfire gambit that has cost many a government unit in the flat rice country of the delta dearly. It works like this:

A small government unit, say 100 men, is moving across a long stretch of flooded rice paddies. The only high ground on which to walk is a straight, narrow path or road atop a wide paddy dyke. It is a strong temptation for any unit to move in a column along one of these little roads. It is exhausting to go for mile after mile in the paddies themselves, pulling one leg after the other out of the knee-deep muck. Especially when an operation has had no contact all day long, the quick, easy way of covering ground is almost always the method of choice.

Now our column is out in the middle of an ocean of these fields, the nearest tree line a mile or more away. Suddenly, heavy machine-gun fire starts coming in from the right side, 400 or 500 yards away.

The enemy machine gun is too far away to destroy the column, especially since it is firing at a long column facing it sideways. All the troops are in position to fire at the lone enemy gun, and the advantage is clearly on the government side. But still, the gun is not far enough away that it can be ignored. Slugs are snapping just overhead or thumping into the right bank of the dyke, and perhaps several of the men have been hit. So the main force does the instinctively correct thing: it jumps off the left side of the dyke into the paddy, so as to get maximum cover from the enemy gun and to use the road as a firing parapet.

But as in so many aspects of this war, the instinctively right thing is the wrong thing in practice. The left side of the dyke turns out to be studded with spiked foot traps, booby traps and mines. And another enemy machine gun, only 100 yards ahead and almost up against the left bank of the dyke, opens fire. This gun has the government troops in what is known as enfilade, which is the worst way to be. It means that only the few troops at the head of the line can fire on the enemy to defend themselves, while the enemy can cover the entire friendly group without having to change his aim at all. If he's lucky, one of his bullets may go through two or three of the defending soldiers.

This is a type of ambush in which the Viet Cong does not need overwhelming superiority of numbers to win. In fact, twenty-five guerrillas stand a reasonable chance of wiping out 100 government troops with minimal losses to themselves. The keys to success are exact planning and perfect camouflage. Camouflage is afforded easily, even in open fields, by such devices as lying under water with one's head protruding under a pile of straw.

On a somewhat larger scale, a Vietnamese government battalion once set out on a "search and destroy" operation within the Viet Cong stronghold known as the "Iron Triangle." There had been intelligence reports that a couple of reinforced Viet Cong companies were camped dead ahead of the government battalion's line of march, and the object was to make contact.

The jungle was dense and movement was slow. At nightfall, the government force reached a deep stream and decided to defer crossing until morning. Scouts were sent out during the night to pick a line of march for the following day. They discovered a bridge made of two logs flung across the stream, and decided the main body would start here in the morning. American advisors said later they felt pretty sure the Viet Cong had put down those two logs to smooth the path into the trap.

So the following morning, 400 troops moved across the makeshift bridge and found themselves on a faint trail. To the left of the trail was dense jungle clogged with vines, and to the right was underbrush which looked a little more open. The troops started cautiously down the trail, alert for ambush.

After a quarter of a mile, fairly heavy small-arms fire opened up on them from dead ahead. By the sounds, at least a platoon and possibly a company was firing. The bullets ticked through the tree branches, but the fire was spotty and inaccurate.

"Aha," the battalion commander told an aide, "they think they've caught us, but they opened fire too soon. We'll turn the tables on them and flank their ambush."

With that, the commander assigned a platoon to stay in the path to continue to fire at the Viet Cong up ahead, while the commander and the rest of the battalion moved off to the right into the scrub. Making a wide arc, the whole government force threaded itself through the underbrush until it had come up abreast of the sound of the enemy firing and about 500 yards to the right of the presumed Viet Cong ambush. Then the roof fell in.

Concentrated machine-gun fire from three sides swept over the battalion, and it was immediately apparent the unit had walked into the open end of a horseshoe-shaped trap. But the worst was yet to come. A few seconds after the new firing began, the first of a series of heavy mortar shells landed right in the middle of the loose battalion formation, killing a dozen men. A hideous barrage of 81-millimeter mortar shells hissed down through the treetops, and each shell had fatal results. There were no marking rounds or "walking in" to bracket the target; the first shell was right on target.

The battalion lost more than one third of its men in the first ten minutes of the barrage. There is no apparent reason why the Viet Cong could not have gone on to annihilate the whole unit, but for some reason the guerrillas decided not to. They broke contact as abruptly as they had begun and faded away into the jungle, probably without a single casualty.

A relief force and the remnants of the battalion later inspected the deserted Viet Cong positions. The Viet Cong had so precisely pinpointed the spot where they would nail the government battalion that their mortars had been zeroed in in advance. And to make sure nothing went wrong with the mortar shells, the guerrillas had even chopped away foliage over their mortar tubes to coincide exactly with the trajectories they planned to use.

That operation was an unpleasant demonstration not only of the sophistication with which the Viet Cong has learned to operate ambushes, but of the real insight of Viet Cong commanders into the military psychology of their Western-trained opposite numbers. More than anywhere else, the doctrines of St. Cyr and West Point led that ill-fated battalion to its undoing.

Part of the effectiveness of Viet Cong ambush tactics depends on lightning speed in engaging convoys in hand-to-hand combat.

The American pilot of an L19 spotter plane was cruising over the Mekong Delta, directly over a marching column of Vietnamese troops. He happened to be watching this column move across a field when suddenly the unit was taken under fire. Men were running and falling, and at 1,000 feet, the pilot said he could clearly hear shooting, but the source of the shots could not be discerned. All at once, a second column of men, clad in black, materialized alongside the government group. The Viet Cong had been so perfectly camouflaged that when they stood up it seemed as if the roadside were turning into men by magic.

The pilot swooped down as he called by radio for help for the stricken unit. He thought of firing his automatic rifle at the attackers from the window of his plane, but by this time the Viet Cong were completely mixed in with the defenders, hacking them to pieces, man by man. Some of the Viet Cong were aiming automatic rifle fire at him, and he was forced to climb to avoid being hit.

Ambushes are not all on roads. Throughout the delta, a vast labyrinth of communications canals actually forms the primary means of travel, both for civilians and for soldiers.

Some of these canals, especially the ones deep enough to accommodate gunboats, are kept closed down by the Viet Cong. The guerrillas, using armies of forced laborers, simply dam up the canals with a lattice of logs overlaid with mud. To make sure the dams stay in place they are usually mined. It takes a team of government frogmen more than a day to demolish one of these dams with underwater charges. And then they are usually rebuilt in a matter of weeks.

But on the other canals, the Viet Cong rely on ambush to keep out intruders. Many canals are not much wider than roads and afford exactly the same ambush potential. Convoys of government boats often are escorted by gunboats armed with machine guns or 20-millimeter cannon, with which they can sweep fields beyond the canal banks. But they are just as susceptible as armored cars to ambush.

In the early years of the war, the Viet Cong invented a gadget they called the "lance bomb," which is just about as destructive as a 3.5-inch rocket. The lance bomb, entirely homemade, has a high-explosive warhead made of scrap iron. Behind the head are four small fins, and trailing back behind is a tube that looks like a stovepipe. This tube contains a propellant charge that is set off electrically. To fire a lance bomb, a stake with a short yardarm is needed. The yardarm is shaped so as to fit snugly inside the end of the rocket tube of the lance bomb. The stake is driven into the ground just before firing, with the yardarm and bomb precisely aimed at the target. The guerrila then runs his wires back to a safe distance and cranks his magneto.

A lance bomb will demolish a brick watchtower or stop a

light tank. It will also pierce an armored gunboat. Lance bombs are often mounted in trees overlooking canals, pre-aimed at just the place where the hull of a passing gunboat would meet the water. A guerrilla hundreds of feet away has only to watch the boat come, wait for it to come exactly abreast of some landmark, and then crank his magneto. Many a landing craft and gunboat are now rusting at the bottom of canals as the result of lance bombs.

Railroad ambushes deserve special mention. The national railroad, which, as I mentioned earlier, runs all the way up the coast of South Viet Nam from Saigon, has been sabotaged at one point or another several times a day for the past two years. It is a marvel to me that it continues to run at all. Big steel bridges are regularly blown up, long trains are derailed by running over torn up track, and a tattoo of sniper fire rolls down at trains from a hundred spots. Occasionally the Viet Cong stops a train, detaches the locomotive, and sends it hurtling driverless down the track at full speed. The locomotive invariably smashes into something, usually another train stopped at a station. But while these incidents make for spectacular destruction and sometimes heavy loss of life, they are not quite the same thing as ambushes. The true ambush involves shooting up and halting a train defended by troops, and then looting it for supplies and equipment.

In any case, train rides in South Viet Nam are not particularly pleasant, even though the passenger coaches are comfortable and good dining cars are usually taken along.

I made one trip from the Central Vietnamese city of Quang Ngai to Saigon at a time near an important Vietnamese holiday, and many of my fellow passengers were troops on pass going home to their families. None of them was in uniform, and each was trying to look as much as possible like a harmless civilian. I noticed that when the train slowed down to five miles an hour or so (which it always did over stretches where derailment could mean a plunge over a cliff) the soldiers would take out their military identification cards and hold them out the open windows of the train. I asked one why.

"If the Viet Cong board the train, we don't want to be found carrying these cards. They would take us away for good," he said.

At one place, near the town of Tuy Hoa, nine soldiers

locked themselves in a tiny lavatory for a solid hour while a trackman checked conditions up ahead of the stopped train. Passengers have grounds for fear.

After leaving Saigon, the railroad goes fifteen miles north to Bien Hoa, and then, paralleling Route 1 all the way, strikes east through part of the jungles of D Zone on its way to the sea. The track then arcs north, and gradually reaches the coastline itself. This stretch of track is where a lot of the worst ambushes occur.

One night, some American advisors were enjoying martinis on the roof of their hotel in Phan Thiet, a small coastal town 100 miles east of Saigon, near which the rail line passes. As the advisors stood chatting about their day's work, a glaring orange fireball billowed up from the distant jungle, followed a few seconds later by a dull boom. The Viet Cong had attacked a large supply train moving north, and a cannon shell had ignited the train's supply of diesel fuel. It proved impossible to send a relief force out to the stricken train that night, but about dawn a relief train loaded with troops moved into the area and was promptly ambushed. The relief train was badly mauled, but most of its troops survived and fought their way to the first train, where guerrillas were still carting off huge stocks of rice and other provisions. It was estimated later that more than 2,000 Viet Cong must have worked on that train all night long, unloading its cargo and padding off into the jungle.

One of the things the Viet Cong found aboard the train was half a boxcar of bottled beer—tens of thousands of bottles. There was an amusing aftermath to the big beer haul.

Phan Thiet itself is more or less under government control, but everything immediately outside the town is in Viet Cong hands. Even the airstrip one mile away is sometimes under mortar fire. One end of the strip is almost in the jungle, and it is dangerous to park planes there. The other end of the strip is at the top of a cliff of red earth that drops several hundred feet to the ocean. Because low approaches over the jungle end of the strip draw dangerous ground fire, planes must land coming in from the sea, something like landing on an aircraft carrier. And they generally take off in the opposite direction, regardless of the wind.

But 500 feet from the end of this runway is a hamlet which at least part of the time is fairly friendly to government

Colt .45 Automatic, M 1911A1

authorities. From one side of the hamlet is a gently sloping field that ends in a cliff over the ocean. This field is full of small game, and several American enlisted men from the Phan Thiet detachment used to like to hunt there.

One of these Sunday afternoon hunters was a sturdy little sergeant first class named Roque Matagulay who had been born and raised on Guam and who knew a lot about guerrilla warfare from Japanese occupation days on his home island. But one afternoon, a Viet Cong squad was out waiting for Matagulay in his hunting preserve, and they jumped him. He held off the guerrillas until his ammunition ran out, and then had to surrender.

Matagulay was in Viet Cong hands about six months, and conditions in the jungle were very bad. A political re-education officer assigned to him worked him over for long hours each day.

"As a Negro, you should understand as well as we the nature of American racist imperialism," the commissar told Matagulay one day.

"But I'm not a Negro, I'm a Guamanian."

"What's that?"

Matagulay patiently sketched a map of the United States on the ground, and another map of the coast of Asia, and in the Pacific Ocean space in between he marked with a dot the island of Guam.

"Ah, then you are an Asian and one of the peoples oppressed by the Americans," the commissar said.

"No. I'm a Guamanian and an American," Matagulay answered.

This kind of thing went on for a long time. Matagulay was fed no worse than his Viet Cong captors, but no better, and they were living on rice and rat soup. He contracted malaria and, later, dysentery. Matagulay held out better than most American prisoners, but his health was dangerously bad. The Viet Cong knew they would have to improve his diet if they wanted him to live, and they already had decided on sending him back to his detachment, so they wanted him to look as good as possible.

One day, Matagulay awoke from a fevered nap to find one of his guards offering him the best dinner he had seen since being captured. There were salted meat, some canned vegetables, canned fruit, and even a nice bottle of beer.

"Where in hell did all this come from?" he asked the commissar. The Viet Cong smiled and said: "By good fortune, it happens that last night the people's forces blew up an imperialist train near here. All this, including the beer, comes from the train."

The Viet Cong have even tried to ambush helicopters by tempting them to land in traps.

Viet Cong radio communications are so good that the guerrillas can very often monitor helicopter frequencies and make effective use of the conversations they hear. On many missions, helicopter pilots ask ground troops to mark safe landing spots with smoke grenades. These grenades produce different colors of smoke used to signify different things. Not long ago a helicopter ambulance was called into a battle area north of Saigon to pick up some casualties. The area was mostly covered with jungle, but there were a few clear patches apparently safe for landing. The pilot radioed to the ground: "I can't see you. Give me some brown smoke."

Almost instantly, a puff of brown smoke rose from one of the patches, and the helicopter settled down into it. The machine was within ten feet of the ground when a fusillade of tracer bullets came spraying out of the woods at it. The pilot glanced around, saw no troops of any kind, and hastily pulled full pitch, rocketing out of the clearing. At a little higher altitude, he spotted another column of brown smoke rising from a patch nearly a mile away. The second patch turned out to be the right one.

Many of the clear fields around hamlets in the Mekong Delta appear from the air to be perfectly safe landing spots, but actually are studded with long wooden spikes that would tear a helicopter fuselage to shreds. Viet Cong units sometimes try to lure "eagle flights" of helicopters into landing in such places.

In summary, it is probably safe to say that the primary distinguishing military feature of the Vietnamese war is the ambush.

Americans tend to despise the ambush as an inferior form of warfare employed by cowards and thieves in the night. This it may be, but it is as effective now as when the American Continental Army used it against the British redcoats. It is a tactic that enables the weak to attack and destroy the strong, particularly when used by highly skilled military tacticians.

Various defenses against ambushes have been developed. Armored railroad coaches called Wickham trolleys now travel with many Vietnamese trains. The Wickham trolleys, used by the British in the Malayan guerrilla campaign, have gun turrets and actually are tanks on rails. And they are often derailed.

To deprive guerrillas along roads and canals of natural cover, the U.S. Air Force put into effect a huge program to spray the jungles along communications arteries with a herbicide spray. After nearly a year of experiments, the Air Force finally got the defoliation program to work, and now broad strips along roads and canals have been cleared of foliage. But the ambushes continue. Unfortunately, skillful Viet Cong guerrillas can mount successful ambushes just as well in open fields as in jungle growth.

Trucks have been armed with all kinds of antiambush gadgets, including one that spews bombs in all directions at the touch of a button in the driver's cab. About thirty trainees were killed by accident in a demonstration of one of these things at a camp near Saigon once, but I know of no instance in which the device was used successfully against a real ambush.

Vietnamese government and American troops are ambushed, most of all, because they are trained as conventional armies in conventional tactics. When they travel, they do so mostly on roads, railroads, canals or trails, all of which can be ambushed.

A guerrilla army such as the Viet Cong and its North Vietnamese Army ally generally travels in two and threes and stays away from regular routes when possible. It comes together only at the precise moment of battle. Thus, the enemy in Viet Nam is usually impossible to ambush.

Of course, the Viet Cong sometimes slips up, especially when it has become overconfident because of a series of successes against American or Saigon troops. American ambushes sometimes turn the tables on the guerrillas, badly mauling the enemy with his own tactics. This doesn't happen often.

Needless to say, the United States has sought to correct the situation, and there have been measures more positive than merely issuing soldiers wallet cards of antiambush instructions.

In 1966, the 3rd Training Brigade at Fort Polk, Louisiana, started a one-week course for GIs on orders to go to Viet Nam, and much of the training had to do with ambushes. Dummy Vietnamese villages were built at the post, and GIs were shown booby traps, typical ambush situations and simulated attacks.

Many instructors at the school, themselves veterans of Viet Nam, felt their efforts were futile.

"Sometimes I think only about half of the recruits really listen," a captain said. "It is inconceivable to me that they don't hang on to every word. What they learn here can save their lives."

Closer to the actual bloodletting, the U.S. Army's 25th Infantry Division set up an "ambush academy" in Viet Nam, under the close watch of General Westmoreland himself.

The ambush school opened at Cu Chi near the dangerous D Zone jungle in July 1966, and Westmoreland was on hand to inaugurate the school. He said:

"We must be masters of guerrilla tactics to a much higher degree than the Viet Cong. We are going to out-guerrilla the guerrillas and out-ambush the ambushers.

"The ambush is the classic tactic of the VC; he excels in it. He is best at this because he is disciplined—disciplined in camouflage, concealment and surprise. We are going to master the ambush and make the Viet Cong play into our hands."

Westmoreland went on to describe to the trainees the Viet Cong ambush slogan: "One slow, four quick."

The slow step is painstaking preparation and rehearsal of all attacks. The four quick steps are attack and open fire; exploit and pursue; clear the battlefield rapidly; and withdraw rapidly.

Unfortunately, the one-week Viet Nam course at Fort Polk and General Westmoreland's four-and-one-half-day ambush academy have not ended ambushes. Neither have all the gadgets and air power which were brought to bear on the problem.

The French fought essentially the same enemy in Indochina that the United States faces in Viet Nam. To the end, the French never found a solution to the ambushes that slowly tore them apart. Even when the Viet Minh shifted from guerrilla warfare to sull-scale "mobile warfare," the basic operating pattern remained the ambush, on a huge scale.

Ambush warfare requires a discipline and a way of thinking that are essentially alien to the United States of the 1960s.

Despite the classes, the gadgets and the think-tank analyses, the Viet Cong has maintained clear-cut supremacy in the tactic of the ambush.

9

TERROR AND
COUNTERTERROR

The agony of Dam Doi began many years ago and is not over. The little hamlet of a few thousand souls has bled and bled and bled, to the point at which it is hard to understand why anyone still lives there. The ties of ancestral bones buried in the alluvial mud nearby must be strong indeed.

I first visited Dam Doi in February 1962 and have been there often since then, always on grim business.

At the southernmost part of Viet Nam is a large tongue of land called the Ca Mau Peninsula which juts down from Indochina, dividing the South China Sea from the Gulf of Siam. Ca Mau, the capital of this region, is the southernmost town of any substance in Viet Nam. There is more land below Ca Mau, much of which is trackless mangrove swamp and practically all of which belongs to the Viet Cong, except for a few pinpoints on the map like Dam Doi (pronounced in Vietnamese as "dom yoy").

To the west of Dam Doi is a forest about forty miles long, running along the coast of the gulf of Siam. This forest is the base of the Viet Cong's notorious U Minh Battalion, one of the most feared units in the nation. To the east and south of Dam Doi are other important Viet Cong base areas, most of which are openly administered by the Viet Cong as "liberated zones."

There is no road connecting Dam Doi with the provincial capital of Ca Mau—only a footpath and a network of canals.

It was a scorching hot February morning when I first arrived in Ca Mau in a light plane which slid into the landing strip right in the center of town. A little river thick with sampans, houseboats and fishing nets curves through the center of town, and the part of the city inside the curve is a thriving market place. Cool maritime winds blow over Ca

Mau in the monsoon season, but in February there is no relief from the merciless heat. No one works any harder than necessary.

Ca Mau is the capital of An Xuyen Province, one of forty-five provinces making up South Viet Nam. Each province is divided into districts, and each district is divided at progressively lower levels into cantons, villages (which are not actual towns but geographical subdivisions), and, finally, hamlets.

Dam Doi, despite its tiny population, is the capital of Dam Doi District.

I mention these trivial administrative matters only because they have a bearing on the horror of life in places like Dam Doi. Each time an urgent plea for help passes from one level to a higher one, it must be processed through the red tape mill at each level. Really important things often have to go all the way to Saigon (which does not work nights or on weekends).

Let me set the stage a little more. At the time I arrived in Ca Mau, it happened that two battalions of Vietnamese marines, that is to say about nine hundred officers and men, were temporarily assigned to the province to guard work crews repairing a road in the northwest part of the province. It takes that many troops to prevent a road crew from being wiped out by the guerrillas.

Of course, as soon as the road crew and the marines leave, the road is invariably ripped up and planted with mines and bamboo groves, but the exercise is presumably good training for all concerned.

An Xuyen Province is poor, remote from Saigon, and at the bottom of priority lists for supplies, military operations, and nearly everything else. Saigon government troops rarely operated there, and American representation was limited to advisors.

But besides its regular army, Saigon had two large paramilitary forces which at the time were called Bao An (Civil Guard) and Dan Ve (People's Militia or Self-Defense Corps).*

*Since then, there have been many reorganizations of Vietnamese forces, including the theoretical absorption of all paramilitary forces into the defense establishment. Since the Self-Defense Corps (SDC) had acquired such a bad reputation with peasants, the name was changed to "Popular Forces" (PF). The over-all size of the paramilitary forces remained about as it was before the reorganizations, and PF units maintained a large degree of autonomy despite the new theoretical chain of command. Most peasants continued to regard the PF as cutthroats and pirates.

In the paramilitary forces, pay and other benefits were smaller than in the regular army. But a man joining the paramilitary forces stood a good chance of being assigned near or in his home community, not having to fight hundreds of miles away.

Thus, Ca Mau had its share of civil guards, self-defense corpsmen and youth corpsmen.

The city of Ca Mau had a few 105-millimeter howitzers that were fired nearly every night, supposedly to destroy Viet Cong as they attacked outlying hamlets. But these howitzers rarely hit anything except an occasional hut, and their range is not great enough to do anything for places like Dam Doi.

In addition to these forces, a Roman Catholic priest of Chinese origin, the Reverend Nguyen Lac Hoa, for several years maintained his own provate army of irregulars at a hamlet called Binh Hung south of Ca Mau. Father Hoa, a refugee from China and a former colonel in the Nationalist Chinese Army, settled his little band of Chinese refugees in about the most desolate and unpleasant bit of land anywhere in South Viet Nam. Almost completely cut off from the rest of the world and surrounded by large and extremely hostile Viet Cong units, Binh Hung nevertheless survived and grew.

Some Vietnamese from the province went to live in muddy Binh Hung, and Father Hoa recruited and trained his own irregular defense force, which he named the "Sea Swallows." More than one thousand men strong, this little fighting unit began to establish a reputation for disciplined and courageous fighting, and its reputation as a thorn in the very intestines of the Viet Cong began to spread.

The American Central Intelligence Agency took a keen interest in Binh Hung, and through its Combined Studies Group in Saigon and the U.S. Army Special Forces, regular airdrops of supplies began to pour into Binh Hung.

Bind Hung actually got some of these supplies before they were issued to anyone else—even the U.S. armed forces Supplies included the new ultralight AR-15 Armalite automatic weapon—the forerunner of the U.S. Army's M16 rifle. The M16 was one of several weapons first tested by Vietnamese forces before being adopted by U.S. forces. Binh Hung also was the first to get the new unsinkable Fiberglas assault boats equipped with outboard motors. U.S. planes flew down to Binh Hung at night whenever the Viet Cong mounted a large attack, dropping flares to help the defenders. An aging Chinese wearing a priest's robes and a steel helmet and pistol belt is a strange study in contrasts, but the combination worked. Since those early days, Father Hoa has given up his military command and the Sea Swallows have been incorporated into the regular national armed forces, but Binh Hung is still fighting.

At any rate, the Sea Swallows in 1962 were a valuable addition to the normal forces of An Xuyen Province. Father Hoa felt secure enough that he would even loan neighboring district chiefs a platoon or two of Sea Swallows, at times when they felt extra shotguns were needed.

In February 1962 a thirty-one-year-old Vietnamese army captain named Tran Van Kha was the chief of Dam Doi District. They say he had a wife in Saigon with whom he didn't get along and this was one of the reasons he welcomed his assignment to Dam Doi. He had been there about three months.

Kha was an ambitious young officer, spoiling for a fight with the guerrillas who ruled the murky jungle. He was also worried about Dam Doi's defenses.

Counting all his civil guards and militiamen, he had only about a score of able-bodied men to hold the hamlet itself. Every night the guerrillas did a little sniping and probing, and you never knew what might come next. So Kha sent word to Father Hoa that he would appreciate some extra men. Father Hoa obligingly sent a platoon of Sea Swallows over to Dam Doi, giving Kha a complement of sixty-four men, counting himself. That was how things stood when I arrived in Ca Mau.

It was long before dawn on a Saturday morning when Kha decided to lead his men out for a foray against the enemy. Two things probably led him to do it. One was his boredom with always sitting behind the barricades of Dam Doi, the initiative always on the side of the unseen but lethal enemy outside. The other was Kha's mistress, a girl of about twenty, in her seventh month of pregnancy. Through "contacts" of her own, the girl had told Kha, she had learned that a squad of Viet Cong propagandists was operating in a cluster of huts about three miles south of Dam Doi, and could easily be caught red-handed by such strong forces as Kha commanded. It has never been established whether or not Kha's mistress actually was a Viet Cong agent. But there is no question that this bit of intelligence she gave him led directly to his death.

By Saturday evening, Kha and his men had still not returned. A village official—a man too old to fight—was worried. He managed to raise Ca Mau by radio.

"The chief and his men have not returned after all this time. The sun is setting, and there are signs the Viet Cong may be planning an attack. Please send help. Please, please, send help," the old man said.

A radio operator in Ca Mau dutifully took down the message and carried it to the duty officer. The duty officer asked for counfirmation of the time Kha had left. Confirmation came back. The duty officer was stuck with a hot potato, and he knew it. But he manfully swung into action to pass the word to higher command.

I was having a flyspecked dinner with a major named Hoang at the time. Two listless sentries with the dark round faces of Cambodians stood at the gate outside. A few school-girls in their ankle-length *ao-dais*—graceful, high-necked dresses slit to the waist, and worn over loose white silk trousers—still stood chatting in the dusk, twirling their conical hats, fluffing their long black hair, and giggling. A steady stream of bicycles hurried people home to their dinners. Somewhere in the distance, a street vendor was yelling for customers for *pho*, a savory noodle soup favored by South Vietnamese.

The house was not the best in town, but neither was it the worst. It was a simple stucco house fit for a deputy province chief, which was the office Hoang held.

On the front porch, a squad of tough civil guards, their skin tanned almost black and all carrying Tommy guns, was settling down for the night, stringing mosquito nets from the railing. But apart from these cutthroats, the scene was one of complete peace.

The dinner was tough chicken chopped in small pieces without regard to the pattern of bones, cold rice, some watery soup and an aging salad. But the major had some good Algerian wine, and we shared it.

There were no cigars or cognac, but there was more wine after dinner. Hoang spoke fluent French and felt disposed to talk.

"You know, the province chief, Colonel Ut, and I were in the same class together at the military academy," he began.

"As a matter of fact, I usually got higher marks than he did. Fate plays peculiar tricks. Here am I in this miserable job in this wretched house, away from my wife and children, and there is he, in that palace of a house, a full colonel, and enjoying a full and happy life. Tonight he is holding a dinner party for some people down from the Interior Ministry. You can be sure it will be a good party! Why don't you go over?"

I said I was tired.

"Well, then. Have some more wine. Perhaps later I can escort you for some sight-seeing around Ca Mau? There's not much to see, but you shall see Ca Mau by night—the pearl of Viet Nam's buttocks."

But Major Hoang did not have an opportunity to show me around Ca Mau. (He was right. There is not much to see at night, although market stalls lighted by little acetylene lamps and fragrant with the smell of tasty soups are attractive places. Most Vietnamese provincial towns are on or near waterways, and it is always pleasant to stroll around them in the evening.)

Major Hoang was interrupted when a jeep roared through the gate, throwing gravel as it braked. The sleepy sentries snapped to attention, and the duty officer strode up to the stone bench in front of the house door where Hoang and I were sitting. He glanced at me suspiciously, saluted Hoang, and handed him a note.

Hoang frowned as he read, and then excused himself without explanation. He was locked in his combination office and bedroom the rest of the evening, and I didn't see him again until morning.

I learned the next day that Hoang had not been able to reach Province Chief Ut during the night, either because Ut was unavailable or Hoang was unwilling to break up Ut's party with bad news. In any case, Ut didn't hear about Dam Doi until more than twenty-four hours had passed since its district chief had set forth into the jungle.

It was a pleasant Sunday morning in Ca Mau. Children were strolling and laughing in the streets, and the sun was not high enough yet to make things oppressively hot. But an oddly mixed convoy of army trucks, rickety civilian buses painted pink with green and yellow dragons on the sides, and a handful of prewar automobiles was rolling into town—loaded to the roofs with marines in battle gear. I asked one of the marine officers what was going on, and he said he had no idea.

"We were out guarding that cotton-pickin' road project," he said, "and nothing's happened all week long. Now, all of a sudden, along comes this convoy of buses and trucks, and we're ordered back to Ca Mau. You never know what to expect in this country."

"Where'd you learn English like that?" I asked.

"Quantico," the officer snapped back. "A marine's not a leatherneck if he hasn't been there, regardless of his nationality."

I went to the province chief's house to find out what was going on.

Ut, looking dapper in camouflaged fatigue uniform with razor-sharp creases, did live in a fine house. A long driveway led to the magnificent portico of the big yellow stucco house. The wide doorway entered on a very large reception room with black and yellow tiled floor, comfortable and fairly modern furniture, an electric overhead fan and a tray of beer and cold soda ready for all comers. On the far wall, a portrait fully eight feet high of President Diem dominated the room, flanked by yellow and red national flags and bunting.

"There may have been some trouble down in Dam Doi, a town about thirty miles southeast of here," Ut said. "We've—well, it seems we've lost contact with the district chief there. We're going to have to have a look, so I pulled back those marines for a look at the area. They'll be leaving in a few hours. Want to go along?"

I did. I loaded my few belongings into my field pack and rejoined the marines, who were resting under the trees of one of the streets.

About 11 A.M., we marched through the streets to the river front, where Colonel Ut had assembled the most incredible armada of boats I had ever seen.

The backbone of our river task force was made up of three or four salvaged and reconditioned French gunboats called FOMs. The FOM is a steel boat about forty feet long. Its armored sides are pierced at regular intervals with gun ports. On the top is perched a slab-sided little machine-gun turret. The ship is painted black, and is altogether one of the most ugly vessels I have ever seen.

Tied up alongside the FOMs were about twenty commercial river boats about the same length. But they were made of wood with high, curving bowsprits. They were painted yellow with red trim, and each had painted eyes just at the bow, staring forward, to bring good luck to river navigators. The squat diesel engines inside their cabins were already belching smoke. Each of the boats in our fleet carried a large national flag—yellow, with three horizontal red stripes—at the stern. It looked like the beginning of some odd regatta.

The marines bundled their packs, rifles, machine guns and mortars aboard the boats, and we chugged off down the river in single file, fifty yards or so apart. The market place, jetties and riverside huts slipped away and were replaced by a dense green wall of palms and bamboo on both sides of the narrow river.

We all knew that the Viet Cong had sunk many a boat—even armored boats—along here, using homemade rocket launchers mounted in trees along the banks. But the marines accepted this knowledge philosophically. Rather than crouching tensely behind their rifle sights, most of them went to sleep.

The convoy threaded its way through progressively more narrow tributaries and canals, passing an occasional outpost, the defenders of which just stared listlessly at us.

It was about 2 P.M. when the convoy reached a fork in the stream along which it had been traveling. The banks at this point were so close together the long palm fronds spreading from opposite banks almost touched overhead. The fork was sharp, and the banks on each side of it were steep. They were also studded with dagger-sharp bamboo foot spikes hardened by fire.

The fork formed the apex of a little triangular outpost defended by a dozen civil guards who had used their pitiful means for fortifying the place as best they could. A big national flag was perched bravely in the middle of the jungle enclave.

"From here on we have to walk," the English-speaking marine officer grumbled to me. By now, the bows of all our ships were jammed into the muddy bank, and the marines filed ashore, many of them muttering "*troi oi*"—a mild oath ("my God") that Vietnamese troops invariably use when strenuous physical exertion appears imminent.

We moved away from the outpost along a path hemmed in by jungle and still as death in the shimmering heat. The whole column was moving single fire and fairly rapidly, with no flank scouts or any other precautions against ambush. The idea now was to get to the relative safety of Dam Doi before sunset. The night belongs to the enemy, Quantico training notwithstanding.

The path ran more or less parallel to a small canal occasionally visible off to our left. Smaller canals and ditches cut across the path every few hundred yards. Some were spanned by single logs. Poles jammed into the mud bottoms of the ditches afforded hand holds on which to balance across, but the logs were slippery, and falls were frequent. Progress was painfully slow.

Every once in a while we passed a lone hut, generally neat, with a large pile of threshed rice in front of the door, a few flowers, and a water buffalo or two tethered in an adjacent shed. But no sign of human life.

It is not healthy to be in an isolated hut when either the Viet Cong or government forces come through, and it's generally safer to go into the jungle and hide for a few hours.

There was not a trace of the enemy, either. No barricades or foot traps across the path at all, for a change.

I should note at this point that I am writing about an incident in 1962. Years have passed since then, and one important aspect of operations of this kind has changed. The Viet Cong eventually became strong enough that it would almost invariably ambush relief columns. These ambushes became so powerful in numbers and firepower they were little short of slaughter.

The shadows grew longer, and the faint stirring of air in the treetops that comes with dusk began. Sunrises and sunsets are short in the tropics, and night quickly follows dusk. By seven every night of the year in South Viet Nam it is dark.

All at once, we began moving past huts in groups, and the path widened. Before us was a fairly wide wooden footbridge. Beyond this bridge was Dam Doi, and we could see even at this distance that a national flag was flying.

Dam Doi, which is on the right side of the canal we had been paralleling, is bisected by a smaller canal that runs at right angles to the main one. The side of the town we were entering included a fairly large circular market place flanked by a few fairly large wooden buildings. Streets, actually paths of well-trampled mud, radiated from this to form the residential district of town. On the other side of the bisecting canal, crossed by another fairly good footbridge, was the military part of the town, including the district headquarters compound.

There were several hundred people milling around the market place, where acetylene lamps were already beginning to cast their harsh white light. The people had clearly heard our approach, and had turned out for a look at their visitors. But they stared incuriously, with no noticeable expression. Most were women and children. None waved or called out. Their welcome didn't seem actively hostile, but they certainly didn't greet us like liberators, either.

The long column moved silently through the heart of downtown Dam Doi, weapons clanking, then over the footbridge, a dozen at a time. Here the main "street" ran right next to the main parallel canal. And facing the canal was the compound where we would spend the night.

District headquarters was a building with, inevitably, yellow stucco walls, black and yellow tiled floors, a small yard in front facing the canal, a flagpole in the center of the yard, and a wooden watchtower about thirty feet high in the back. A smaller building facing the courtyard, a kind of shed, was festooned with gaudy paper stars and bunting left over from an observance of *Tet*, the lunar New Year that had passed a few weeks earlier. *Tet* is by far the most important holiday in Viet Nam, and even the Viet Cong quits fighting during the four-day holiday.

But the holiday decorations looked wrong. Inside the shed, men were hammering planks together into what were obviously coffins, and the smell of death was heavy all around. A handful of women wearing white bands of mourning around their heads were wailing in front of the main building; all of them had babies in their arms.

The smell of death was coming from the canal, where an FOM gunboat was tied up. In a small sampan the FOM had towed in were two bodies in a ghastly stage of mutilation and decomposition. They were so bad that the FOM crew had not been willing to take them aboard the big boat itself, but insisted on towing them back. Two families in Dam Doi had recognized what remained of the faces as their own. These two had gone out with Captain Kha that black Saturday morning forty hours ago.

Inside the bared wire of the headquarters compound,

marines everywhere were setting up their mosquito nets and boiling rice in the pots they always carry with them. Captain Kha's dry-eyed mistress was pouring tea for the officers inside the headquarters building.

If I said that Dam Doi was completely isolated from Saigon, this was not quite accurate. Saigon's government radio station has repeater stations all around the country, so that it is possible to receive the station any place. Very few peasants own radios of their own, but every hamlet of any consequence has a radio (from the U.S. AID Mission) hooked up to a large loudspeaker which blares away all day long. Dam Doi's loudspeaker was mounted in the watchtower. I remember that it was playing an old recording of "In the Blue of Evening" that evening. The mourners went right on wailing.

Kha's mistress gave orders for dinner to be served to all the officers (and to me) and had cots set up indoors for all of them. This was a bit of unexpected luxury, but the word had already got around that this girl might have had something to do with Kha's disappearance. Every man slept with his service automatic in reach, and took turns posting guard.

There was no idea of going out to look for Kha and his men at night, who, by this time, had been missing about forty hours. For one thing, the night is risky even for large units, and for another, Dam Doi itself had to be protected.

Kha's girl friend showed us pictures of her man, and her eyes finally began to show signs of misery. He was young and strong and ambitious, she said, and had been terribly anxious to be able to report a victory. If only he had not been so headstrong. One of the pictures showed Kha talking into a microphone in front of the big picture of Diem over the front door of the headquarters building. It was probably a rally of some kind given for some visitors from Saigon.

All through the sweltering night, the geckos (lizardlike creatures that eat bugs) trumpeted their love songs, but otherwise the night was still. Apparently the Viet Cong had no appetite for a fight with a force of marines this large.

By sunrise we had all gulped down some cold rice and were ready to move again. The direction was the same, farther down the parallel canal. It would only be a matter of three miles or so before we would reach the place where Kha had gone.

Crowds of women chattering excitedly and looking worried now crowded the compound courtyard. They were waiting for word about their husbands, sons and fathers who had gone with Kha. Outside the barbed wire, children trudged along with the marines for a few hundred yards before turning back.

The jungle was very thick again, and the path narrower than ever. We slogged along about two miles, and then sent out some scouts to the right.

The scouts moved a few hundred yards through the trees, their rifles and Tommy guns at the ready. Then they stopped. They had smelled something that could only mean we were headed in the right direction.

The whole column turned right to follow the scouts. We were soon on another path, very muddy and heavily tracked and rutted. The smell of rotting human beings was almost overpowering as we moved along, and a few marines tied pocket handkerchiefs over their noses. This does no good whatever, by the way.

The jungle thinned out a little, and we came to some huts—the hamlet. All of them were deserted completely; there weren't even any chickens or buffalo. Behind the huts was a water hole about thirty feet in diameter with mud sides that sloped down to the filthy water. Neatly ranged around these sides, like spokes in a wheel, were thirty bloated corpses, all in the uniform of government troops. The hot sun had hastened the decomposition of two days, and intestines had forced their way out of gaping belly wounds, making yellowish piles atop each body. Tracks showed that the bodies all had been towed to the place by ropes tied to buffalo.

From a small bamboo flagpole a few feet away fluttered a large Viet Cong flag—red on top, blue on the bottom, with a large yellow star in the middle. The enemy had left a display for us.

Someone found a rope, and all of us got out of the way while the flagpole was pulled down. The precaution proved to have been wise. The flagpole disappeared in a geyser of mud, and grenade fragments snapped through the trees. Booby trap.

The Viet Cong had no doubt held a fine victory celebration before we arrived, with drill formation, salute to the colors, photographs of the war booty, and all the rest. But now they were gone.

BAR

Under trees and in clumps of weeds we found more bodies. Among them was the body of Kha. But we could not find Kha's head, which apparently had been hacked off with a machete. Perhaps the Viet Cong stuck it on the end of a pole and took it parading around some other hamlets, as they sometimes do.

Beheading is a terrible thing to do to a man in Viet Nam. Most people believe that the loss of the head damns the spirit to an eternity of restless wandering. It is the worst way to die.

We found a little store in the hamlet, boarded up with folding, louvered wooden doors. The marines ripped the doors off and found a large stock of joss sticks—the long, tan sticks that burn like incense and are said to please the spirit world. The whole stock, several thousand sticks, was stuffed into jars and lighted. The burning joss didn't improve the odor of things much, but perhaps it made things better for the spirits that had left the carnage at the water hole.

We ripped the door sections from their hinges to make litters, and began the revolting job of picking up the bodies. A half-dozen marines were retching as they worked. A large sampan had pulled up to the hamlet along a creek, and the bodies were heaved aboard like sides of beef. I noticed that some of them wore the shoulder insignia of Father Hoa's Sea Swallows.

The sampan, water almost up to its gunwales, moved off, and we started probing the jungle around the hamlet in a futile quest for the enemy. Someone spotted a lone figure in black, running through the trees a few hundred feet away. The marine snapped his BAR and emptied a whole magazine at the figure, but I don't think he hit him.

Nothing much happened from then on, and eventually we marched back to Dam Doi. The corpse boat had preceded us there, and the bodies were now all laid out on the ground in front of the administration building, wrapped in the mats that are used in Viet Nam as both mattresses and shrouds. Scores of women, all in the white dress of mourning, were wailing and prostrating themselves before the bodies of their dead men. The coffin factory was going full tilt, with old men and boys filling the little building with lumber and hammering away. Some coffins were finished and mounted on sawhorses, a candle or two on their lids.

The sun was setting again and Pat Boone was singing something or other from the tower loadspeaker. I asked an officer if he couldn't turn the damned thing off.

"Sure, but it's better not to. Our people here don't care. And for the Viet Cong out there, it's a sign we're still alive and still able to resist. With that thing playing and the flag flying, we still have something."

I left Dam Doi, but somehow every few months I found myself back there. Each time it was somewhat the worse for wear. American advisors and helicopters began to arrive in Viet Nam, and at least it was easier to get to Dam Doi each time it was hit.

The low earth fighting walls around the district headquarters compound were scarred with countless bullets and the courtyard was pocked with scores of mortar shell craters. None of the shells and bullets seemed to have gone into the residential side of town across the little canal, though.

But the last time I went to Dam Doi, more than two years after my first visit, the place was almost unrecognizable. In the administrative compound, all the smaller buildings were flattened in a tangle of bamboo. The administration building was wrecked, its walls blasted with huge holes by 57-millimeter recoilless cannon shells. The watchtower was destroyed, and for the first time, the loudspeaker was silent. I almost missed it. The flagpole was gone.

Twenty or thirty huts built behind the administration building for the wives and children of the defense force were burned to the ground. I nearly stumbled over the charred bodies of four pregnant women as I walked through the embers. The bodies were so badly disfigured that no one had claimed them and picked them up. On the tiled floors of the building, dozens of corpses were lined up, a few propped in seated positions around the walls. More bodies were laid out in front, most of them on litters made from sections of corrugated iron blasted from roofs. They were covered with rattan mats and tagged. A lot of them were small—the bodies of children. One live child of about five clung to one of the large bundles, screaming uncontrollably. It was his mother.

The National Liberation Front had come stealthily in sampans at about two in the morning. They had cut some of the barbed wire, and were inside one corner of the compound before anyone knew what was happening. The fight had lasted several hours before the little garrison was finally wiped out. Brass cartridge cases were scattered everywhere, and some of them were Russian or Czechoslovak submachine-gun ammunition. Their bases were dated 1962.

Among those who had died was the district chief—the third in a row to die at his job in Dam Doi. He, too, had lost his head. Some Viet Cong unit must have quite a collection of heads.

Tile was blasted from some of the roofs of the houses in the residential section across the canal, although most of that part of town, as usual, showed little damage.

But this time a lot of survivors, mostly women, had had enough of Dam Doi and its never-ending bloodshed. Their bedding and pots over their shoulders, they had clustered around a flight of American helicopters that had landed behind the hamlet, pleading to be taken out, anywhere. I think a few of them finally did leave, but most of them are still there.

"I shall leave my bones in Dam Doi," an old woman told me. "Where else have I to go? The fate of this place is black, but so is my own. My husband was killed during the French war, and both my sons died here in this one. Death means nothing to me any more."

The same day, I visited another distict capital hamlet about twenty miles away, called Cai Nuoc. The same thing had happened at Cai Nuoc during the night, and here, too, the district chief was dead. More than forty defenders had been killed.

The pattern was always the same—the officials, soldiers and their families were brutally slaughtered, but the rest of the townspeople generally were not touched, except by stray bullets.

In this same province of An Xuyen there used to be two tiny hamlets, called Thoi Binh and Cha La, up in the northwest part of the province along a canal. Both places were at the edge of the big forest I mentioned earlier in the chapter, occupied by the Viet Cong's fierce U Minh Battalion.

Another hamlet called Thoi Binh still exists, but the Thoi Binh farthest up the canal is gone.

There used to be a little garrison there, with about a score of militiamen to defend the place. As usual in such cases, the men had their wives and children with them. There were sniping and probing by the Viet Cong nearly every night, but the post held. It held, that is, until Thoi Binh's last night, when the Viet Cong swept in, in a mass attack.

The following morning, a post farther down the canal had a ghastly visit. A large sampan came down the river. In it were the bodies of all the Thoi Binh defenders, mutilated by bayonets and acid poured over the faces. Also in the sampan were the surviving widows and children, who had been forced by the Viet Cong to ride the sampan downstream. Slogans were painted on the sampan saying, "Don't get in the way of the National Liberation Front or the same will happen to you."

The hamlet of Cha La on the same canal was wiped out

and leveled the same night. The only thing left standing was a sign bearing the name of the hamlet. Later that day, U.S. Air Force fighters ran an air strike on the sign to blow it out. It seemed like bad propaganda to leave only the sign standing.

At another hamlet farther north in the Mekong Delta, a hamlet chief (newly arrived and inexperienced) had been trying to collect government taxes and get young men registered for the national draft.

One night the Viet Cong came in, tied him to a stake in the center of the market place, and forced all the other villagers to come and watch. Among them were the chief's pregnant wife and child. They all watched as the man was slowly disemboweled. The child was then decapitated. Finally, the widow was tied to the same stake and also disemboweled.

I could fill up many more pages of similar incidents I have seen, but it would be merely repetitive, and besides, I don't like remembering them. The noteworthy thing about all of them is that they show a clear pattern of terror directed against those who oppose the National Liberation Front in one way or another. But beyond this, the terror is directed on general principle against officials—especially energetic or competent officials. Perhaps each dead district chief means relatively little in himself. But the mortality rate of district chiefs in some places, such as Dam Doi, is not conducive to recruiting civil servants. A district chief is paid about $40.00 a month, and the only other financial incentive is graft. The corrupt civil servant is swiftly singled out by the Viet Cong for assassination, if only to please the people. In any case, assignment to places like Dam Doi in the past has generally been the result of incurring the displeasure of officials in Saigon, and has happened in many cases as punishment or even personal revenge.

It is a cruel assignment which in some cases is tantamount to the death sentence.

Politics often are merely an excuse for terrorism.

I know a young woman named L. whose family was trapped in the cross fire between the French and Ho Chi Minh's Viet Minh, with tragic results. The case is typical of what still goes on.

L., who was ten years old in 1946, was the daughter of a Vietnamese civil servant under the French colonial province chief in Ben Tre, a Mekong River Delta town about fifty miles south of Saigon. Her mother was a schoolteacher. The family was fairly well off, and had a fine house near the center of Ben Tre. Things were happy for the family, even during the Japanese occupation of World War II. L. remembers making tourist trips up the Mekong into Cambodia during the occupation, and sharing the lunches of friendly Japanese troops. Japanese occupation reached the southern part of Viet Nam only late in the war, and was never very oppressive. The hatred for the Japanese felt in North Viet Nam never had time to develop in the south.

L.'s father, a man named Tet, worked for the French, but his sympathies were on the side of the nationalists. He began to cooperate with the Viet Minh.

Tet had a neighbor in Ben Tre who was jealous of his nice house and prosperity. There had been bitter feelings for years between Tet and this neighbor.

After the end of World War II, a seesaw battle began between the returning French and Ho's Viet Minh, which was now operating in the open (with Japanese blessings) as the legal government of Viet Nam.

The battle swept repeatedly over the Mekong River Delta, and never was really resolved there. But in one of the French advances, Tet and his family moved back with the Viet Minh, out of Ben Tre. They went to live in a small, peaceful hamlet where the Viet Minh held complete sway.

L. remembers many happy days living, for the first time in her life, as a peasant girl. She, her sister and five brothers enjoyed living under a thatched roof. They liked playing with livestock, and the whole family relaxed in the lazy apolitical peasant atmosphere.

The Viet Minh used to hold daily song rallies in the back of the hamlet, marching around and saluting the big red flag with the yellow star every morning. Tet was one of them, and was even armed with a fine big hunting knife he had bought on one of the family vacations in Cambodia.

There was always the rumble of distant artillery, but the war got no closer. The situation began to stabilize into definite areas of control. But what the family didn't know at the time was that their old enemy from Ben Tre was now a fairly high ranking Viet Minh officer. One day he denounced Tet to the local commissar as a French spy. Tet was arrested by the Viet Minh and taken to a jungle jail.

He was not particularly badly treated, and Tet's frantic wife was permitted to take food to his cell. After a few weeks, he was released, with no more explanation than he had been given when he was arrested.

Time passed, and there was no more trouble, but the family was uneasy. They knew they were being watched.

One day, an old friend of Tet came to him and asked him to accompany him to Ben Tre on a business matter. Ben Tre by now was in French hands. There was some worried discussion, but in the end Tet went. The business was finished in several days, and Tet came back safely to his family in the hamlet.

But again, the old enemy denounced him, saying Tet had gone to Ben Tre to carry information to the enemy.

L. was asleep, her head resting against her father's shoulder, when they came. It was about 2 A.M., and they dragged Tet roughly from his bed. He was not permitted to take any clothes. Mrs. Tet pleaded with the men in black, and the children screamed. But Tet was gone. A muffled shot sounded somewhere off in the dark jungle.

As a postscript, Mrs. Tet managed to raise the family with her earnings as a teacher. Some of the children went to Europe to take degrees. At this writing, two of the sons are in the Vietnamese army, fighting the new enemy—the Viet Cong.

But usually there is no happy ending. Strnagely enough, Viet Cong terror is often blamed on the Americans. The reasoning is that the Americans have the power to stop the terror but refuse to do it.

Once I was driving back from the Mekong Delta to the capital, and stopped at a hamlet called Go Den on the main delta highway, only fifteen miles south of Saigon. The night before, a police check point on the road had been destroyed by Viet Cong rocket launchers and machine-gun fire. The guerrillas had then poured into a militia training camp on the other side of the road and killed about forty of the trainees in their beds.

The militia post was typical of outposts all over the nation.

Built in the old French style, the post was triangular with mud walls on all sides and a small mud tower with gun slots at each corner. The whole thing was surrounded with tangles of barbed wire, and could be entered only through a barbed wire gate in one wall, leading over a little moat by footbridge. Inside were half-a-dozen long wooden barracks buildings and a locked concrete arms room.

The Viet Cong had not come through the gate. They had smashed each of the corner towers with rocket launchers and set up machine guns at two of the corners. Between the two guns, the whole post was covered.

About ten of the militiamen, some of them wounded, dashed from their barracks when the shooting began and ran for the gate. But a Viet Cong had set up an automatic rifle trained on the gate, and each man who came through tumbled into the moat, a burst of slugs through his body. The leftover defenders were all either shot or bayoneted by the Viet Cong clean-up crew. The guerrillas shot the lock off the arms bunkers, and carried off about one hundred good American weapons, including several machine guns and mortars.

In all the shooting, the town of Go Den was not touched, and there were no accidental casualties.

While I was sorting through the remains, a Vietnamese policeman came running up to me, tears streaming from his eyes.

"My God, why didn't they come to help us?" he said in French. "They were so close. When the attack began, I called them by radio, and they answered, but they never came until this morning. Why couldn't you Americans with your helicopters have come to help us, at least, if our own soldiers wouldn't come? If you can't help us, why don't you get out of Viet Nam completely and leave us to die quickly?"

After a while, I learned that the "they" the policeman was complaining about were two full battalions of crack Vietnamese paratroopers, a battalion of regular army troops, some other smaller units and a good supply of armored cars and tanks—all no more than ten minutes' drive away down the road. These units were all bivouacked in the area as part of the government's ambitious "pacification plan."

There is no question that these units were available at the time of the Go Den massacre, and I have never been given an explanation by any of the responsible officers as to why they didn't come. But that is the way this war goes.

Oddly enough, while peasants often blame America for Viet Cong slaughters, it works the other way around, too.

A U.S. Army helicopter was flying over the same province in which Go Den is located, and drew heavy enemy ground fire from a hut in a small hamlet. The helicopter wheeled around, dived at the hamlet, and emptied its rocket pods into it. The whole community became an inferno of explosions and flame. Five civilians, definitely not members of the National Liberation Front, were killed.

Later, American civilian field workers moved into the hamlet to make some reparations.

"I'm sorry this happened," an American told the hamlet chief.

"Oh, we understand," the old man said. "Your helicopter was right to fire. It was the Viet Cong's fault for starting it.

"The Viet Cong will be back tonight, but this afternoon we shall hold a protest rally against the Viet Cong to express our anger."

Viet Cong terror is not confined to government officials and soldiers and their families. Many a schoolteacher has been dropped from his bicycle by Viet Cong bursts. Teachers, unless they are neutral or pro-Liberation Front, are regarded as dangerous elements by the Viet Cong. In Viet Cong "liberated areas," the Front has its own schools and teachers. These schools are always clean and orderly, and bedecked with paper Viet Cong flags cut out by the children.

Rural Catholic priests are sometimes shot down, although they generally are first given several warnings to leave their parishes. Even Buddhist monks have been assassinated.

There is a word used in Viet Nam a great deal by the experts on guerrilla warfare (or, rather, on "counterinsurgency"). That word is "infrastructure."

Broadly speaking, "infrastructure" means all organized authority. Presidents and politburo chairmen, province chiefs and province commissars, armed forces and their command structure, petty officials all the way down the line, secret agents, terrorists and propagandists, doctors and aid men, public works employees and communications technicians, even teachers and religious leaders—all of these are considered part of the over-all "infrastructure."

As a general definition, infrastructure is the people and machinery essential to holding a government and a nation together.

The Saigon government has its infrastructure (or at least tries to) and the Viet Cong has its own separate infrastructure.

From the beginning of its operations in the late 1950s, the Viet Cong has made its primary objective the cutting apart and dissolving of the government system of authority, and substitution of its own. It is a slow process that has been compared with dripping acid on the steel frame that holds a large structure together. It is highly selective, since, according to the rules of Viet Cong warfare, the acid must not spill any more than necessary on the bulk of the structure, only on the supporting frame.

Officials and "cadres" must be killed, but the mass of the people must not be hurt. Fortifications, canals, roads, and offices must be blown up, but installations that will be useful after an anticipated Viet Cong victory must be left alone. For instance, the Viet Cong could easily have sabotaged or even destroyed the big Japanese-built hydroelectric plant at Da Nhim. Instead, they chose to knock out the power line from the dam to Saigon after the dam was completed in 1964. Saigon was thus deprived of an enormous and badly needed source of power, but the power plant itself was preserved. Similarly, French plantation men were regularly kidnaped for ransom in the early 1960s, but the rubber trees themselves were left alone.

The Viet Cong rarely harmed their French prisoners, and usually released them after payment of ransom. The reason was that each French planter employed several thousand Vietnamese plantation workers. The closing of a big plantation would be a staggering economic loss for thousands of workers, who would blame the Viet Cong instead of helping it.

One of these plantation managers, Claud Salvaire, manager of "Catecka," the largest tea plantation in Viet Nam, told me of his own experience with the guerrillas.

"During the height of the picking season, we hire about five thousand workers who get paid by the bushel. They make good wages. A few hundred more work in our processing plants [at a hamlet near the Central Vietnamese town of Pleiku].

"A lot of these men and women are Viet Cong, of course. I know who some of them are. One day, one of my workers complained to me that he and all the others were not getting any sleep, because the Viet Cong kept them up late listening to propaganda lectures.

"I went to see a man I knew to be a high-ranking Viet Cong organizer, and complained to him. He smiled and said he would see what he could do. A few days after that, the nightly lectures ended. But daytime lectures began, right in the fields. Production sagged. There's nothing much I can do.

"The government and the Americans would like to help. The Americans at their camp over in Pleiku often come here to my house for dinner. But I have to be careful.

"We needed power for our processing machinery, and it happens that there is a good river on this plantation. So we built a little hydroelectric dam that works beautifully and gives more power than we need. The government province chief sent me several companies of his civil guards to protect the dam and the powerhouse.

"Of course, I never had any faith in the civil guards. Their noncommissioned officers are all lowland Vietnamese, but the privates are all montagnards [primitive mountain tribesmen of different ethnic origins from the Vietnamese].

"The montagnards and Vietnamese have always hated each other. These NCOs treat their men like dirt, sitting around playing cards with each other all day long. Naturally, the men hate them and refuse to take this job seriously.

"At any rate, when American advisors first started moving to Pleiku, they had almost no equipment for their camp, no generators or anything. They were nice people, and I wanted to be friendly. So I offered to run a line out to their camp from my hydroelectric generator, at least until they got settled in. They were pleased, and it was done.

"But two days later, my hydroelectric plant was blown to bits by a huge bomb, practically under the noses of the civil guard. And a note was left on my door saying: 'Power for the plantation, yes, power for the U.S. aggressors, no.'

"Eventually, I had the generator rebuilt, but without a line to the American camp. It hasn't been disturbed again.

"You see how I live. I am in the hands of God—or, rather, of the Viet Cong."

That was a long time ago in 1962, in the wind-swept, open prairies of Pleiku Province. Salvaire survived all that, only to meet a killer in Saigon. A plantation worker Salvaire had fired caught up with him in Saigon one weekend, and planted a knife in his stomach. Salvaire lived, but went back to French to recuperate.

Viet Cong terror extends to the big towns and cities as well as the countryside. The key tools are bombs and grenades.

The object of a city bombing generally is both symbolic and practical. Americans are the most frequent targets of such bombings.

A major object of Viet Cong terror bombing is to isolate American advisors and officials from the Vietnamese by making Vietnamese afraid to associate with Americans. The bombings are therefore as much for propaganda purposes as they are to destroy people and things. The technique is fairly effective.

On February 18, 1964, Tran Nam Trung, chairman of the Viet Cong's military committee (and commander-in-chief of Viet Cong forces), issued the following communiqué, which was broadcast by "Liberation Radio":

> For more than two years, the U.S. aggressors' army has continually enlarged the crime-studded war against the patriotic movement of the South Vietnamese people. The U.S. troops have not neglected any savage act to terrorize and massacre our compatriots.
>
> The situation has now become more serious than ever. The South Vietnamese people have no course other than to resolutely devote all strength, at any price, to carry out to the end the armed, comprehensive protracted war of resistance in order to defeat the U.S. imperialist aggressors and the traitorous lackeys to attain the final goal: Peace, independence, neutrality, democracy and prosperity in the country.
>
> In order to create favorable conditions for the liberation troops and the People's Armed Forces to attack the enemy more strongly and intensively, and to destroy the enemy forces as much as possible, and with a view to sparing our compatriots and foreign [neutral] nationals living in South Viet Nam, as well as officers and enlisted men of the lackeys' armed forces who actually are one the side of the people, the National Liberation Front's Central Committee's Military Committee announces the following:

1. Effectively immediately, the compatriots from all walks of life living in areas under the enemy's temporary control are requested to stay away from places where there are U.S. aggressor troops, such as billets, restaurants, dance halls, clubs, theaters and so forth. Let the compatriots positively join the liberation troops and People's Armed Forces in destroying and annihilating the enemy.

2. Foreign nationals should not collaborate in any way with the U.S. aggressor troops. In other words, they should not, under any circumstances or in any place, fraternize with or live with the U.S. aggressor troops. Foreign nationals should also not use any means of transport of a military type.

3. Officers and enlisted men in the southern [Saigon] army and the personnel of the southern administration who are patriotic but who have not had occasion to contribute to the people's struggle for the liberation of South Viet Nam should seek to stay away and refuse to take part in the criminal acts of the U.S. aggressor troops and their lackeys.

The military committee earnestly calls for patriotism from the compatriots, for understanding from the foreign nationals, and for clear-sightedness and awareness of the situation from the officers and enlisted men in the southern army and the personnel in the southern administration. Let them seriously comply with the points set forth in this communiqué.

Many Vietnamese are in fact nervous about being in public places with Americans. Vietnamese bus drivers generally will not take Americans as passengers, and if they do, most of the Vietnamese passengers get off. Terror works.

Even concerning Americans, the Viet Cong is reasonably selective in its targets. "Liberation Radio," the Viet Cong's clandestine propaganda transmitter, has said that American women, children and civilians will not be targets of bombings unless they frequent military establishments. Viet Cong leaf-

lets even apologized after a number of American women and
children were badly wounded in 1964 in two huge bombings—
the American community theater and the American baseball
park.

After February 7, 1965, dependent wives and children of
American officials and military men were evacuated from Viet
Nam. The American school was closed down, along with all
other dependent facilities.

But dependents or not, the bombings go on. Grenades
fly over the hedges around American-occupied villas, and
bombs are heaved into American military buses and jeeps,
barracks and billets, and, most of all, bars.

Bar bombings almost always are grisly.

I was especially moved by one, at which I arrived just a
few minutes after the explosion. This particular bar had a
very good five-piece combo, and was well known as a good
place to dance. None of the five Americans seriously hurt by
the blast died, but seven Vietnamese—most of them taxi
girls—were killed.

One wall was blown out of the bar. The party decorations
hanging from the ceiling lay in a smoky jumble with chunks
of bodies, and the whole floor was slick with a mixture of
blood and shattered glassware.

Next to the orchestra stand in the corner, a foot still
wearing a fancy high-heeled shoe was standing upright, its
body somewhere in the jumble on the other side of the room.

Tragic irony is an integral part of all wars, and terror
bombing in Viet Nam has contributed its share.

U.S. Army Master Sergeant Al Combs went to the
Indochina area in 1959 in the Special Forces. Combs, a young
wisecracking native of Brooklyn, New York, had spent most of
his life as a wanderer. He had a wife back in the States, but
was separated from her.

At first, Combs was in the jungles of Laos fighting the
Pathet Lao guerrillas, but later was assigned to Special Forces
in neighboring Viet Nam. He loved the country and ended
up spending nearly five years there—possibly a record for a
U.S. serviceman in Viet Nam.

To do it, Combs pulled all kinds of wires, getting exten-
sions of his tours, brief transfers back to the States with
immediate reassignment to Viet Nam, and so forth. Combs's
jobs in Viet Nam were always dangerous. He served for a

while at the Ranger training base at Trung Lap, for a while as an advisor in the Mekong Delta, and for a while as a paratroop advisor in Central Viet Nam. He had thousands of close shaves.

Combs had a Vietnamese girl friend in Saigon who became his common-law wife. They had two children to whom Combs was devoted. On weekends when Combs could get to Saigon, he could often be seen happily strolling the boulevards with his wife and children. Saigon had become his home, and his roots were solidly planted there.

On June 25, 1965, Combs's wife was nearly due to have their third child, and rather than ask her to cook at home, he decided to take her out to dinner at one of the most romantic restaurants in Saigon—the My Canh. They took the two children along.

The My Canh is a floating restaurant on the bank of the Saigon River, as described in an earlier chapter. At night sampans glide past diners, and the lights of the port sparkle in the water.

That night, the Viet Cong set off a mine that killed forty-three people at the My Canh, and wounded many others.

Among the dead were Combs and his wife. Surgeons tried in vain to deliver the baby from Mrs. Combs's lifeless body.

The two children survived. Army friends of Combs took up a collection to support them.

Besides this kind of bombing, there are many bombings for personal revenge or even by accident. Deserter soldiers turned robbers often use grenades against the houses they intend to rob. Grenades sometimes drop from their pins by accident when soldiers go to movies. Fragmentation grenades in crowded movie theaters result in awful casualties.

Many people dabble in bombing in Saigon, and the Viet Cong is by no means always the culprit. Bombing in Saigon has been for many years an accepted mode of political expression.

In French colonial days, there were notorious bombing factions everywhere, including some of the French themselves. Nor has the Saigon government itself, in recent years, been above an occasional discreet bombing. U.S. intelligence men are certain that a good many of the low-power bombs that exploded in Saigon during Diem's last year in power were actually of government origin. Such bombings can always be blamed on Viet Nam, Buddhists, or anyone else against whom a government wishes to stir up American wrath.

In late 1964, a huge bomb in Saigon's plush Caravelle Hotel blew out the entire fifth floor of the building. A number of people were hurt, but no one died. The Caravelle is the usual hotel for wealthy visiting foreigners—diplomats, high-ranking military officers, rich tourists, congressmen, visiting news correspondents, and so on. It also houses the Australian and New Zealand embassies.

The bomb was apparently planted by a well-dressed Vietnamese who had rented an entire corner suite of the Caravelle (at about $30.00 a day). He left the bomb in a closet of the suite in such a way that damage would be heavy but loss of life probably minimal. This kind of bombing is not the Viet Cong style. For one thing, it is expensive, and the Viet Cong prefers bombing on a shoestring. But it happened at a time the government was in chaos and there was rioting in the streets. Any one of a dozen factions, including the Nguyen Khanh government itself, might have stood to reap some psychological advantage from the Caravelle bombing.

Some of the Viet Cong bombers have been caught. Most have been students in their teens.

The Viet Cong has a youth organization called the "Volunteers for Death," for which Cell 65 and Cell 67 have been identified as the primary troublemakers in Saigon. Bomb throwing is considered an honorable and worthy occupation by these people, who show no remorse whatever if they are caught.

Up to this point, I have concentrated on Viet Cong terror. But terror in Viet Nam is a two-way street. It probably would be unfair to describe the Vietnamese as an unusually brutal people. But at the same time, I have personally witnessed more brutality in Viet Nam than in any other country of Asia.

Torture has been an adjunct to interrogation for many years in South Viet Nam, and there are no prospects that this pattern will change in the foreseeable future.

To the average American, all forms of torture are revolting. But given the situation in Viet Nam, distinctions must be made between degrees of torture.

The Vietnamese police probably use the mildest forms in interrogating political (or Viet Cong) prisoners.

There is a small American field generator used extensively in Viet Nam for powering pack radios. The device is mounted on a tripod and is operated by hand cranks on both sides, turned by one man. The generator produces a high enough voltage to produce a severe but not fatal shock.

The "ding-a-ling" method of interrogation involves connection of electrodes from this generator to the temples of the subject, or other parts of the body. In the case of women prisoners, the electrodes often are attached to the nipples. The results are terrifying and painful, but subjects are not permanently damaged. This technique is often applied at provincial interrogation centers by police, and in the field by soldiers.

Another method involves the near drowning of the subject. In late 1963, a young Vietnamese woman working as a secretary at the British Embassy in Saigon was arrested on grounds that she had provided shelter for a Buddhist monk wanted by Diem's police. She described her experience this way:

"I waited in a room with some other prisoners, who were led off one at a time for interrogation. Finally my turn came. I was taken to a bare office where there were two desks and a bench. The man interrogating me was seated at one of the desks.

"He asked me if I knew anything about the monk. Actually, I did, but of course I denied it. Then two other large men came into the room. They ripped off my dress and forced me to lie down on the bench, tying me tightly to it with pieces of rope. Next to the bench was a bucket of filthy water. Some of this was poured over my face and I choked and vomited. Then a big cloth was placed over my face—tightly—and the water was poured on it. I couldn't breathe. Just as I was about to lose consciousness, the cloth was taken off. Then one of the men beat me on the soles of my feet with a heavy club. I screamed terribly from the pain. The other began beating my stomach with his fist. The cloth was put over my face again, and this time I passed out. When I came to, I was ordered to dress and clean up the room. They told me I would be questioned again tomorrow."

It happened that this woman was not questioned again, because the following day, Diem was overthrown in a bloody coup.

But the wet-cloth interrogation technique is still used. It has at least the merit that it is not fatal and leaves no physically harmful effects.

Presumably, the "mild" forms of torture sometimes leave psychological effects, however. Years after the coup of November 1, 1963, in which President Diem was overthrown, nearly a dozen former political Buddhist prisoners were patients at the Cong Hoa Hospital, Viet Nam's main military hospital. All were highly disturbed mental patients when they were released from Diem's prisons after the coup.

Major General Nguyen Khanh, one of the military premiers who followed the Diem regime, visited these patients more than one year later. They screamed and went berserk. Khanh was told by embarrassed hospital attendants that the patients always reacted that way at the sight of a military uniform. Khanh left, promising to return later in civilian clothes.

But some of the forms of torture employed are more sinister, in that they maim or disfigure. Most of these are used in the field by Vietnamese troops on Viet Cong prisoners or suspects, and the object is to extract tactical intelligence.

They can involve beating and cutting, or worse. Many a news correspondent or U.S. Army military advisor has seen the hands whacked off prisoners with machetes. Prisoners are sometimes castrated or blinded.

In more than one case a Viet Cong suspect has been towed after interrogation behind an armored personnel carrier across the rice fields. This always results in death in one of its most painful forms.

Another common torture was the use of truncheons designed not to cause marks on prisoners but to induce internal hemorrhaging. According to acquaintances of mine in America's various intelligence services, this type of beating was often applied at the interrogation center of the Vietnamese intelligence agency on the beautiful Quai Bach Dang. My sources say it was considered proper etiquette for Vietnamese interrogators to ask American intelligence officials to leave the interrogation room before the frequently fatal types of torture were applied.

Americans themselves rarely used anything worse than their own fists when interrogating prisoners.

I must observe here that if the United States ever had had a really serious objection to the torture of Viet Cong prisoners, the practice could have been swiftly halted. On the one hand, the United States dominates Viet Nam's armed forces, and on the other, it contends it has no control over such matters as the torture of prisoners.

It appears that American pilots taken prisoner in North Viet Nam receive generally much better treatment than do Viet Cong prisoners in the South. The Americans are subjected to indignities, they must wear red and black striped pajamas, and they are forced to labor at filling in bomb craters. But there is no evidence from any visitors to North Viet Nam that U.S. prisoners are physically tortured.

In South Viet Nam, too, a number of American servicemen have escaped or been released from Viet Cong captivity in the jungle. Conditions were generally harsh. In several cases, Americans were shot while trying to escape, or as hostages in reprisal. But none of the Americans who have returned has reported any evidence that the Viet Cong tortures American prisoners.

It seems that in wartime Americans can accustom themselves to cruelty with relatively little difficulty. I shall return to this subject in a later chapter.

Vietnamese troops have taken their share of enemy heads over the years, and many Americans have adjusted to the idea. At one point, many of the American advisors returning from Viet Nam brought photos of themselves holding aloft freshly severed heads given them by Vietnamese colleagues. The Americans in these pictures generally were smiling at their heads, as they would at a good catch of fish.

Interrogation has taken many forms. I have talked to American servicemen who swear they have seen the "long step," although I personally have never uncovered direct evidence of the existence of this gruesome practice. In the "long step," two or three prisoners supposedly are taken up several thousand feet in a helicopter and questioned. If answers are not forthcoming, one of the prisoners is shoved out to fall to his death, and the others are told a similar fate awaits them if they remain silent.

Americans have learned to be suspicious of Vietnamese claims of victory over the Viet Cong, and are usually satisfied with the validity of these claims only when they see visual evidence, such as bodies.

One day, an American battalion advisor was seated in his headquarters shack in the Mekong Delta when a grinning Vietnamese officer walked in and said, "Big victory. We killed seventeen Viet Cong today." The American smiled doubtfully, and said, "Where are they?"

"Oh, out there near the road, about five kilometers from here."

"But, Nhut, you know we have to have evidence before we can report that on the American side."

Nhut scratched his head and walked out. The American thought the matter was ended. But an hour later, Nhut returned and asked the American to step outside. Outside, a truck had parked, surrounded by grinning Vietnamese Rangers. In the truck were seventeen bloody heads, stacked like melons.

But by and large, things like this in the field appear to be more acts of revenge and hatred than merely adjuncts of intelligence interrogation. Many soldiers enjoy beating up Viet Cong prisoners. The subjects of interrogation so often die under questioning that intelligence seems to be a secondary matter.

In 1963, the American advisory command began experimenting with small, field lie detectors for use by Vietnamese troops on Viet Cong suspects.

The innovation drew wide international publicity, most of it unfavorable. Leading American publications attacked the little lie detectors as nothing more than toys, which in the hands of unskilled operators could result in nothing but injustice. The criticism was probably valid.

But seasoned field men in Viet Nam regarded the criticism as wholly irrelevant.

"Stuff like that gives me a pretty good idea of how little Americans know about the war we're fighting here," a U.S. Army Special Forces officer told me.

"Sure, those lie detectors would be no good in a U.S.

court of law, but this ain't a U.S. court of law, it's Viet Nam. I figure it this way. These little lie detectors must give the defendant a clean bill at least some of the time. As it is, when the Rangers or Airborne get their hooks into some guy, he doesn't stand even a chance. The lie detector would give him some chance. And it might cut down the unpleasant preliminaries to the executions."

American advisors in Viet Nam generally don't like the torture they see applied almost daily. They are required to report what they see on special forms through the American command chain. Occasionally, they actively interfere with proceedings, sometimes offering a cigarette or a candy bar to the captive. But they cannot interfere too often without provoking the hostility of the officers and men they are supposed to be advising. And, like it or not, they must learn to make distinctions between various degrees of torture.

Some Vietnamese regard Americans as hypocritically softhearted.

"You don't like the methods we apply to prisoners and the way we do business in the field," a Vietnamese commander told me once. "But you have nothing against the use of artillery barrages, and air strikes using heavy bombs and napalm. Have you ever visited a hamlet hit by napalm after your planes have finished?"

I have visited such hamlets, and there is no question that the results are revolting. Unfortunately, the Viet Cong builds bunkers so skillfully it is rarely touched by aerial bombs or napalm, except in cases of direct hits. But huts are flattened, and civilian loss of life is generally high. In some, the charred bodies of children and babies have made pathetic piles in the middle of the remains of market places.

Artillery also causes heavy accidental casualties.

Most Vietnamese officers have been trained in French or American patterns. A young infantry officer leading his company across an open field that is suddenly taken under fire from a tree line tends to react instinctively. His men are in the greatest danger, and pinned down helplessly, so he calls for artillery support or an air strike on the tree line. The barrage or strike comes. Almost invariably, behind the tree line is a hamlet which is destroyed, with heavy civilian casualties. The Viet Cong plans things this way, and reaps a substantial propaganda harvest every time it happens.

The nonselective terror of artillery and air strikes led one American infantry officer to say: "This is a rifleman's war, and I'd be happy if they took every plane and every cannon out of the country. They do more harm than good. To pick a needle out of a haysack you need tweezers, not a bulldozer. And the best tool for picking out Viet Cong is the rifle."

This attitude was expressed even more forcefully by Father Hoa, the seventy-five-year-old fighting priest mentioned earlier in this chapter whose men were butchered by the Viet Cong at Dam Doi and elsewhere. Father Hoa, who received the Ramon Magsaysay Award for outstanding service in Asia in 1964, said at his acceptance speech in Manila:

> When fought as an international war, we have no chance to win. How can we explain to a mother when her child is burned by napalm? And how can we expect a young man to fight for us when his aged father was killed by artillery fire?
>
> Indeed, how can we claim to be with the people when we burn their homes simply because those homes happen to be in the Viet Cong controlled territory?
>
> Many have asked me why are we not winning in Viet Nam? My answer is simple. The misplacement of the order of importance. The Magsaysay way is: Winning the people first, winning the war second. I am afraid in Viet Nam today, the order is reversed.
>
> I can talk plainly like this because I am a soldier as well as a priest. Fighting is necessary in order to protect the people from being physically harmed by the armed communists. But arms are useful only for defensive purposes. Our offense is to rely solely on winning the people because as soon as the people understand what communism means, and as soon as they have faith in our ability to protect them, and as soon as they have confidence in our integrity, the battle is won.

Personally, I'm inclined to agree with Father Hoa and others who oppose the use of terror as a weapon of war. Still, there is no doubt that it can be effective in limited ways.

In 1964, hand-picked Vietnamese troops were organized

by American agents into experimental assassination squads. These squads worked in secrecy, in cooperation with rural agents who had infiltrated the Viet Cong.

Viet Cong officials in "liberated" enemy areas began dying mysteriously in their beds, usually with daggers in their throats. On their bodies were nearly always attached four-inch-square slips of paper printed in black with the white outline of a grotesque human eye.

The U.S. Information Service in Saigon printed 50,000 of these sinister death notices, which started turning up on the doors of houses suspected to be tenanted by Viet Cong. They no doubt frightened a lot of people.

But, then, the fear of assassination is nothing new to Viet Nam. More than one Saigon government in the 1960s has almost certainly used assassination as a political weapon, and not always against the Viet Cong. A lot of ugly things happen in the shadows of Viet Nam, and fresh bodies turn up in the Saigon River nearly every morning.

My wife, who was born in the Mekong Delta, recalls that in one of the hamlets in which she lived as a child there were waterways abounding with large and succulent lobsters. The people avoided eating the lobsters in those days because the lobsters were believed to feed on the corpses floating everywhere.

One wonders whether there will ever be a day when North and South Vietnamese lobsters no longer dine on fresh corpses.

10

RED, WHITE AND
BLACK PROPAGANDA

It was dusk when ten strangers arrived in town. The sleepy little hamlet of Ap —— rarely had visitors, and this was something worth investigating. For many years the war had been far away, and life had not changed much at this hamlet in the past thousand years. The day's plowing was over, and the water buffalo were back, tethered in their open sheds next to the huts. Rice was steaming in big aluminum pots over charcoal fires, and the smell of *nuoc mam*, the ubiquitous Vietnamese fermented fish sauce, was heavy in the air.

The strangers all carried guns, but they were smiling as they walked into the cluster of huts. As they came into town, their leader passed an old, bearded resident and deferentially saluted, one fist in the other closed hand. *"Chau bac. Manh gioi?"* ("Hello, Uncle, are you well?") the stranger politely inquired.

The old man responded with equal politeness, but looked the strange group over closely. The leader, who called himself Thuan, was wearing a wide-brimmed bush hat, a black shirt tucked into khaki military trousers, and sandals made from sections of automobile tire and leather thongs. A rifle was slung carelessly over his shoulder. Thuan was a bright-eyed, intelligent-looking man of about thirty whose face was deeply tanned.

One of the others wore a white shirt and gray trousers. He also had a rifle, but incongruously squinted through spectacles. He looked more like an impoverished student than a peasant. Several others wore the black, baggy trousers and blouses of farmers, and conical palm-frond hats.

The only one in the party without a gun was a young

woman of about twenty-five, also dressed in black farm clothes and rubber-tire sandals, but with a guitar over her shoulder. Her face was serious, but her wide eyes were warm and friendly.

"My people have not had anything to eat in two days, and we are very hungry. I wonder, Uncle, if we could impose on your hamlet for a little rice? We would be happy to work for you in exchange," Thuan said.

A dozen or so villagers had gathered around the group.

"Certainly," the old man said. "You shall eat your fill."

A stranger with an empty stomach is never turned away by a Vietnamese farmer, whose hospitality to poor people is almost limitless.

There was some talk as the old man made arrangements as to which strangers should be entertained by which family. The strangers were obviously tired and ready to relax, as they unslung their guns and leaned them against palm trees.

"It is very kind of all of you," Thuan remarked. "Earlier today we passed through a hamlet where we hoped we could get something to eat, but while there was plenty of food, it was impossible."

"Why not?" someone asked.

"Oh, the same old story," Thuan went on conversationally. "The Americans had dropped poison all over everything. No one can eat the rice there without a terrible death."

The strangers made agreeable guests. Each family was warmly complimented on its excellent cuisine. Besides, the strangers, who obviously traveled most of the time, had all kinds of interesting stories about faraway places, even the great city of Saigon.

After dinner, Thuan suggested that the visitors repay their hosts with some entertainment. The strangers gathered in one of the larger huts, and the young woman sang and played her guitar. She had a soft, sweet voice, and her songs were the sad, old-fashioned songs of lonely fishermen poling sampans. The eyes of some of the older villagers were moist with nostalgia, and quite a crowd gathered around the hut to listen. Someone produced a few bottles of strong "33 Export" beer, and it was a nice party.

At length, one of the villagers asked the pleasant strangers if they would care to stay overnight.

"No, many thanks all the same," Thuan said. "We must keep going. But perhaps we shall return again before long."

The ten strange travelers slung their rifles and disappeared into the night. But a few days later, they did return—this time, during the midday siesta. They were greeted with smiles and were offered rice.

"No, thank you," Thuan said, "we have eaten. But we came to repay our debt to you. We noticed some of your houses need repairs, and we would like to work on them. Also, we noticed the last time we were here that some of your children look sick. Miss Nga, the girl who played her guitar for you, is a nurse, and this time she has brought some medicine."

This time, the young woman carried a kit bag over her shoulder instead of a guitar, and was wearing a Red Cross armband.

"All of us must be able to do many things in order to help the people effectively. We have had to learn these things in the National Liberation Front," Thuan said.

The woman turned toward a group of children and singled out one whose face and scalp were covered with sores and scabs. She gave the boy a light kiss on the head and then applied some ointment to the bad spots.

As Nga busied herself with other children, five of the men wandered over to a clearing where an old man was cutting bamboo and building a frame for a new roof panel.

"Let us lend a hand," one of the friendly men with guns said. Quickly and expertly, the free labor force hacked lengths of bamboo to size, and lashed them together.

Thuan wandered from house to house, exchanging greetings with each occupant. The man who looked like a student also wandered around the hamlet, stopping to chat with all the young men.

At two thirty, the squad gathered as if by signal in the middle of the hamlet.

"We must be on our way again," Thuan told a bystander. "Before we go, we should like to sing a song together, our song of freedom. Some of you may know the words and may join us, if you like."

In a circle, standing at rigid attention, the ten visitors began, "Viet Nam Men Yen..." ("Beloved Viet Nam"). As the old Viet Minh song rambled along, the glint of recognition shone from the eyes of most of the villagers. It was a song they used to sing but had not heard since 1954.

The agitprop ("agitation and propaganda") squad moved away in single file across the paddies. But they came back again and again and again. With successive visits, the squad began holding "group meetings" for discussion of important problems. At first the meetings were all in the middle of the hamlet, but later they began to separate into groups. The young woman, Nga, gathered around her most of the women in town. Thuan talked to the men. The student talked to the young people.

The talks were always short and informal on simple themes.

One day Thuan would tell the people, "We had to shed our blood to destroy the French devils and throw them out. The fighting spirit of the Vietnamese people proved too much for the colonists. But sadly for us, the fight was not over in 1954 when the People's Army stormed into Dien Bien Phu. A new aggressor came, with bombs and germs and poison. But the Liberation Front will destroy the new aggressor, too! *Da Dao De Quoc My!* (Down with U.S. Imperialism!)"

And the student said: "The Americans are trying to spread hatred between the religions of Viet Nam so that Catholics and Buddhists will kill each other, so that Hoa Hao and Cao Dai will kill each other, so that Vietnamese will destroy Vietnamese, and the Americans can drink our blood. How do you like that? *Da Dao De Quoc My!*"

And Nga said: "My sister, who was only sixteen, died because of these Americans. They raped her eighty-two times, and then cut off her breasts and hung them from a tree. The Liberation Front is the only hope for Vietnamese women. *Da Dao De Quoc My!*"

And one of the men in conical hats said: "After the war of liberation, I was given five hectares of land by the Viet Minh, and I lived happily with my family. But the Americans and their lackeys came and threw me out. Now a rich man who lives in My Tho owns my land and I have nothing. The only hope of the farmer is the Liberation Front. *Da Dao De Quoc My!*"

And another man said: "The Liberation Front grows every day, and all civilized countries recognize it as the only legitimate government of Viet Nam. Only the Americans and their lackeys oppose us. The world is on our side. *Da Dao De Quoc My!*"

And so it went, day after day. The villagers listened and said little.

But one day, Thuan and his group arrived at about dusk, laughing among themselves and talking excitedly.

"I have something very good to tell you today," Thuan told the villagers who quickly gathered. "Today the Americans and their puppet troops tried to destroy a hamlet twenty kilometers from here that had been liberated by the People's Self-Defense Forces. But the puppet troops got a nasty surprise. Our people killed three hundred of them, including fifty Americans. It was a glorious fight."

Thuan's face suddenly clouded. "But of course," he added, "I'm afraid they will be back. And I'm afraid they may even strike here. Our people need so many things that are so hard to get . . ." he trailed off. "Of course, if you could help us a little—it wouldn't involve fighting, or anything—just some help from all of you, as we have tried to help you."

"What is it you need?" someone asked Thuan.

"We need things to defend ourselves. Most of all, we need foot traps to snare and wound the enemy, halting his advance. They are easy to make. You take ordinary nails, hammer barbs into the ends, and sharpen them. Then you plant four or five nails upright in a board or a block of concrete. Even a child could make one. Would some of you children help us defend our homeland?"

Several children stepped forward, and the demonstration began. The visitors sang as they worked and made a kind of game of it. A few of the women joined in.

At the end of a week, most of the hamlet was involved in making nail boards. A makeshift forge had been set up, and two children delighted in pumping the bellows as the charcoal fire glowed cherry red. The agitprop team had brought several large bags of American cement to the hamlet, with which they made concrete blocks for the nail boards. The children loved it. The cememt bags were still marked with little American "hands-across-the-sea" stickers.

For several days, Thuan's team failed to return. When it finally came back, two of the men were carrying a body on an improvised litter.

"This poor woman was murdered by the puppet troops in her hamlet a few kilometers from here," Thuan announced. "She must have a decent burial, but it is not safe there. We shall bury her near here."

The villagers watched the burial, and some of them were plainly angry. "Damned Americans," one of them muttered. "Everything was peaceful around here until they showed up."

After the ceremony, Thuan called the villagers together. He spoke persuasively and was such a familiar figure that he was by now regarded as something of a village leader. His gallantry and good looks had softened several feminine hearts.

"I have something important to tell all of you," he said. "The aggressors probably will come here. They have heard that we are making nail boards and that we are angry at the atrocities they have committed. We must be ready to save ourselves. We can do it easily, but we must prepare. If we do not prepare there will be terrible bloodshed and suffering. For your safety, we must show you what to do.

"First, they may try to come to collect taxes. You must not let them, because they will use the rice you give them against us. Tell them that rats have destroyed your stores. Hide most of your rice, and give some of it to us for safekeeping.

"Second, they will try to round up all of your young men for conscription into their puppet army. Many of our people have cut off their own fingers and toes to avoid this, but this is not necessary. The main thing is that all the young men should be ready to hide somewhere away from the hamlet when they come. You young men should have a leader to help you avoid the pirates. You, Xuan, would you like to accept that responsibility?"

Flattered, the peasant youth nodded his head in agreement.

And so it began. Each day, Thuan held drills for the young men, who would scatter into the fields and jungle. Some hid in rice paddies, and Thuan showed them how they could breathe under water through a straw without being seen. Others hid in secret tunnels that were beginning to honeycomb the hamlet.

The agitprop team worked as hard as anyone else on the tunnels and some other fortifications they decided might be useful. Mud embankments with gun ports began to go up, so skillfully camouflaged they looked like normal paddy dykes. Sharpened bamboo stakes bristled from these embankments, and nail boards were planted in the water fields around them.

And the visitors were out in the fields, too, helping with the plowing and the business of keeping the farms going.

"We have a saying in the Liberation Front that '*tam dong*' will save us all," he told the villagers once. *Tam dong* means likeness of thought and action.

"We work together, eat together and live together. Sometimes, we must fight together," Thuan added.

The songs and rallies continued, and the slogans were repeated and repeated.

One day, Thuan pointed out to the villagers that they would be better off if they could defend themselves while the Liberation Front team was away.

"Xuan, you and your men are tough and brave. Isn't it too bad that all you can do if the enemy comes now is run away in the face of the running dogs?"

Xuan agreed that it was.

"Wouldn't you prefer to have some self-protection, like these guns of ours?"

Xuan, who was only seventeen, strongly agreed. He had been interested in those shiny guns ever since he had first seen them. It would be nice to have a pistol stuck in one's belt.

"Well, unfortunately, the People's Self-Defense Forces don't have any to spare. We have to make everything we use, or else seize it from the running dogs. We shall show you how to make some swords and daggers, which are certainly better than nothing. We can also make some good grenades."

More weeks passed as Thuan's group taught the young people the rudiments of weaponry. And now, the youths held a little parade every morning with their homemade swords. They stood in ranks, proud as peacocks, and sang the patriotic songs in front of a brand-new flagpole. On the pole was a huge red and blue flag with a yellow star in the center—the colors of the National Liberation Front.

Early one morning Thuan and his team came into town with a prisoner whose hands were tied behind his back and who staggered along with a rope around his neck. It was the local government district chief. He was bloody and bruised, and his khaki uniform was slashed and torn in a dozen places.

Three of Thuan's men dragged him to the flagpole and lashed him to it.

"Comrades, come here. I want to show you an enemy of the people," Thuan shouted. People gathered curiously.

"This man," Thuan said, "is Lieutenant Nguyen Dinh Thao, the U.S. lackeys' district chief. We caught him last night while he and his men were raiding a hamlet not far from here. They were arresting all the young men to put in the puppet army, and were stealing rice from the people. You all know him, I'm sure. His pocket is bulging with the money he has extorted from you and the rest of the people."

Several villagers grunted as they recognized the hated tax collector.

"This man has had many chances. We have warned him many times," Thuan said. "But the Liberation Front can extend mercy and charity only to those who are on the side of the people. This is one of the running dogs—and he must pay the penalty."

Thuan nodded in the direction of two men in black standing near the bound district chief. One unsheathed a dagger, stepped in front of the struggling office, and spat in his face. Then, with a series of swift strokes, he plunged the knife into the district chief's belly five times.

The officer screamed and pitched forward, hanging from his bindings. The second man in black, carrying a heavy sugar-cane axe, stepped up to the dying man. Three strokes of the axe and the district chief's severed head lay in the mud at his feet. A sharp groan came from the watching villagers.

Thuan turned to two village youths who had been watching with their mouths open. "Take him down and bury him in the fields somewhere. We shall take care of the head. It will go back to his district headquarters as a warning to others." There was something new in Thuan's tone. He was commanding, not requesting. The two youths hesitantly walked up to the bleeding body and began their assignment.

The days passed at Ap —— and life underwent changes. One night the roar of artillery interrupted the peaceful croaking of the geckos, and ten shells landed in and around the hamlet. A man, three women and two children were killed. Thuan's team was not there at the time, but arrived at sunrise.

"It is horrible," Thuan said sympathetically. "But we

must let others know what the aggressors have done here. I want all the women in this hamlet to join with other women in a demonstration planned for Saturday to denounce the imperialist atrocities. Ten thousand women will march in the province capital with banners showing the people's indignation against these cruel shellings. Miss Nga will tell you about the arrangements, and we will provide sampans for you to get into town. You need not worry about the running dogs making trouble for you in the province capital. They are afraid of the people seeing them brutalize defenseless women. Those of you with babies and young children should take them along. They also can carry banners."

At the demonstration, things worked out exactly as Thuan had predicted. There were not quite ten thousand marchers. In fact, there were only about three hundred. But they made an impressive sight as they straggled through town, their handpainted cloth banners burning with indignation and their eyes streaming tears. Finally, police chashed them out of town, but not until everyone had seen the women and their banners.

Thuan and his team were not there, but had remained at Ap —— to discuss a new project with the men of the village.

"It is not enough to run from the aggressors every time," Thuan was yelling from his usual place in front of the flagpole. "When we can, we must hurt him. It is our duty to defend our fatherland by force when we can. But we need weapons and we need men. I know that there are many young heroes here who are eager to undertake this work. You, Xuan, for example."

Xuan grinned and saluted. He felt he already had been accepted by this glamorous group of leaders, and was proud of his status.

"I want you to gather the self-defense squad you command for an important secret meeting tonight, at which we shall discuss the most important mission you ever have had. It is time for us to prove our steel."

Xuan was tense. He had suspected for some time that the daily drilling with homemade swords and clubs was leading to something, and now the time of decision had come. After all, he must not show cowardice.

At eight o'clock that night, Xuan and nine other badly frightened hamlet militia boys arrived at the hut Thuan had designated. None had wanted to come. But none had wanted to show fear or cowardice. All were curious and excited.

Inside, a single candle flickered. Pieces of cloth had been hung around the thatched walls to prevent light from leaking through. Thuan and two other men dressed like him, both strangers, sat at a large table on which several bottles stood. In the middle of the hut was another table on which an enormous tray filled with mud had been arranged. Miniature buildings, walls and watchtowers had been built out of mud in the tray, rows of bamboo toothpicks marked fences and barricades, and threads were stretched to represent barbed wire. The whole thing was obviously an exact model of a government outpost, complete with miniature flag.

"Ah, my friends, it is good to see you are punctual. We have serious business to discuss tonight, and two of our comrades from the People's Army have joined me to help explain things. But why do you look so serious? This is a joyful occasion. Let us celebrate your initiation into manhood with a drink."

The bottles contained *ba xi de*, a powerful rice liquor distilled in the Mekong Delta, the taste of which is suggestive of diesel fuel and which burns all the way down. Each of the youths choked down a swallow or two and felt better about the whole thing.

"The job we are about to give you is really not difficult, because our comrades of the National Liberation Front have planned everything to the last detail. If you act like the revolutionary soldiers you now are, your mission will be completedly successful. And you will have good weapons as your reward.

"There is one thing you must remember, though. From this point on, everything you do must be in secret. You can't turn back now. If you betray your comrades through cowardice or malice or by accident, the Liberation Front will deal with you as traitors. The government district chief we brought to your hamlet was a traitor to the people. Do not forget what you saw."

The recruits fidgeted but said nothing. Then Thuan turned the meeting over to one of the two strangers—a man who spoke with a hard, nasal voice and who seemed interested only in the model on the table.

"There are ten aggressor troops in this post," he began.

"In each of the watchtowers at the three corners of the triangle is a sentry with a rifle. Each sentry has a bamboo log on which he knocks once in a while. When this happens, each of the other two sentries knocks on his bamboo in reply, to signal that everything is all right. Actually, all of these men have been living in the post for nearly ten months. In all that time, nothing has happened to them, and Liberation forces have kept away. Therefore the sentries are usually asleep.

"As you see, the watchtowers are connected by mud walls on each side of the triangle. The outside of these walls is covered with bamboo spikes. In front of the walls is a moat filled with water and mud. Outside the moat are three concentric barbed wire fences.

"Inside the post, six other soldiers sleep in this building, and their officer sleeps alone in this one. Their ammunition and extra weapons are kept in this small building, which has a padlock on the door.

"The only entrance to the post is through a gate facing this canal. The gate is blocked by a movable barbed wire barricade, and boards crossing the moat are pulled in every night.

"Our plan is simple but depends on strict discipline, silence and camouflage. We shall take two sampans, approaching the hamlet from opposite directions. The sampans will stop two hundred meters from the post, and we whall crawl the rest of the way. Three of you will have wire cutters with which you will make corridors through the barbed wire at three different points, each one close to a corner tower but to the rear of the sentry inside. Each sentry has a chair and this chair always faces forward, so you need not worry about being seen.

"Three others will carry explosive charges through the fence and place them against the walls of the towers. They will not be spotted, because you will be working so close to the sentries you will be under their fields of vision. At exactly 2 A.M., the fuses of each charge will be started. These fuses burn for only eight seconds, so you must get out of the way quickly. When the charges go off, everyone will throw all the grenades we shall give you into the post. Then you will wait while three of us from the People's Army clean out the running dogs with machine guns. When we give the signal, you will all go over the wall into the post and finish off anyone left with your daggers. One of us will shoot the lock off the arms hut, and then we shall all leave carrying everything that seems valuable to us. Besides their weapons, they have a radio we want. We also want their documents, money, food and everything else."

The lecturer paused and looked around.

"From this moment on, you are under the discipline of the People's Armed Forces," he said. "You know what that means."

All of them did. Each night for weeks on end, various members of Thuan's squad had lectured them until they almost were falling asleep on the fifteen points of secrecy, the twelve points of discipline, and the ten-point soldier's oath. Each knew the whole catechism by heart.

The whole group left the hut and marched along a dark trail to a clearing where a full-scale dummy post had been marked out on the ground. There were no walls or buildings, but stakes and lengths of string marked the outline of the towers, moats and walls. A canal ran nearby.

All night long, Thuan, the two strangers and the ten recruits practiced assaults on the dummy post. After each rehearsal, one of the strangers would criticize the exercise, lacing his remarks with sinister irony.

"Well done, Duc," he told one recruit. "You moved in bravely. Of course you are now dead, since you approached the tower from the wrong side and your guts were shot out by the sentry. But I'm sure your mother will be proud of you."

Finally, the instructor was satisfied, and the recruits marched home to bed. They were under orders to sleep all day, since the following night would be the real attack.

Two mornings later, as a glaring red sun was just slanting up over the flat horizon, the ten recruits straggled back into town in twos and threes. Their black clothing was torn to rags, and they were covered with ugly cuts.

But each one was grinning broadly, and each one was carrying a brand-new weapon. Xuan, the recruit leader, had a Tommy gun slung over his shoulder, a pistol stuck through his belt and four American grenades hanging from the belt. The operation had been a complete success, and the enemy post had been wiped out without a single Liberation Front casualty. Mothers and sisters rushed to embrace their returning soldier boys with relief. Nothing had been said about the operation, but everyone in the hamlet had known more or less what was going on. Thuan and the two strangers had not returned with the recruits, but had said they would return to the hamlet in a few days.

Each recruit had a war story to tell, and each was strutting like a peacock with his new weapon. Each was ready for a new operation of some kind.

Thuan and his team did return again and again. There were more and more lectures and meetings, and schedules were worked out for every resident of the hamlet. Two new buildings were placed in the central market area—an information booth and a new primary school. Miss Nga was assigned to take care of both of them as a combination teacher and information officer. On inauguration day, the two buildings were decked out with paper Liberation Front flags made by hamlet children, and there were speeches and songs along with a hamlet feast. Thuan's group even presented a musical play in which Thuan acted out the part of an American helicopter, flapping his arms around his head like rotor blades. Thuan fell crashing to the ground when Xuan and Miss Nga pointed dummy rifles at him, and the whole crowd laughed at his antics.

Xuan, the hamlet recruit leader, was obviously fond of Miss Nga, and was always bringing her choice pieces of fruit. In return, she would often sit with him under a tree reading to him aloud from one of her Liberation Front books. It was rumored that she was allowing Xuan to call her *em* (Little Sister, or Beloved).

Work went on constantly. Big clay pots were buried up to their lids in most of the huts for use as air raid shelters. Secret hiding places also were dug under most of the hamlet, often under the charcoal stoves of the mud floors. One large hiding place could be entered only by diving into the canal and swimming through an underwater tunnel in the bank. The roomy hiding place had air vents skillfully concealed by bushes. Each man and woman was drilled daily on the procedure to be followed in case of an enemy attack.

For a while, Thuan personally supervised some recruits in the building of a rather large underground chamber with a bell-shaped roof pierced by three ports aboveground, each facing in a different direction. Thuan was very fussy about the exact shaping of the interior of their chamber, and explained that a sentry must occupy it all day long, listening closely. The shape of the walls would amplify sounds coming through the ports in such a way that an approaching helicopter could be heard from a distance of up to fifteen miles, he explained. Furthermore, the sentry would be able to tell exactly the direction from which the helicopter was coming.

So little by little, Ap —— became a Viet Cong "Combat Hamlet." Of course, there were residents who didn't like the idea. Older people, especially, were afraid that all these preparations would expose the hamlet to war.

But it was too late to object. Thuan's crowd controlled everything, and the young recruits ruled the roost. Every man, woman and child was somehow committed to the new way of things, and to back out would mean banishment from the hamlet, or worse.

Besides that, everyone had been organized into cells, mostly of five persons each. There were self-defense cells for the men, first aid cells for the women, flagmaking cells for the children, work cells, building cells, agricultural cells, and, above all, political study cells. Nearly every cell included one member from Thuan's group who kept a close eye on things.

Thuan and the steady stream of strangers now passing through town had insisted that the membership of each cell be kept secret. At first, it had seemed like a game, and many refused to take the thing seriously. But those who failed to turn up for cell meetings were punished. Usually, the hamlet central committee would confiscate rice stocks from the uncooperative cell member.

Each cell chairman was a member of the hamlet committee, but somehow the committee always seemed to go along with what Thuan proposed. And Xuan, who now was chairman of the self-defense cell, had a lot of say in things too, despite his youth.

In all this time, a period of a year or so, the National Liberation Front was unhindered in its work at Ap ——. No government official ever came around, and the war never touched the hamlet itself, except for the shelling incident.

The self-defense cell, initially only ten recruits, grew to more than fifty men under arms, all of whom had participated in occasional forays on government posts. Casualties were light, and most of these operations were successful.

Xuan and a few others eventually left the hamlet. They

had been spotted by Liberation Front talent scouts as tough, reliable soldiers, and had been asked to join a higher echelon of fighters—the regional liberation guerrillas. These guerrillas ranged throughout the whole province and were assigned missions much more important than merely knocking out isolated enemy posts. They specialized in big ambushes, often taking on even enemy armored columns.

If Xuan did well in the regional forces and showed continuing political development, he probably would graduate into one of the regular main force battalions, such as the famour 514th—the scourge of the upper Mekong Delta.

Good news and encouragement were continuously pouring into the hamlet. Several transistor radios were kept at the information hut, all tuned to "Liberation Radio." The news reports each day gave glowing accounts of victories by the Front against Saigon forces and the Americans. There were lots of statistics—how many enemy helicopters shot down, how many Americans killed or captured, and so on. One report said that 90 per cent of Central Nam Bo (Viet Cong terminology for the central Mekong Delta area) had been liberated, and residents of Ap —— were prepared to believe it.

But reports each day also told of ghastly new atrocities being committed by the Americans—disemboweling women, violating children, eating the livers of peasants, dropping napalm over whole communities, and—most of all—spreading poison over crops.

Even neighboring Cambodia was complaining at the United Nations about American planes from Viet Nam dropping deadly yellow powder over border villages.

The graphic accounts of American atrocities inevitably brought blood to a boil. Many of the hamlet residents had seen the French Foreign Legion in action, and were prepared to believe anything of the big-nosed alien troops.

Besides the radio, news bulletins were circulated in the hamlet each day—at first, on mimeographed sheets, but later in the form of a six-page printed newspaper. The newspaper apparently was published in the delta capital of My Tho, right under the enemy's nose in some city print shop.

The radio and newspapers also told each day of the support the outer world was giving the National Liberation Front. Professor Nguyen Van Hieu, the Front's ambassador at large, was given a standing ovation in Jakarta or Prague or Havana. The English aristocrat, Lord Bertrand Russell, had come out against the imperialists in Viet Nam. Even American college students were demonstrating in favor of the Vietnamese National Liberation Front in Times Square in New York City. Most of all, the fraternal socialist bloc—North Viet Nam and People's China—was standing by to help.

So, all in all, it looked from Ap —— as if things were pretty well sewed up for the National Liberation Front. In any case, Ap —— was now prepared to fight the imperialists and their lackeys to the death, and Thuan's mission had succeeded to the last detail.

I have not mentioned the name of the hamlet where all this happened, for the reason that I have drawn the details from several hamlets as a kind of composite. But I want to assure the reader that none of it is fiction. I have a real hamlet in mind for most of this story, and the protagonist of the story, Thuan, was real.

I saw Thuan's shattered body among others that fell at Ap —— one afternoon when a government task force happened to take them by surprise. The hamlet had fought well, and its defenders managed to shoot down three American helicopters. All the huts in town were burned down, but the artillery and bombs never touched the underground hiding places, and casualties were comparatively light. When Saigon troops came in, they found, as usual, only women and children and a handful of old men.

But Thuan had made one of his rare slips and had got caught out in the open. Next to his body I found a bloodstained pocket notebook with his name inside and a photograph of himself with a pretty girl. The book was meticulously written in longhand, and obviously had been dictated by some instructor from a handbook on insurrection.

In common with all such field manuals, Thuan's notebook had several homespun remedies for curing the diseases of oxen and men.

I have no idea whether any of these remedies work, but they are all standard elements of Viet Cong medical lore, and their application presumably makes propaganda agents more popular with the people.

Thuan's book was a kind of how-to-do-it summary of Viet

Cong insurgency. The most important section had to do with propaganda.

The reader may be familiar with the writings of Mao Tse-tung, General Vo Nguyen Giap, and the other standard writers on Asian "people's welfare." But there are writers at lower levels who must translate the theory into more practical instructions. These writings cover every practical subject to which a guerrilla is exposed, and generally are given in question and answer form, like a kind of catechism.

Since the cutting edge of the Viet Cong is political propaganda, let me introduce here a translation of most of the section of Thuan's field manual headed "Propaganda Mission." Thuan himself was a highly successful agitprop team leader, and there must be something to the instructions.

PROPAGANDA MISSION

Question: What is the importance of a propaganda mission? What should you do in carrying out this mission with people in general and youths in particular?

Answer: A propaganda mission is designed to attract people's interest and stimulate their thoughts, and also to expand our party's policy and ideology.

Question: What are the four ways by which this mission is carried out?

Answer: 1. Increase feelings of discontent on the part of the people before trying to mobilize their patriotic sentiments; 2. Explain to the people the efforts being made by the enemy to divide us from the population; 3. Educate the people about our struggle in South Viet Nam; and 4. Stress the importance of our Front for the liberation of South Viet Nam (which already has legal status in Viet Nam and throughout the world). Also, educate the people about our party's basic policies, about North Viet Nam, about socialism, and other world news.

Question: What are the consequences of widespread application of propaganda at meetings and so forth, which, however, lacks work in depth?

Answer: No valuable result can be obtained if a propaganda mission is carried on in width only, that is, superficially, but not in depth. The public can never understand the subject well, because at most meetings you cannot explain everything in detail. Only by carrying out your propaganda mission secretly and at the grassroots level can you succeed. You should divide your work according to three separate zones: The liberated zone, where you can push hard in width as well as depth, the contested zone, where most of your operations must be in depth and in secret, and in the enemy zone, where all must be secret and in depth.

In towns, do as much as you can, but do it in depth using maximum caution. Avoid wasting the time of our people. In places where the enemy has strong fortifications, work only in depth.

Question: How should youths be approached on the question of joining our forces?

Answer: Revolutionary spirit among our people is now high. Now is a favorable time for talking our young men into our army and into reporting enemy activity to us, for educating youths about our policy, for teaching them about the struggle of the classes, about present and future victories, and about the sacrifices of a revolutionary combatant.

Before the departure of a recruit, a ceremony should be arranged and a meeting of a Liberation Front cadre with the recruit's family should take place. Front committee members will arrive later to work out personal problems for the recruit. At the recruit's request, his family will have support from our group and from the people.

Question: How should propaganda be carried out opposing enemy military conscription?

Answer: Explain to the people the deep significance of the current drafting of youths by the U.S. imperialist clique. Opposition to the draft should be carried out in three ways: Refuse to comply with the draft notice, desert after being drafted, or get the people themselves to prevent the drafting of a youth. If a youth is drafted, a dramatic and tragic departure ceremony should be arranged by the Liberation Front.

Question: How should religious subjects be handled?

Answer: Denounce religious leaders who ally themselves with the imperialists. Our policy is to separate them. We must tell the people that no soldier should be a member of any religious organization. Among religious persons, organize a system whereby traitors working under the cover of religious robes are denounced. We must, however, be very careful in our judgments.

Question: How should you react to enemy propaganda in your area?

Answer: Enemy propaganda techniques sometimes have a bad influence on the people. We should react promptly to this, leading the people's thinking in the opposite direction, and instilling in the people a spirit of mutual assistance and mutual struggle. Revolutionary counterpropaganda and counterattack should be carried out simultaneously.

For example, if religion is mentioned in enemy propaganda, we must plead for freedom of religion. We must point out to the people that it is the policy of the U.S. and its lackeys to exterminate religion, and we must give some concrete evidence of it. Thus we not only are rejecting the enemy's propaganda but we are attacking him directly.

Question: What is our policy concerning cultural matters?

Answer: The performance of popular shows for the public is one of several ways for carrying out propaganda after attracting popular interest. The Front should promote this type of work and organize programs. But be careful in choosing the actors for such shows.

Question: How should the agitprop team approach the problem of educating children?

Answer: The mission undertaken by the team to educate children is most important. The main goal is to bring immediate educational benefits to the children, to help build the future of the nation. Schools should be built in conformity with our new type of life—well ventilated, neat and clean, but cheap. Teachers must be well educated because they are the engineers of future generations.

Programs of education should include political, social and domestic topics. The program of mass education should be pushed.

Question: What is the proper behavior of the propagandist?

Answer: A propagandist should be modest, he should learn from the people, and he should teach what he has experienced to the people. This helps to consolidate his position. He should be patient and his behavior should be exemplary.

Question: What is the current role of the party and popular organizations compared with the time of the resistance war against the French?

Answer: Throughout the history of our revolution, events usually have been initiated by the people. Only a popular organization can defeat the enemy. Our giant party organization originally was formed from large popular gatherings. We must always work closely with the people, for the people, and in the interest of the people.

During the days of the Resistance [the Indochina War, which ended in victory for the Viet Minh in 1954], popular organizations constituted the rear lines of our forces. *But in the current fight, which centers so strongly on the political field, any mass organization should be regarded as a combatant unit*. (Italics are author's).

Thuan's manual continued for many more pages, but I think this suffices to indicate the tone. It is similar to many other manuals captured in battle, although there often are regional differences in propaganda themes.

Because of extremely primitive communications in many parts of South Viet Nam, Viet Cong propaganda can contradict itself from one area to another without danger of exposure. An interesting and dangerous instance of this developed in September 1964 when 2,000 mountain tribesmen, trained and armed by American Special Forces as irregular guerrilla troops, rebelled against the Saigon government.

In itself, the incident was actuely embarrassing to the United States. For three years, Americans had been training the tribesmen to be crack soldiers, capable of fighting in well-disciplined units.

The mountain tribesmen of Viet Nam are racially very distinct from the lowland Vietnamese, and all of their thirty-odd tribal languages are linguistically different from Vietnamese. Communication between the tribesmen and the lowland Vietnamese is normally in French, the only language universally understood.

The tribesmen and the lowlanders have been mutually hostile for centuries. Most Vietnamese regard their highlanders as savages and treat them accordingly. The highlanders don't like it, and feel that total foreigners—French or Americans—are likely to treat them with more dignity and respect.

It happens that the highlanders are the dominant racial group in many of Central Vietnam's sparsely populated provinces. Hamlets often are separated by many miles of trackless, jungle-covered mountains, where only the tribesmen know their way around. These provinces happen to be prime infiltration routes for Viet Cong from Laos and Cambodia, and the guerrillas generally have been careful to keep their fences mended with the tribesmen.

Years ago the Viet Cong understood the necessity of having friendly or at least neutral tribesmen in these areas, and began cultivating friendships. Viet Cong organizers frequently settled down in tribal hamlets, marrying the daughters of hamlet chiefs.

Recognizing the potentialities of the hostility between the tribesmen and the lowlanders, the Viet Cong managed to put the feud to practical use. Rather than preach unity of highlanders and lowlanders, the Viet Cong propagandists talked of creating an autonomous tribal kingdom, completely independent of lowland Viet Nam, in the event of a Liberation Front victory.

The first serious threat to Viet Cong dominance in the highland jungles came directly from America in the early 1960s. The American Special Forces troops had a knack of working with the highlanders, and turned many of them against the Viet Cong. Of course, the highlanders remained anti-Vietnamese in general. The irregulars were delighted to kill Viet Cong for the Americans, but they probably would have been just as happy killing any Vietnamese.

American efforts to transfer their training and leading role with the highlanders to the Vietnamese largely failed. And in September 1964 five tribal camps revolted from Saigon authority. At three of them, the tribesmen butchered Vietnamese officers and officials, but made it plain they wanted the Americans to stay on to lead them. This was a direct slap in the face to Saigon, and had a chilling effect on relations with Washington.

Premier Nguyen Khanh was all for blasting the rebel camps to destruction, but the Americans objected. For one thing, American officers were being held more or less as hostages at one of the camps. For another, the Americans felt that many of the tribal demands were justified. But at the same time, America was committed to supporting Saigon against rebellion, and therefore faced an ugly dilemma.

Finally, Saigon laid down an ultimatum to both the rebels and the Americans: If in twenty-four hours the main rebel camp had not surrendered, it would be attacked and destroyed, with or without Americans inside.

In the end, American officers inside the camp persuaded the rebels to surrender after extracting a promise from Saigon that no reprisals would be taken. Then the Americans pulled out the Vietnamese troops poured in.

The net effect of this was that both the tribesmen and the Vietnamese were angry at America. And the Viet Cong agitprop men were quick to capitalize on the situation.

The tribesmen were told that this was clear evidence the Americans could not be trusted and really were just as bad as the Vietnamese. If the Liberation Front wins, the agitprop men said, both the Americans and the Vietnamese will be thrown out of the area, and the tribesmen will be free to build their own nation.

But in propaganda beamed at Vietnamese, other agit-prop teams took precisely the opposite line. The Americans for years had been arming and training the savages as part of a plot to exterminate Vietnamese, they said. Even after twenty-nine Vietnamese were slaughtered, the puppet Saigon government was powerless to take strong measures against the insurgent savages because of Uncle Sam's meddling in Vietnamese affairs, the line went.

During the summer of 1964, Saigon saw a simple and striking demonstration of Viet Cong agitprop technique applied to religious dissension.

For several days, there had been rioting between gangs of predominantly Buddhist and predominantly Catholic youths. The government had adopted a hands-off policy, and security police and troops were under orders not to interfere in the street fighting. The apparent idea was to let the gangs fight themselves to exhaustion, at which point resumption of government controls would be welcomed. But the fighting grew worse, and a dozen or so youths were slain with machetes, hammers and hatchets.

One afternoon, an army jeep equipped with loudspeakers was stolen from one of Saigon's compounds. A few hours later, two men in military uniform were seen driving the jeep slowly past the main Buddhist headquarters compound. The loudspeaker was blaring a warning that Catholic youths from a suburban community called Ho Nai were coming to burn down the compound that night. The jeep next turned up about three miles away in front of the North Vietnamese refugee settlement at Ho Nai, which is predominantly Roman Catholic in faith. Here, the loudspeaker warned that Buddhist gangs were coming that night to attack the settlement and burn its church.

According to the best police and intelligence information available, neither the Buddhists nor the Catholics had any intention of fighting each other that night, until the mysterious jeep passed their respective strongholds. But after that, both sides were off and running, armed with clubs, spears, torches, axes and pushcarts filled with bricks.

Police managed to halt both mobs peacefully and turn them back, but bloody chaos was averted by only 500 yards. There is every evidence that the jeep (found later parked in a back alley) had been hijacked by two well-known Viet Cong agents.

Viet Cong propaganda has been known to appeal to the Vietnamese instinct for savage humor.

For many years, Saigon legends have linked Mme. Ngo Dinh Nhu, the once powerful sister-in-law of the late President Ngo Dinh Diem, with various amorous adventures. One perennial story has to do with Mme. Nhu and a U.S. Army colonel. Another links her in a tragic adventure with one of South Viet Nam's leading young generals whose wife is supposed to have shot Mme. Nhu through the arm.

I have never seen a shred of documentation for any of these yarns, but Saigon's cocktail circuit intelligentsia accepts differing versions of the Mme. Nhu stories as established fact.

In any case, the Viet Cong evidently saw grist for its mill in the stories. One morning, traffic on a key road out of Saigon was halted by a bigger-than-life display in the middle of the pavement. The display consisted of enormous dummies made in the likenesses of the American ambassador and Mme. Nhu, lying compromised on a layer of gigantic dollar bills. The themes of capitalism, miscegenation, current rumors and the idea of Viet Nam being sold out to the American imperialist all were wrapped up neatly. To safeguard the handiwork, a small sign had been placed in front of the figures reading: "This monument is mined."

Buses, cars and boats are regularly stopped by agitprop teams and passengers get lectures. In a typical incident, two large ferryboats headed in opposite directions across a main branch of the Mekong were stopped, and all their passengers were taken ashore. The crews of the boats served at gunpoint as chefs and hosts to a picnic, while agitprop actors put on a political skit for the passengers. The passengers were twelve hours late getting home.

These interludes do not always have pleasant endings. On the highway north of Saigon to Dalat, two missionaries once were driving with their wives and children when they were halted at an agitprop roadblock. The Viet Cong agents had just begun questioning the carloads of people they had halted when an approaching American helicopter was heard. The Viet Cong fled, but not before machine-gunning the missionaries to death.

Viet Cong propaganda works both secretly and openly, and has many outlets. Some of its techniques seem subtle and clever, others seem childish and stupid. But it works.

It is practically impossible to measure the effect of any single piece of propaganda. But one thing that can be more or less measured is recruiting. The success of a recruiting campaign is directly related to the effectiveness of the propaganda of the side doing the recruiting.

Since 1960, the fighting strength of the Viet Cong has grown dramatically, despite heavy casualties. A relatively small part of the increase is owing to infiltration from North Viet Nam.

In 1961, American experts estimated Viet Cong strength at around 18,000. By late 1967, they estimated Viet Cong strength at about 113,000, including 50,000 infiltrated North Vietnamese troops, but not including an estimated 170,000 Viet Cong reservists who could be called up at any time.

At this writing, American intelligence men believe that up to 30 per cent of the men in each newly organized Viet Cong unit are infiltrators and the rest are local recruits. As units reach fighting and political maturity, the infiltrated organizers move on to new units. The infiltrated organizers work only with the Viet Cong's "main force" units—the equivalent of the regular army. Regional guerrillas and local hamlet defense groups, numbering between 60,000 and 80,000 men, are all locally recruited. From this it can be seen that on a national basis the percentage of Hanoi-trained infiltrators in the Viet Cong army is probably quite small, say about 15 per cent at most.

The rate of infiltration of agents in South Viet Nam is believed to have been more or less constant over the years.

But at the beginning of 1964, for example, Viet Cong

"main force" strength was rated at around 27,000 men, with up to 80,000 other guerrillas and local forces under arms.

In the following six months, according to the most reliable intelligence estimates, the Viet Cong suffered an estimated 10,000 battle casualties. But its main force strength reached about 34,000, with the other groups under arms still rated at about 80,000. This represented a net gain for the Viet Cong of 7,000 fighters in a six-month period, or a gross gain (allowing for the casualties) of around 17,000.

The Viet Cong has never hesitated to use force or coercion in drafting young people into its armed forces. But experience in North has shown that it is not enough to draft a man to make him fight. The kind of military successes achieved by the Viet Cong is not suggestive of bands of unwilling, frightened draftees, but rather of hardened soldiers.

From the beginning, the Viet Cong has laid much heavier stress on rice-roots propaganda work than have either the Saigon government or American propaganda agencies in Viet Nam.

In late 1964 the Viet Cong felt that it controlled seventy-seven out of South Viet Nam's 237 administrative districts so completely that agitprop activity no longer was required. But the other 160 districts were considered "contested," that is, up for grabs by both sides. In each of these contested districts, at least two Viet Cong agitprop teams of about ten men and women each were at work.

To counter the Viet Cong, Saigon's Information Ministry fielded information teams of about ten members each, equipped with three-wheeled scooter trucks, loudspeakers, movie projection equipment and various "visual aids." Saigon initially had about twenty of these teams in operation.

In itself, that gave the Viet Cong a sixteen-to-one numerical edge in personnel assigned to propaganda work. Over the years, Saigon added more teams and more staff workers in Saigon. But the techniques remained essentially the same, and the quality of government workers was very low.

Saigon information teams are supposed to spend their time in the countryside, especially in contested areas. This is dangerous work. The Viet Cong regards its own agitprop teams as the basic cutting tools of the National Liberation Front, and looks on enemy propagandists as prime targets, even ahead of regular troops.

It probably would not be just to say that Saigon's field propaganda workers are dragged in off the streets, given a few thousand piastres and told to go to work. But this is not far from the truth.

The work of these teams is not really very difficult. On a typical mission, the team is sent to some hamlet with its scooter truck, sets up its movie screen and projector, shows the movie, passes out brochures and leaflets, and leaves as quickly as possible. Most of the leaflets and brochures are printed by the U.S. Information Service in Saigon or Manila.

Rarely if ever do government propagandists stay around for more than a few hours, and the whole approach is based on mass communications rather than the "living together" and audience-participation techniques of the Viet Cong. Viet Cong propagandists generally are peasants, but the government men are not.

To American ears, propaganda is a bad word, and Americans often feel a little queasy about using either the word or the technique. This reticence is reflected at every level in Saigon's programs.

In the U.S. Army there is an organization devoted to "psychological warfare," and an exact counterpart of this has been designed and built in the Vietnamese army. It is primarily a force of technicians who know such arts as printing aerial leaflets, recording tapes for loudspeakers, and so on. As such, it has about as much prestige as a fighting organization as, say, the chaplain's corps, or the special services section for troop recreation. The emphasis is on electronics and machinery rather than on direct contact with the "target people."

On the civilian side, the U.S. Information Service has what it terms "information programs." These, again, are essentially duplicated by information programs of the Saigon Information Ministry.

These programs are different from propaganda campaigns, their administrators say, because they are predicated on truthful reporting rather than distortions and lies. The theory behind this approach is that eventually the truth will out, and it is better to keep things clean rather than face exposure and possible humiliation later.

Unfortunately, in Viet Nam, where communications are so poor and people get so little chance to travel very far and check things for themselves, the truth rarely does out. The

average propaganda lie is very apt to go unchallenged
indefinitely.

It is simpler and safer for the poorly trained and paid
government propaganda worker to make his rounds and hand
out his presents than to get really involved in hamlets.
Presents include school notebooks in which a few pages of
government "message" have been inserted, pencils stamped
with Vietnamese flags, and children's tee shirts printed with
big Vietnamese flags. (The Viet Cong regularly tears the
offensive pages out of the notebooks, cuts the flags out of the
pencils and dyes the tee shirts black.) The most acceptable
USIS item is a monthly magazine called *Huong Que* (*Rural
Spirit*) which consists mostly of helpful hints to Vietnamese
farmers on agricultural problems. It contains no propaganda
(except for the fact that it is available only at government
information centers) and the articles, written exclusively by
Vietnamese, apparently are really useful.

After February 7, 1965, North Viet Nam was bombarded
with American propaganda, but as usual the approach was
mechanical rather than personal. Efforts were measured in
terms of tons of leaflets dropped rather than real salesmanship.

It became customary, during each of the holiday pauses
in the bombing of North Viet Nam, to drop gift packages over
major North Vietnamese cities. Each unit was a plastic bag
hung from a parachute a little larger than a handkerchief. The
bag's contents, assembled by the Saigon Information Ministry, consisted typically of a calendar, a child's sweater, needles
and thread, some plastic toys, a small Saigon flag and a
handwritten letter from a resident of South Viet Nam telling
how good conditions in the South were.

These gift packages customarily were followed the next
day by 1,000-pound bombs, and it is difficult to assess their
effects.

Needless to say, there were no American or Saigon
propaganda teams working on the ground in North Viet Nam.
The efforts over the years to introduce even simple commando teams into North Viet Nam were generally unsuccessful,
because such teams were generally turned in to the Hanoi
government very quickly by the peasants themselves.

Atrocity propaganda, for better or worse, has an important impact on Viet Nam. In a war, there never is a shortage

of dismembered bodies and other horrors to photograph for such use.

The Viet Cong has always made constant use of atrocity themes, and eventually the Saigon government and USIS (or, as it was renamed, the Joint U.S. Public Affairs Office—JUSPO) began also using atrocity propaganda.

For instance, a bus ran over a Viet Cong mine about twenty miles south of Saigon, and more than twenty civilians, mostly women and children, were killed. Before the blood had clotted, Saigon cameramen were flown to the scene, and the result of their work was printed by USIS on tens of thousands of leaflets. Within hours, planes were sprinkling these leaflets over the province, with appropriate captions.

There was an immediate reaction. At the province capital of Tan An, several hundred peasants staged what appeared to be an authentically angry demonstration to denounce Viet Cong atrocities. Several days later, two ranking officers of a local Viet Cong battalion defected to the government with their weapons. They said they were disgusted that the Front had wantonly blown up the civilian bus. (In fact, the mining probably was an accident, but the Viet Cong was nevertheless successfully saddled with the responsibility.)

This kind of thing was repeated many times, especially in the Mekong Delta. If nothing else, government atrocity propaganda seems to have made the Viet Cong more cautious about accidental attacks on civilian vehicles in the area.

An American propaganda expert summed up the essential differences between red and white propaganda in Viet Nam this way:

"There is a basic rule, applicable to all Vietnamese propaganda from whichever side, called 'tam dong.' Freely translated, 'tam dong' means "likeness in thinking and ideology.'

"The Viet Cong propagandist breaks it down into the slogan 'live together, eat together, work together.'

"This means that the Viet Cong propagandist is expected to spend all his time with his psychological targets, blending in completely with their whole existence. Too many of the people on our side are just not willing to do this. They like to wear white shirts and sleep in soft beds. We send out our Vietnamese field workers on dangerous missions, and more often than not they go on sick call instead, or find some other excuse not to go. When they do go, they spend as little time in the target area as they can get away with. These workers are not peasants themselves, and they don't like or understand peasants.

"Too many American officials, especially those at USIS, have assumed for too many years they can cover the field using mass communications methods. You can count on your fingers the number of Americans devoted to propaganda activity who actually get out in the field on any regular basis.

"Within these limitations, our propaganda program has to be divided according to three basic groups—the Vietnamese who have had virtually no contact with Saigon authority in thirty-five years or more, the Vietnamese who have had little or no contact with Saigon since Vietnamese independence in 1954, and the others.

"For the first group, most of whom live in Viet Cong base areas, the only kind of propaganda with which we can reach them is threatening. We drop leaflets saying, in effect, surrender or die. We mention that this year, 20 per cent of the men in this or that village were killed by government troops, and say that next year another 20 per cent will die unless resistance ends.

"For the second group, we concentrate on the meaning of Vietnamese independence and nationalism. We point out that Viet Nam is no longer under the foreign domination of France, and we concentrate on the responsibilities of free citizens in building a new country. This group makes up about half of the Vietnamese population, incidentally. That's some indication of how much control the Saigon government has over its population.

"For the last group, centered mostly in the larger towns, our main approach is bringing people up to date on what has happened since the end of the Ngo Dinh Diem regime. For one thing, people are no longer forced to give their labor and time, building the hated strategic hamlets. We point out all the benefits being offered by the new revolutionary regime, and describe its aspirations for peace, prosperity and democracy.

"But obviously all this is done by mass communications.

"The most important thing is the thing our side is not doing nearly enough of—getting out and talking and living with the people. What's really needed is the personal touch, and that's where the Viet Cong is beating us so badly."

Some years ago, the Saigon government opened an agency called the Ministry of Civic Action. In successive coups, the ministry was closed down, but its functions remained on the books. In brief, civic action is the sending of propaganda agents skilled in social service work into contested or enemy areas following military operations. Civic action workers are supposed to build schools, dig wells, help harvest crops and so forth, while putting the message across.

On the American side, U.S. AID Mission civilian officials and military S-5 officers are supposed to work with the civic action people. In 1963, the former minister of civic action, Ngo Trong Hieu, was in jail on charges of gross corruption. At best, the average civic action agent looks down on the peasants he is expected to convert as inferior beings.

But beyond reluctance to face dangerous situations, unwillingness to take initiative and flagrant corruption, civic action officials often have shown lamentable lack of planning and coordination with related agencies.

I once visited a hamlet near the southern tip of Viet Nam where a civic action team was at work. The day before there had been a bloody firefight, and the hamlet was still reeling from the effects of war.

It was clear that the brunt of the civic action job had been shouldered by a young American Negro army captain. This captain with one interpreter was wandering throughout the hamlet outskirts, talking to peasants and trying to form an idea of what was needed in the area. His polite manners and obvious sincerity apparently were softening up a lot of the peasants, especially the older ones.

One peasant told him rats were eating most of the rice reserves in the hamlet. He promised to get them rat poison within a few days. Another said water supplies were desperately short, partly because government soldiers had smashed most of the clay reservoirs in which rain water is kept. (Most of the surface water in the area is brackish because the canals are tidal and near the sea.) The captain promised to investigate the possibility of bringing down deep well drilling equipment.

One woman complained that her son, a government militiaman, had been arrested by district authorities recently, after his post had been wiped out by the Viet Cong. He had managed to run into the jungle while all his comrades in the post were slaughtered. The American said he would try to get the youth out of jail.

He talked to an old and obviously influential villager about building a new market place for the hamlet. Wherever he went, he seemed to be making friends.

But in late afternoon, someone must have reported seeing a small group of Viet Cong moving through the opposite end of the hamlet from where the American was working. Without warning, two A1H fighter planes swept in with rockets and cannon, and blasted half of the hamlet to splinters and embers, with charred pieces of bodies strewn in all directions. From then on, the American found it impossible to talk to anyone in the remains of the hamlet.

In other cases, civic action teams have been sent to innumerable hamlets on the heels of regular military units to find the hamlets robbed blind. Vietnamese soldiers are not issued food on operations but are expected to pay for the food they confiscate. They rarely do pay, especially when they are in areas considered Viet Cong territory, but help themselves to all the chickens, ducks, eggs and rice they can carry away. This makes things tough for the propagandists.

Vietnamese peasants like to be shown respect by the soldiers even in government-dominated areas, and they don't like doing anything free for the army as a matter of principle. Complicating matters, most soldiers are Central Vietnamese, while the war is hottest in the south. Central and Southern Vietnamese don't like each other.

A large group of peasants interviewed by an American team in a Mekong River Delta province disclosed that they would not willingly carry even battle casualties for the Saigon troops.

"They force us to do this work, and they have no right to," one peasant said. "If they would pay us even a little for it, we wouldn't mind. That way we would be equals."

The Viet Cong also confiscated food and labor, of course, and this is a strong point for government propagandists. But the Viet Cong very often makes a show of issuing receipts or worthless pay certificates for the things it takes, which sometimes mollifies the peasants.

The jarson of the propaganda specialists includes the

term "black propaganda," which should be mentioned at least in passing at this point, because it is so close to the Vietnamese way of life. In substance, black propaganda is the art of putting words in the other guy's mouth and then blaming him for them.

The "signed confessions" obtained by the Viet Cong from American and Vietnamese prisoners are a crude sample of the technique. Such confessions invariably attest to atrocities, the use of poison gas and germ warfare, and so on.

At a slightly more subtle level, government agents dressed to look like Viet Cong (complete with battle flags) have sometimes come roaring into coastal towns, firing in the air, and throwing around leaflets denouncing God, motherhood and the local province chief. The idea is to make the Viet Cong look bad and local authorities look good.

Local residents are rarely fooled by these shows, but American military advisors (who never are given the word in advance) have sometimes had some nasty shocks. On a few occasions, Americans actually opened fire on the "Viet Cong" before officials hastily told them what was going on.

Many American experts believe black propaganda is dangerous because it can easily misfire if handled with clumsiness.

This writer had an irksome exposure to black propaganda once during a period when the Ngo Dinh Diem government was particularly angry at foreign newsmen.

A document purporting to have come from the Saigon Central Committee of the National Liberation Front was quietly circulated to most embassies in the city. The document consisted of instructions to Viet Cong agents as to how to get in touch with "sympathetic" foreign correspondents in the city, and there followed a list of ten names and addresses. My name headed the list.

Copies of the document had come from the government Information Ministry. Because of certain internal details, it was immediately clear to American authorities that the document was phony and even traceable to a specific functionary in the ministry. But clumsy or not, it was enough to start rumors going, which was one of the main objects of the exercise. Incidentally, for the record, I never have knowingly met or been approached by any Viet Cong agent in Viet

Nam, although it is probable that I have met some of their undercover people. I have also met Viet Cong officials outside Viet Nam, in Laos and Cambodia.

There is strong evidence that terrorist grenades sometimes are used as black propaganda. Many American intelligence officials believe Saigon agents have from time to time exploded grenades and then blamed the Viet Cong to generate a public reaction.

Saigon residents are used to this kind of thing. When something happens in town, residents often suspect black propaganda at work, or even double black propaganda ("The Viet Cong threw that grenade, knowing that we would suspect the government of throwing it with the idea of blaming it on the Viet Cong.") South Viet Nam is a nation in which twisted, devious thinking is the rule, and nothing is accepted at face value. Another sample:

"The government deliberately lost that battle in order to alarm the Americans into giving us more aid." And conversely,

"The Viet Cong deliberately lost that battle to give the Americans a false sense of security."

Americans are widely regarded as gullible people ready to swallow all black propaganda. Perhaps we have, on too many occasions.

In any case, if Americans are gullible, it is my judgment that Vietnamese are probably the least gullible people in the world. They tend automatically to reject all official statements as lies, regardless of the source. Furthermore, they assume that every organization and every person acts wholly out of selfish motives. It is utterly inconceivable to the average Vietnamese that America might be trying to help Viet Nam in any genuinely altruistic way. The more altruistic American aid looks, the more suspect it is. If a Vietnamese is told that some American has volunteered to serve another tour in Viet Nam, he is apt to reply, "Yes, our girls are pretty, aren't they?"

On July 29, 1964, Vietnamese Foreign Minister Phan Huy Quat formally charged the Viet Cong with making black terrorist propaganda to stir up trouble between Viet Nam and neighboring Cambodia. His charge appears to have a lot of supporting evidence.

Certainly, the Viet Cong is interested in keeping rela-

tions between Cambodia and South Viet Nam bad. Two of the
effects to be realized from this are that Cambodia is more
likely to remain a fairly safe haven for anti-Saigon guerrillas,
and that Cambodia and South Viet Nam are not likely to
undertake joint action to patrol the frontier. Besides this, the
madder Cambodia gets at Saigon, the more likely it is Cambodia
will move away from an ostensibly neutral international position to one more closely aligned with North Viet Nam.

In any case, somebody attacked a string of Cambodian
border villages in July 1964 with fairly heavy loss of life for
the villagers. The Saigon government occasionally raids
Cambodian border hamlets, but almost always apologizes
afterward. From the evidence I saw, it is very unlikely that
any Saigon units were near the area in question when the
attack happened. There is no question, on the other hand,
that there was an attack. Cambodian villagers in the wrecked
hamlets said they were certain the attacking troops wore
Saigon uniforms. This mystery probably never will be solved
to the satisfaction of everyone but I think it is quite likely that
Quat was right in deciding that the Viet Cong, disguised as
government troops, pulled off the raids.

This kind of thing leads Vietnamese to mistrust everything, even if they see it with their own eyes.

I think it is indicative of the lack of trust Vietnamese
have in each other that the bodyguards of the president (or
prime minister, or whoever happens to be in power) frequently are Cambodians, not Vietnamese. Also, Vietnamese
hire Chinese as cooks, maids and domestics. They do not hire
Vietnamese, unless they are too poor to afford anything else.
Most Vietnamese families believe that Vietnamese servants
cannot be trusted.

It is my opinion that this deeply ingrained suspicion,
skepticism and cynicism make the average Vietnamese almost
wholly immune to any propaganda that depends on mass
communication techniques.

Airplanes with loudspeakers, for instance, are an amusing novelty in Viet Nam, but have little effect. A ghostly voice
coming from high in the clouds is always an attention getter,
but I have yet to see a Vietnamese taking the words themselves very seriously. The attitude seems to be that the
Americans have come up with another impressive gadget, but

that one shouldn't read too much into it. After all, the plane is miles away from·my hamlet, my jungle, and my whole frame of reference.

South Viet Nam is a professional propagandist's nightmare. Everywhere he turns, he faces apathy, mistrust and hostility. His biggest chance of success seems to lie in making friends with individuals on a personal basis, establishing his credentials, and then, cautiously, putting his point across. It is slow and often frustrating work, but no short cut is apparent.

The Viet Cong lacks technology, but it more than makes up for the shortcoming with its propaganda skills. Furthermore, the Viet Cong and its prototypes have had a quarter-century head start in their propaganda operations over the United States.

The Viet Cong has repeatedly said at its organization meetings that it does not hope to win a victory by military means alone. Most of all, the Viet Cong expects a political victory. And in this, propaganda is by far the most important weapon.

It appears so far that the Viet Cong has outgunned Saigon and its American ally in this field.

11

WAR ON THE FAMILY PLAN

It had been raining hard every day for several months, and the Plain of Reeds forty miles west of Saigon was an almost unbroken sheet of water. From the air, there is a peculiar beauty in this kind of landscape, especially at certain times of day or night. There had been a particularly heavy series of helicopter raids on the area at that time, and one image in particular sticks in my mind: a vast expanse of flooded fields just before dawn, a great full moon mirrored in the glassy surface of the fields, and the dark silhouette of a flight of helicopters speeding across the face of the moon in the fields.

Of course, from the ground, the whole thing seems much less attractive. The Chinese-scroll quality of the setting becomes a mass of neck-deep mud, and the helicopters no longer look like wild geese but merely the instruments of destruction they are.

There is a town called Go Dau Ha in this area that stands only a mile or two from the Cambodian border. It is a very busy, prosperous town, largely because of the tremendous smuggling trade between South Viet Nam and Cambodia that goes on nearby. The buildings are the substantial yellow stucco kind that characterize Viet Nam's affluent society, the streets are paved and fairly clean, and the downtown section has many open air coffee shops, a number of billiard parlors and a few movie houses. Just outside town, the smugglers' market flourishes. On the Vietnamese side, one can buy Cambodian silver, and various Chinese medicines and foods not available in Viet Nam. On the Cambodian side, popular items are good Vietnamese cattle and cigarettes.

The Plain of Reeds also is one of the strongholds of the National Liberation Front, and I had come to Go Dau Ha to watch an operation against the Front.

The operation commander had set up his headquarters in a large, two-story wooden house in a compound at the edge of town. The small compound was bulging with troops, and a pair of 105-millimeter howitzer emplacements had been dug in next to the back porch. A column of thirty M113 amphibious armored personnel carriers stood pulled up in the road outside the compound gate waiting for opening of the operation in the morning. They were under especially heavy guard, because two nights earlier a child had wandered up to the gate with a big metal box that looked something like a pie tin. No one paid much attention to the boy and his box, although someone had noticed him putting it down next to an armored car parked outside the gate. Ten minutes later, a heavy explosion ripped open the armored car, killing its dozing four-man crew.

The operation commander liked the plans for the new operation and was confident of a victory in the morning. Reports had it that a battalion of Viet Cong was operating out in the open about fifteen miles away from Go Dau Ha, and since M113s had never been used in this sector before, he was counting on giving the enemy a nasty surprise. At dinner in town that night, he was a model host to his officers and the American advisors, and he broke open four bottles of a delicious Vietnamese strawberry wine he had been saving.

After dinner, under the light of a gasoline lantern on the porch of the headquarters house, the commander spread out his maps once again for a final conference with his officers and advisors.

Final intelligence reports were plotted on plastic overlays, and lines of march laid out in red crayon. Every once in a while, a large wriggling gecko would lose his footing on the wooden porch ceiling and come slapping down on the map, to the extreme annoyance of the strategists.

The officer and American advisors were sleeping inside the house. They had glued newspaper over the walls and ceilings of the rooms to keep plaster dust from falling over them every time the howitzer battery fired.

The howitzers kept firing all night long at intervals of about twenty minutes. Each time, the guns fired only six or eight shells. But to a man sleeping only a few yards from a howitzer muzzle, each shot is like an electric explosion in his brain, and there is a feeling of panic and unspecified horror every time.

The task force was tired as the men slapped cold water in their faces at three thirty the following morning. A thin drizzle was falling, and breakfast was cold rice and glasses of hot, weak tea.

By 4 A.M., the column of clanking M113s, each loaded with about fifteen soldiers, was moving down the road with lights out. Five miles out of town, the column stopped. Someone off in a dark field to the left of the road had been signaling with a flashlight. A squad of troops dismounted and went out into the field to investigate. Twenty minutes later they were back, having found nothing. By 6 A.M., the column reached a point on the muddy road where the operation was to jump off across country. Drivers have to see the dykes and holes they must drive across, and cross-country travel is impossible at night. So the column halted until the sky became light a little before 7 A.M.

At length, we began moving abreast across the fields. I was in the M113 on the extreme left of the line, seated behind the gunner so as to have a good view.

Abruptly, firing began somewhere off to the right. Someone had seen movement in a tree line about two miles away and started shooting. Our vehicle surged ahead at full speed toward a hamlet the outlines of which were barely visible in the tree line. Plunging up and down dykes, we narrowed the distance from the hamlet to about 800 yards, and then our gunner spotted two tiny figures in black running in front of one of the huts. The big gun began hammering out tracers. The mixture of powder smoke and exhaust gas from the M113 engine was nearly suffocating as we charged on. Geysers of mud and water were spurting in the fields ahead as the slugs hit. Now we were only 200 yards out, and could see the two figures running fast to the left, apparently aiming for some protective scrub growth. We altered course slightly to head them off. The gun continued to pour out tracers, but because of the lurching motion of the M113 none of it was very accurate.

At 100 yards out, the geysers of water finally were spitting up all around the two running figures, and we evidently had the range. Any second now they would go down in the mangled pulp of flesh and shattered bone.

The two figures suddenly stopped and threw up their arms in surrender. The lieutenant commanding our vehicle ordered the gunner to cease fire as we closed on our captives. The troops leapt out to grab them.

Our two guerrilla prisoners turned out to be brothers, eight and nine years old. One had fallen or been hit by something, and his hand was broken, a spear of bone protruding through the muddy skin. Both boys looked at us incuriously, and neither face registered any trace of emotion. One boy had a coil of electric mine-detonating wire over his shoulder, and the other had two grenades slung from a rope around his waist. The boys were roughly stripped of their gear.

The hamlet ahead of us was deserted, except for one old man. The boys were given a rope and ordered to tie the man's hands behind his back. They did it.

The lieutenant in charge of our platoon walked up to the boys and asked them where the Viet Cong had gone. No answer.

"Well, then, where have they hidden their weapons and supplies?"

No answer. One of the boys spat into the mud in front of him.

"You'll answer my questions, or you'll be sorry," the lieutenant said. No answer. The officer pulled out his .45 automatic and pointed it in the face of the older boy.

"Where did they go?" The boy did not answer, but gazed straight into the officer's eyes.

Furious, the officer fired three quick shots into the ground in front of the boy's feet. The boy did not flinch or answer.

The lieutenant snorted and walked off, shouting to a subordinate: "Have them help search the ponds for weapons." The boys were led off, and began sullenly wading through the hamlet ponds as ordered. I don't think they were very helpful in the search. After twenty minutes of combing fruitlessly through the hamlet, the troops climbed up on their vehicles, and the boys and the old man were shoved through the back hatch of one of the M113s.

None of the new passengers had ever ridden in one of these machines, and none knew that you must hold on to nylon straps hanging from the ceiling or there is danger of being badly hurt. Pieces of machinery and loose oilcans fly around the interior of the vehicle every time it hits a bump. So our three captives were pretty badly scraped and banged up as we moved on to the next hamlet, and soldiers laughed when the bedraggled trio was hauled out again. The boy's broken hand had been hurt some more, and was now bleeding profusely, but his face was still emotionless.

The hamlet, too, was deserted. But from one of the huts, a soldier let out a whoop. He had found a huge silk Viet Cong flag. Another soldier, poking a stick in muddy holes he passed, also hit it lucky. One of the holes contained a young man with a rifle, who popped up like a jack-in-the-box when the stick gouged his shoulder. Here was an authentic prisoner, and four or five soldiers took turns beating him up until he was bloody and unconscious. They shot him later, but not until the American advisors were safely out of the way.

By this time, the M113 crews felt a certain satisfaction with their operation, and the Viet Cong flag had been attached to the radio mast of one of the vehicles. The huge red, blue and yellow banner looked rather strange flapping over the vehicle.

It was time to leave, and there seemed no point in taking along the three prisoners. The two boys were ordered to untie the old man, which they hastily did.

"All right, go home, and let this be a lesson to you," the lieutenant told the boys. The old man sat down on a log and watched as the M113s prepared to leave. The two boys trudged off across a field without a backward glance.

Those two boys were tough little guerrillas. If they survive, they will grow up to be tough big guerrillas.

War is a family matter in Viet Nam, and a Viet Cong family has Viet Cong children.

There is nothing extraordinary about women and children getting involved in wars. Most wars claim civilian lives. In some wars, women and children are active participants. History has seen many phenomena like the Children's Crusade of the Middle Ages. Women and children seem to have a particular tendency to get involved in guerrilla operations, and played major roles in the undergrounds of Europe during the Nazi occupation.

But there seems to me a peculiarly personal quality to family war in Viet Nam. Fighters on both sides very often take their families with them, right up into the front lines.

I saw another incident in the Plain of Reeds that struck me as poignant in a characteristically Vietnamese way.

Viet Cong guerrilla tactics are not always letter perfect. The enemy sometimes makes bad mistakes, too, which cost him dearly. It happened once that a battalion of Viet Cong was moving rapidly from one province to another across the Plain of Reeds, and made the fatal mistake of moving in large groups without adequate camouflage.

The battalion was under the command of a Viet Cong brigadier general who had the reputation of being an excellent guerrilla officer, but who had spent most of his combat career in Central Viet Nam and who was new to the Mekong Delta. It often happens that when Viet Cong move from one area to another they take their families along. This general had brought his young wife and infant son.

The general had not counted on being spotted as quickly as he was. The Vietnamese army swooped down in helicopters and M113s, and cut his battalion to pieces. The fight was such a disaster that for months the National Liberation Front continued to issue critique papers on the mistakes made and how they should have been avoided. Some of these secret critiques happened to fall into American hands, which is why I know of them.

In any case, one government unit even managed to catch the Viet Cong command post in a hut, flat footed. A machine gunner spotted four men running through a thicket behind the house, and cut all four of them down with one burst. They were the general and his three top aides. It was a brilliant coup for the Saigon forces.

A half hour later, the shooting was over and the troops were collecting their war booty—an impressive pile of enemy bodies and weapons. While this was going on, an American captain heard a whimpering sound in the direction of the spot where the Viet Cong officers had been killed, and saw a flutter of movement in the thicket. He walked over, his Tommy gun at the ready.

Huddled on the other side of a dyke was a young woman stripped to the waist, her blouse wrapped around an infant that she was trying to nurse. The blouse was covered with blood, and it turned out that the baby had been shot through the belly.

The pathetic pair was the family of the dead Viet Cong general.

The American hastily stripped off his field shirt and put it over the shoulders of the young mother. Within minutes, a helicopter on the ground had been ordered to take the mother and baby to a Saigon hospital as priority casualties. Some of the Vietnamese officers were angry in a polite way about this display of American softheartedness, but did nothing to interfere.

Tears were running down the woman's face, but she nodded when told to get aboard the helicopter with her baby. That was the last I saw of those two, but I learned later that the baby survived, and the softhearted Americans were taking care of mother and child financially.

I think it is quite likely that the mother remains a hard-core believer in the National Liberation Front, and the baby probably will grow up to be a guerrilla. But that is one of the tragedies of this kind of war.

It works both ways. Thousands of little government posts manned by militiamen dot South Viet Nam, and most of them have brassieres and diapers hanging out to dry on the barbed wire. Each post actually is a little community of military families, leading an existence quite isolated from the rest of the countryside. I know of one such post in eastern Kien Hoa Province that went without supplies or contact with the outer world for six solid months in 1964. The post was literally forgotten, and not a cartridge or a piastre reached it during the whole period the mighty leaders in Saigon were fighting among themselves for control of the capital. Somehow, this little post of ten men, seven women and a liberal sprinkling of children went right on with its war routine, even doing a little fighting.

In the center of the sea of Viet Cong domination, this post could easily have been annihilated by the guerrillas at no cost to themselves. It is difficult to understand why this didn't happen, unless by some unlikely chance even the Viet Cong felt some pangs of compassion.

More often than not, the Viet Cong feels no such qualms. The guerrillas do not make a point of killing women and children, but in overrunning a post, it is difficult to avoid.

Accidental civilian casualties are much more often caused by the government side than the Viet Cong, because of artillery and air strikes. The usual justification given for this is that if civilians persist in living in Viet Cong zones they have to be prepared to take the consequences. But the consequences can be ghastly.

On the other hand, there is a tendency among Westerners to regard women as the frail sex. The Vietnamese do not so regard their own graceful and beautiful women, nor should they. Women make dangerous guerrillas.

Women make up an increasingly important part of the enemy's fighting ranks in Viet Nam as the years pass.

In North Viet Nam, many women carry rifles to work and use them against American planes. Hanoi propaganda frequently speaks of Miss Nguyen thi Hang, a girl commander of an antiaircraft unit near Thanh Hoa, who has supposedly downed some U.S. planes.

In the South, many local Viet Cong militia units had up to 30 per cent women guerrillas in 1967, according to intelligence estimates.

American troops increasingly faced women Viet Cong in battle, and many of the enemy girls proved tough and courageous. Paratroopers of the 173rd Brigade had some especially difficult firefights with all-girl Viet Cong units just north of Saigon.

The Viet Cong girls, often wearing steel helmets, got into the same habit as their male comrades of going into battle with a piece of cable or wire knotted around one leg. This makes it easier for one's comrades to haul off the corpse, if one is killed.

Americans found it hard to shoot women at first, but got used to it fast when bullets from the women began causing GI casualties.

For that matter, the deputy commander of all Viet Cong fighting forces was, from the beginning, Miss Nguyen thi Dinh. Miss Dinh is not good looking, but she is a highly effective commander.

There is one woman in particular who has become a legend in the upper Mekong Delta, especially Long An Province where she most often operates. Her name is Kim Loan; she is a small woman in her mid-thirties, and she commands a large Viet Cong combat team in one of the most bitterly contested areas of the nation.

Kim Loan used to be a family woman. She was the wife

of a Viet Cong district commissar and the mother of two small children.

In 1963, Kim Loan's husband was killed in a clash with government troops. She is said to have identified his mangled body without betraying a sign of emotion. A few days later, she took her children to the home of her dead husband's sister in Tan An, twenty miles south of Saigon, and disappeared.

From then on, Kim Loan went on a one-woman killing spree, even sometimes tackling groups of soldiers singlehanded. On various assassination jobs, she captured first one pistol and then another. Since then, she has always worn two pistols.

At first, the Liberation Front assigned her mostly to tax-collection chores, which she carried out with brutal enthusiasm. She once visited a government official at his home in the dead of night and demanded money. The official refused. She whipped out a pistol and slammed it down on a table in front of her.

"Talk to my pistol," she said. The man trotted off to his bedroom and brought back a wad of bills. Kim Loan spat contemptuously and slammed her other pistol on the table.

"Talk to my other pistol," she said. "I want everything you've got." The man went off for a second trip and brought back a more satisfactory sum.

Kim Loan quickly gained a reputation for extraordinary daring, shrewdness in military tactics, and dedication to exterminating Saigon authorities. She rose rapidly through the ranks, and in little over a year after her husband's death, she was placed in command of all Viet Cong intelligence and subversion throughout a large sector of populous Long An Province. As a sector military commander, she headed a Viet Cong politico-military machine that made continuous progress during a period when Saigon and Washington were bringing maximum pressure to bear on precisely the same province. An entire government division was assigned to the area, and all kinds of special civilian aid and propaganda teams went to work in the province, but Kim Loan and her legions gained increased mastery of the countryside.

As a Viet Cong bigshot, Kim Loan was assigned two permanent bodyguards, each armed with a submachine gun. She also generally traveled at the head of a twenty-man assault platoon. One month, she returned to her home village in a remote part of the province, and recruited thirty-three men into the Viet Cong army.

Kim Loan's brutal but colorful style began to become a kind of latter-day Joan of Arc legend on both sides. She was regarded with a mixture of awe and delight, and anecdotes about the female gunslinger have become favorite conversation pieces in the cafes of Tan An.

There is even a touch of the miraculous about it all in some eyes. Kim Loan has had so many hair-raising narrow escapes that there are those who say she turns into a monkey if cornered in a tree, or turns into a fish if boxed in near a canal.

But legendary or not, Kim Loan was kept under sharp surveillance by Liberation Front political commissars. Basically she was a vengeful fanatic rather than a coolheaded leader, and, besides this, her methods were often a little too brutal. These qualities do not rate high in Viet Cong field manuals.

And one day in 1964, Kim Loan went too far. A minor Viet Cong official had failed in a mission assigned by Kim Loan. She told him quietly that he was a coward, and then shot him down in cold blood.

Top-ranking Viet Cong commissars relieved Kim Loan of her command, and packed her off to a base area on the Cambodian border for several months of political indoctrination. For one thing, Kim Loan was not a communist, and the leadership felt she could not be trusted without initiation into the party.

Evidently Kim passed her course, because after a few months she turned up again in Long An Province. But this time she was stripped of her pistols and troops, and apparently was assigned as a full-time intelligence operative. She was reported to be dressed as on old woman, using a fourteen-year-old boy as her lookout.

The boy's mother was deeply worried about her son's association with the terrible Kim Loan, and one day actually approached an American civilian operative in Tan An on the matter.

"I don't want my son killed," she said, "and he will be, if he stays with Kim Loan. If there's anything you could do, if you ever see him, you will have a mother's thanks."

It will probably come to pass that Kim Loan is caught in

some trap or betrayed into government hands. But her legend is likely to persist long after she is gone. She is perhaps more responsible than any other single individual for the frustration of Saigon and Washington efforts to "pacify" one of the most critical provinces in the nation on Saigon's back doorstep.

The women of Viet Nam are as tiny and fragile looking as any in the world. They stand about five feet high, their waists are likely to be eighteen inches or less around, their legs are slim and in proportion, and their features sweet and gentle. But the impression all this creates is a living lie.

These same gentle little women rule their families and husbands with an iron hand, and in the cities women control an enormous share of all commercial enterprises as well. The traditions of Viet Nam are entirely different from those in Japan and North Asia, where the women have a decorative but somewhat subservient role.

The fiery Madame Ngo Dinh Nhu gained enormous international notice during the last two years of her late brother-in-law's reign over South Viet Nam. But she is not a particularly extraordinary Vietnamese. Madame Nhu could crush a political opponent with the flick of an eyelash, and often did. Even while smiling demurely, her eyes often shone with a deadly hardness that could mean prison or death for someone. And when addressing crowds, her cold fury sometimes reminded me of the Hollywood versions of ancient pagan goddesses demanding a blood sacrifice. I have seen the same stigmata in many another Vietnamese woman.

I always had the feeling that Madame Nhu despised and hated men, including those closest to her.

One afternoon, I was ushered past a pair of stuffed tigers into her sumptuously furnished reception parlor at Saigon's Independence Palace. The First Lady entered, wearing, as usual, a gorgeous *ao-dai*, cut low at the neck in the style she always affected. The *ao-dai* is one of the most beautiful and graceful feminine garments ever devised.

We talked over tea for three hours that afternoon, mostly about politics. I was struck by the frequency with which she attacked or criticized this or that man, always suggesting some approach to a problem she felt was better.

At one point, we were discussing the corruption of some ranking government officials, and she said:

"The President [Diem] is much too softhearted. He will always protect his friends, even if they betray him by doing wrong things in the government. The President is like a child, and sometimes I get so angry with him I could slap him."

I could hardly believe my ears. I had met Madame Nhu only two or three times before at receptions, and was, for all practical purposes, a stranger to her and her family. Furthermore, this conversation was not a casual social call. I was there as a foreign correspondent, working on a story for The Associated Press. She read my story (in which I quoted her exactly) and she sent me a note saying she had liked it. I don't know whether or not Diem read the story, but if he did, it is safe to guess that he did not like it.

Another time, Madame Nhu was playing hostess to an American television crew, and felt the parlor was not an appropriate place for the interview. She wanted the presidential reception room itself. It happened that Diem was using the reception room to entertain some state visitors, but Madame Nhu strode in rather coldly and ejected the whole party, President and all.

There was a spark of fanaticism about Madame Nhu. With a stroke of a pen, she outlawed divorce, dancing, beauty contests, gambling, fortunetelling, cockfighting, prostitution, and a hundred other things dear to the hearts of Vietnamese men. Neither her husband nor his brother, the President, ever dared interfere with these amazing legislative decrees.

She spoke wistfully sometimes of her blighted childhood in Hanoi, her teen-age marriage to Ngo Dinh Nhu, and the life of danger and struggle that followed.

She even declared war on her family. In 1962, she drove her sister to attempted suicide by forbidding the sister to see the Frenchman she loved. In 1963, Madame Nhu disowned her parents, Tran Van Chuong, the Vietnamese ambassador to Washington, and Madame Chuong, the Vietnamese observer at the United Nations. Both of them had bolted from the Diem regime after Saigon troops raided insurgent Buddhist pagodas, and both of them resigned from their posts. A bitter public feud between Madame Nhu and her parents immediately followed, which, as far as I know, has never been healed.

Madame Nhu organized her own party, the Vietnamese Women's Solidarity Movement, and her own army, the Vietnamese Women's Paramilitary Corps. Her daughter, a sixteen-year-old slip of a girl at the time, was one of the first to join. Little Le Thuy swiftly learned the manly arts of judo, marching and shooting, and I have seen her shoot balloons out of a man's hand thirty yards away with her .45 automatic.*

Madame Nhu tried during her last year in Saigon to destroy the integrity of the free foreign press, and in the process she made life extremely dangerous and difficult for my colleagues and me. I think if she had had completely free rein, she would certainly have arranged for at least some of us to die. I know from personal experience that Madame Nhu could be the most dangerous enemy a man could have.

But for all that, Madame Nhu had (and has) a breed of daring and courage that must always command respect, even when it is aimed against principles that Americans hold sacred.

I have written at some length of Madame Nhu because I think there are elements of her in many Vietnamese women, albeit on a less spectacular scale. And a lot of these women are Viet Cong. Men and women revolutionary guerrillas have been meeting and marrying in the jungles of Viet Nam for the last thirty years or more, fighting government forces side by side, and raising children to do just the same thing. For such families, revolution is not merely a campaign, or even a war. It is a way of life.

A good many attractive and talented Vietnamese girls have been siphoned off by the Viet Cong recruiting machine not as guerrillas but as spies. There are tales about some of these girls that make the Mata Hari legend seem pallid.

One is worth recording, in that it involved an American tragedy, and somehow typifies the tangled, wretched relations that can develop between Vietnamese and Americans. I happened to know some of the people involved in this one.

A certain American officer named B. was sent to Viet Nam as part of a group of experts in strategic military intelligence. For a long time, he was stationed in a horribly

---

*Miss Le Thuy, whose father was slain in the 1963 coup, went off to college in France, where she became a radiantly attractive young woman. She was killed in an accident at the wheel of her car in 1967, while returning to college after a vacation.

desolate jungle post in the mountains, where it is usually cold, almost always drenched with rain, and where supplies must be dropped by air when the weather is good enough for flying. It is one of the least agreeable places in Viet Nam. There are no diversions, and the work is lonely and usually frustrating.

B. was pleased to be reassigned to a mountain detachment in more civilized surroundings, but on his arrival there he found a letter from his wife back in the States. She wanted a divorce.

B. had always been a hard-working and conscientious officer, and he had a keen mind. But he was really miserable about the news from America.

The weeks passed, and B. struck up a friendship with a very attractive Vietnamese girl in town. The girl was not only beautiful, but extremely intelligent and able to talk with the officer almost as an equal. The friendship warmed into romance. The girl and her family were hard up, and B. began helping them out financially. B. seemed to be a happy man again, and more weeks passed.

Somehow, B. got involved in directing a counterintelligence operation at his new duty station that began paying off. The object of this investigation was to crack a dangerous Viet Cong espionage ring. The evidence looped in many directions, but B.'s inquest finally led him directly to the girl he loved. There was no question that this girl and her family were important Viet Cong secret agents.

I have no idea how long this terrible conclusion had been forming in B.'s mind before he did what he did. But it is a fact that one night, in the privacy of his quarters at the American detachment, B. blew out his brains.

Vietnamese families themselves often are tragically split by politics and war. There are thousands of officials, officers and soldiers in South Viet Nam with brothers or sisters or fathers or sons fighting for the Viet Cong or serving in important posts in Hanoi. Sometimes, during *Tet*, the lunar New Year festival in January or February, divided families get together for secret reunions. *Tet* is a time when both sides stop fighting completely, and there have even been instances of Viet Cong squads joining government troops for dinner.

The Vietnamese war is fratricide, in the most literal sense. I know very few families in Saigon or the provinces who do not have at least some distant relatives on the other side.

Situations like this are regarded by Americans as tragic ironies. There is a general impression that Vietnamese are fed up with incessant war and political strife, and would be happy just for a little peace and security. This is unquestionably true in many cases.

But Saigon and Washington planning is largely predicated on the conclusion that the Vietnamese peasant wants security more than anything else. To this end, various "pacification plans" have been put into operation, and Vietnamese are told they can have security only if they will cooperate.

I think there are two flaws in this reasoning. One is that the Viet Cong also offers security, and the guerrillas view the Saigon government and the Americans as the forces disrupting security.

The other and more important flaw is that security is apparently not the primary motivation of a Viet Cong guerrilla and his wife and children who go out to do battle together against the Saigon forces. If security were the prime goal, a life in the Viet Cong could hardly be less attractive. But as Viet Cong casualties increase, so does its recruiting, at an even greater rate.

This is the nature of what the great Asian communist theorists call "people's warfare." It means nothing less than mobilization of every man, woman and child. The man who engineered the Viet Minh defeat of France at Dien Bien Phu in 1954, General Vo Nguyen Giap, described the total involvement of "people's warfare" this way:

> The application of this strategy of long-term resistance requires a whole system of education, a whole ideological struggle among the people and party members, a gigantic effort of organization in both military and economic fields, extraordinary sacrifices from the army as well as from the people, at the front as well as in the rear. . . .
>
> Each inhabitant is a soldier, each village a fortress, each party cell and each administrative committee a staff.*

---

*People's War, People's Army, by Vo Nguyen Giap, Foreign Languages Publishing House, 1960.

More than any other aspect of the new face of war, the involvement of entire families is critical. The practitioners of "people's warfare" do not distinguish nearly so sharply as the West between terms like soldier and civilian, politician and officer, front lines and rear lines, or any of the pigeonholes into which conventionally trained tacticians slice up their campaigns.

The new enemy may just as easily be an eight-year-old boy with a mine as a helmeted soldier in jack boots.

12

BUDDHISTS, COMMUNISTS
AND POOR PEOPLE

The long brown joss sticks that burn at Buddhist holy places and homes throughout South Viet Nam generate a pleasing fragrance said to find favor with ghosts. But the smell of joss sticks is one that I shall never be able to dissociate from the ghastly smell of burning human flesh.

The two odors mingled June 11, 1963, at the intersection of two busy Saigon streets to create a political explosion the effects of which are still felt in Washington and elsewhere. I was there, and it happened like this:

On Monday, June 10, I got a telephone call at my office from a young Buddhist monk named Thich Duc Nghiep whom I had known for some time. Duc Nghiep became well known to Western newsmen later as official press spokesman for the Buddhist rebels, by virtue of his fairly fluent English.*

"We shall hold a meeting tomorrow at eight A.M.," Duc Nghiep said. "I would advise you to come. Something very important may happen."

For nearly a month, top Buddhist monks had been holding marching street demonstrations and hunger strikes in Saigon, all aimed at wringing concessions from the authoritarian Ngo Dinh Diem regime. Demands included one for government permission to fly the five-colored Buddhist flag in public. The Buddhists also wanted an end of alleged government favoritism to Catholics, an end to arbitrary police arrests, and "social justice for the nation."

The whole thing had been touched off on Tuesday, May

---

*He later spent two years in the United States studying theology under a U.S. scholarship grant. There was speculation at the time that one of the reasons for the grant was an intense desire by the State Department to get this troublemaker out of Viet Nam for a few years.

8, 1963, when Buddhists observing the birthday of Buddha were forbidden to fly their flag in the streets. A pagoda protest meeting organized by the powerful young monk Thich Tri Quang had been tape-recorded, and the Buddhists demanded permission to broadcast their recording on the local government radio station. Permission was denied, and several thousand Buddhist marchers led by monks headed from Hue's Tu Dam Pagoda for the radio station in the center of town.

As the marchers approached the radio station and surged around its entrance, the local military commander, a major named Dang Sy, had a bad case of jitters. He ordered troops and armored cars to move in.

Several grenades, apparently thrown by trigger-happy soldiers, exploded in the midst of the crowd. A few of the marchers (including children) were crushed under the tracks of the armored vehicles. Eight persons were killed on the spot, and, of the scores wounded, several died later.

The people who died in the Hue incident became the first of the Buddhist martyrs in what was to become a fierce struggle to destroy Ngo Dinh Diem and his family.

The Diem government, rather than back down, applied increasingly harsh measures against the Hue Buddhists, and the pleasant little city on the banks of the Perfume River became an armed camp. In another indicent later in the summer, marchers with arms folded were blocked at a street barricade and staged a sit-in on the pavement. Troops dispersed them by hurling glass containers of acid, which splashed over demonstrators and sent more than seventy of them to the hospital.

The masses of the nation were stirring, and the showdown was nearing.

In Saigon, demonstrations by monks during the first month after the Hue incident were orderly and staged with military precision. Monks would converge at key parks around the city in taxicabs and bicycle taxis with such perfect timing that formations of three or four hundred saffron-robed Buddhists appeared to materialize from thin air, under the noses of security police.

Street marches, especially on Tuesdays, became so frequent they appeared to be losing their impact. Tuesday was the day of choice, because the ascension of the spirits of the dead from the Hue incident was said to be marked by seven-day intervals, and the victims had died on a Tuesday.

Sometime in late May, one of the English-speaking monks at the cluster of concrete buildings known as An Quang Pagoda had given a visitor a piece of blood-chilling intelligence. He said that two monks were planning to commit suicide publicly in support of Buddhist demands—one by disembowelment and the other by burning. The Buddhist high command (consisting of about ten monks, including Tri Quang) had not yet authorized the suicides but was considering them, the informant said. Nothing further was said about this plan, and many people wrote it off as an idle threat, on grounds that the nonviolent Buddhist faith would never condone suicide.

But something special was in the air the morning of June 11.

I arrived about a quarter to eight at the small pagoda off Phan Dinh Phung Street where I had been advised to go. The concrete pagoda building was set in about thirty yards from the street with a muddy alleyway as an entrance. In the rear was a small courtyard, jammed with yellow-robed monks and gray-robed nuns. Loudspeakers nailed to trees and corners of the pagoda building were blaring in rapid Vietnamese.

More monks and nuns, all of them standing, were jammed in the main pagoda room, where another loudspeaker was howling.

I was shown to an alcove in which a large gilded Buddha statue stood and was asked to sit down at a low table. Six or eight women wearing the white dress of mourning were busy preparing tea. One of them brought me a steaming glass cup of tea, and she tried to smile politely, although tears were coursing down her face.

My monk informant, Thich Duc Nghiep, spotted me and came over. He whispered in my ear, "I advise you to stay until the very end of this, because I think something very important will happen."

At exactly eight o'clock, the jabber of Vietnamese from the loudspeakers stopped and the chanting of prayer began. One monk led the chanting with a microphone and another one next to him kept time, beating rhythmically on a gourd.

"*Na Mo A Di Da Phat*," the ancient prayer begins, each word equally accented on the same monotonous note.

It is the most hypnotic kind of chant I have ever heard, and on that hot June morning, clouds of incense in the air, I found even myself affected. All the monks and nuns joined that chant, quietly at first, then with rising, hammering volume, as the verses were repeated over and over, the tempo speeding up slightly.

Eyes all around me were fixed straight ahead, almost glazed in the absorption of fervor. But at exactly 9 A.M. it stopped.

Monks and nuns who apparently had drilled their procedure many times lined up in the alleyway, moving out into the street in two ranks. Some unfurled banners in Vietnamese and English calling on the government to answer the Buddhist demands. In a minute or two, the procession of 350 or so monks and nuns was formed and moving. At its head was an innovation in the street marches—a gray sedan with four or five monks riding inside. It seemed strange to me at the time that monks were now riding instead of walking.

Police ahead of the procession cleared the streets as usual, keeping clear of the marchers and not interfering, except to shunt traffic and crowds away from the line of march. Preceding the Buddhist car by about a half-block, a white police jeep kept pace. At that time, the main crackdown on Buddhists by government officials was in Central Viet Nam, not the Saigon area.

People leaned from shopwindows along Phan Dinh Phung, and children stared at the passing procession.

The marchers reached the intersection of Le Van Duyet Street, one of the most important boulevards in Saigon, always jammed with heavy traffic. On one corner of the intersection stood the massive gray Cambodian consulate building, with its stone lion statue. On two other corners were apartment buildings, and on the fourth corner, an Esso service station. At precisely the center of the intersection, the Buddhist car stopped, apparently stalled. The police jeep was already halfway down the next block.

The marchers began to move past the car, and then abruptly turned left into Le Van Duyet, quickly forming a circle about thirty feet in diameter, of which the car formed a link. It was now nearly 9:20 A.M.

The monks in the car had got out, and one of them had opened its hood. From inside, he pulled a five-gallon gasoline cane made of translucent plastic, filled to the brim with pink gasoline. Three other monks were walking from the car side by side to the center of the circle. One of them placed a small brown cushion on the pavement, and the monk in the center sat down on it, crossing his legs in the traditional position of Buddhist meditation known as the "lotus posture." This monk was the Venerable Thich Quang Duc, destined to be known throughout the world as the primary saint of modern Vietnamese Buddhism.

The three monks exchanged a few quiet words. The two who had flanked Quang Duc brought the gasoline container quickly to the center of the circle and poured most of it over the bowed head and shoulders of the seated monk.

The monks stepped back, leaving the gasoline can next to the seated man. From about twenty feet away, I could see Quang Duc move his hands slightly in his lap striking a match. In a flash, he was sitting in the center of a column of flame which engulfed his entire body. A wail of horror rose from the monks and nuns, many of whom prostrated themselves in the direction of the flames.

From time to time, a light breeze pulled the flames away from Quang Duc's face. His eyes were closed, but his features were twisted in apparent pain. He remained upright, his hands folded in his lap, for nearly ten minutes as the flesh burned from his head and body. The reek of gasoline smoke and burning flesh hung over the intersection like a pall.

Finally, Quang Duc fell backward, his blackened legs kicking convulsively for a minute or so. Then he was still, and the flames gradually subsided.

While the monk burned, other monks stood in positions at all four entrances to the intersection, holding banners reading: A Buddhist Priest Burns for Buddhist Demands.

City police at first watched in stunned horror, and then began running around aimlessly outside the circle of Buddhists. One of them radioed headquarters, and three or four fire trucks arrived with a platoon of helmeted riot police carrying fixed bayonets. The riot police charged down the street in a wave, but stopped short in confusion a few yards from the circle. As the fire trucks moved down the street, several monks leaped in front of their wheels, and other monks chocked themselves behind the rear wheels, making movement impossible without crushing someone.

All the while, leading monks with portable electric loud-speakers harangued onlookers, both in Vietnamese and English, with a highly emotional explanation as to why the suicide had taken place.

A black delivery truck with large Buddhist flags painted on its sides arrived, and monks unloaded a wooden coffin. The flames by now were completely out, and monks tried to transfer the charred body to the coffin. But its splayed arms and legs were rigid and could not be forced into the box.

Seven monks shed their saffron robes (wearing brown robes underneath) and made a kind of sling to carry the body. The circle broke and formed into a procession once again, the body at its head. Marching a few blocks more, the group arrived at Xa Loi Pagoda, the main Buddhist pagoda in South Viet Nam, where a bell was tolling mournfully from the concrete tower. It was 10 A.M. sharp, and the demonstration was finished.

Quang Duc was the first of the Buddhist monks to die by fiery suicide the summer of 1963. He also was the only one to die with such elaborate public trappings. The other suicides all were sprung by surprise without processions. In Saigon, one young monk arrived in a taxi at Saigon's central market place, walked to the center of the traffic circle and set himself afire. Three American newsmen attempting to photograph the incident were badly beaten by the police. Another young monk, his clothing apparently impregnated with gasoline in advance, died on a street corner facing Saigon Cathedral one bright Sunday morning as Catholic worshipers were arriving for mass. A policeman tried to beat out the flames, but without success.

Two monks in Hue burned themselves to death inside their barricaded pagoda, with no outsiders as witnesses. Another monk burned to death in front of a soldiers' memorial, completely alone, in the coastal town of Phan Thiet. And a thirty-three-year-old nun died in flames near her pagoda outside another coastal town, the seaside resort of Nha Trang. In all, seven died, all with the blessings of the Buddhist high command.

Thich Quang Duc's body was taken for cremation at the Buddhist cemetery just outside Saigon, and monks in charge of burning the body claimed that Quang Duc's heart would not burn. A singed piece of meat purporting to be the heart was preserved in a glass chalice, becoming an object of worship.

Quang Duc's ashes were distributed to pagodas throughout the country. The yellow robes in which his body had been carried were cut into tiny swatches and distributed to Buddhist followers everywhere. Pinned to shirts and dresses, these bits of cloth were thought to have miraculous healing properties, and also were symbols of the Buddhist uprising against the government. At one point, police tried to crack down on wearers of the yellow cloth, but there were too many of them.

Tidings of miracles spread throughout the land. In the evening sky over Saigon, thousands said they could see the weeping face of the Buddha in the clouds. Traffic was jammed everywhere as crowds of people stood gazing into the sky.

Tens of thousands of followers poured through Xa Loi Pagoda each day to worship before the heart in the glass chalice.

The series of pictures I took of the death of Thick Quang Duc came to have an existence of their own as they circulated around the world. They meant many things to many people.

An acquaintance in Lisbon wrote me that my photographs of Quang Duc's death were being sold in back alleys by hawkers of "feelthy pictures." A group of prominent American clergymen used one of the pictures as the basis for full-page advertisements in the *New York Times* and Washington *Post*, over the heading: "We, too, protest." Their protest was aimed against American support of the Diem regime.

Communist China reportedly printed millions of copies of one of the pictures for distribution throughout Asia and Africa. These pictures were captioned: "A Buddhist monk gives his life in the struggle against U.S.-Diem imperialism." Someone in Dares-Salaam, Tanganyika, wrote me a long letter praising my "revolutionary spirit" in taking the pictures. It was not long after that the communist movement in Tanganyika began to attract international interest.

In a conference with U.S. Ambassador Frederick E. Nolting, Jr., President Diem asked if it was true that I had bribed the monks to set up the suicide so as to get an eye-catching picture. The question, absurd though it was, may have been sincere. It was an indication of the suspicion and hostility Diem entertained for the foreign press in general. Actually, I suspect this particular idea was planted in Diem's mind by his brilliant and ever-scheming younger brother, Ngo Dinh Nhu. Nhu certainly knew better, but he hoped to discredit both the Buddhists and the foreign press.

It was characteristic of Diem in those days that he had such slight contact with the realities of his exploding nation and the war that he tended to accept as fact anything told him by his ruthless brother, the "political counsellor."

The Quang Duc pictures also had an impact in Washington. I have been told that when Henry Cabot Lodge went to see the late President Kennedy about being assigned as ambassador to Viet Nam, Kennedy had a copy of the Quang Duc photograph on his desk. Quang Duc's death probably was one of the factors that finally turned the State Department and White House against Diem, altering the course of Vietnamese history to some extent.

Things in Viet Nam changed after that. The Buddhists were solidly established as a force.

The retiring Central Vietnamese monk named Thich Tri Quang, who masterminded the 1963 campaign, became a powerful national figure, and played a role in upsetting more than one of the chiefs of state who followed Diem.

Tri Quang leaned toward pacifism and anti-Americanism, and was regarded by many American leaders as a very dangerous agitator. Other Americans regarded him as moderate compared with Buddhist peace movement leaders such as Yale-educated Thich Quang Lien.

In any case, Tri Quang's power lasted only briefly after the 1963 coup. Soon after that, a deep split developed between Tri Quang and his nearly equally powerful coreligionist, Thich Tam Chau. Tam Chau, a moderate generally willing to bargain and compromise with the government, was more popular with American and Vietnamese officials.

Tri Quang had some allies in the Vietnamese armed forces, but his prestige suffered a smashing blow in 1966, when he staged a hunger strike in an effort to bring down the government of General Nguyen Cao Ky. The hunger strike lasted for weeks (Tri Quang allowed himself fruit juice and sugar water), but it failed to gather wailing crowds of faithful Buddhists. People appeared to have lost interest. In the end, Tri Quang began eating again, having gained nothing.

The same hunger strike in 1963 would have produced an immediate public response.

The entire high command of the Buddhist activists became fragmented. The Buddhist youth movement (dominated by pacifist Thich Quang Lien) was still a potential paramilitary force in the country, but nothing like the force it seemed to be becoming in 1963.

When President Diem died, much of the strength of the Buddhist movement died too. Diem was needed, as the common irritant and enemy of many normally dissident factions, to pull them all together.

But the potential strength of the Vietnamese Buddhists remained, and no government after Diem, either military or civilian, could ignore it. Buddhist political strength remained second only to that of the Viet Cong.

In neighboring Cambodia and farther west in Thailand, Buddhist monks have long cast their shadow on the political scene. When Prince Norodom Sihanouk, fiery young ruler of Cambodia, holds any important public ceremony, a stall is always reserved for the monks, to whom Sihanouk pays his respects before beginning. This is such an institution that it is taken for granted. Buddhism is a much more embracing faith in Cambodia than in Viet Nam. It has been estimated that something like 90 percent of all Cambodian males shave their heads and enter monasteries for a period of time at least once during their lives. The stay in the pagoda may be only a few weeks during a summer vacation, or it may be many years.

It is not difficult to become a monk in either the Hinayana or Mahayana branches of Buddhism that dominate Viet Nam, Cambodia, Thailand, Laos, Burma and Ceylon. No special credentials are required, and novitiates are fairly short. Even a few Westerners have become Buddhist monks in these countries.

Some of these Westerners are among the most bizarre and colorful types I have ever run across outside a Greenwich Village coffee shop, by the way.

One of them, a German who had taken the Buddhist name of the Venerable Anaruda, arrived in Saigon in late 1963 from India for a look at the crisis. He stayed for several weeks at Xa Loi Pagoda, where he was treated much like the army *oberleutnant* he once had been. Despite his yellow robes, he looked more like a Prussian officer than a monk as he ordered the little Vietnamese novices around and had them shave his head.

Anaruda disliked newspapermen in general, but one afternoon while he was having his head shaved, I got him talking. Before World War II he had joined the French Foreign Legion in North Africa, from which he eventually deserted. Making his way through a series of desert adventures reminiscent of those of Lawrence of Arabia, Anaruda was conscripted into the German Navy, in which he fought until the middle of the war. Later he went into the regular army. I'm not sure what happened then, although I suspect he was assigned to the Eastern Front and eventually deserted. In any case, he wound up in India after the war and became a Buddhist monk. He never explained what he was doing in Viet Nam, but spoke vaguely of carrying important messages to and from India. He finally left as a steerage-class passenger aboard a French ship, returning to the flow of strange, homeless men and women who drift endlessly around the Far East.

Among this legion of permanently displaced persons who roam Asia—Europeans in particular—there are many professional agents of various governments. Laos, Cambodia and Viet Nam—the three former associated States of the French Indochina colony—are havens of a particularly large share of these adventurers. Some, often hangovers from the departed but not forgotten French Legion, have found employment in the more unsavory occupations open to foreigners. This particularly applies to the opium industry.

There is, for example, a Corsican named Frondizi who lives in Laos and has a fleet of two-engine Beechcraft planes known throughout the area as "Air Opium." Pilots of this "airline" say they have no difficulty penetrating the radar picket around South Viet Nam at low altitude, flying at night to within visual distance of Saigon, where they make their drops. A large porportion of their "packages" are lost, they say, but for every one reaching its addressee the profits are large enough to exceed handsomely all the losses.

Laos is one of the world's primary sources of raw opium. Opium from the poppy fields of the Laotian highlands is technically illegal in Laos. But in Vientiane, particularly in the neighborhood surrounding the French Military Advisory Assistance Command compound, the opium dens thrive quite openly. Many are cheerful, family-style establishments, brightly lighted and offering Coke machines and jukeboxes as well as the standard opium benches and pipes. For less than one dollar, a patron can smoke ten or twelve pipes at such an establishment, reeling into the street at the end of the evening as high as a kite.

But Laotian opium finds its main outlet abroad. Opium smuggled into Thailand is shipped to every nation in the world. Opium, transported by small planes, is flown in large quantities to neighboring Cambodia and South Viet Nam. It is believed that a good deal of opium finds its way into the hands of the Viet Cong, which uses it as currency or credit. With gold, opium is one of the two most stable commodities in Southeast Asia, and is therefore extremely useful for guerrillas traveling constantly across national frontiers.

In South Viet Nam, the Viet Cong sometimes prints its own paper currency or chits. This currency is in piastres (or dong) which the Viet Cong claims are freely and equally convertible with Saigon piastres. In fact, however, the Viet Cong found it necessary to give this money some kind of backing of its own. Gold smuggled into Viet Nam became the primary backing of the money. It is believed that opium is similarly used as backing for paper currency in some cases.

It is possible that the Viet Cong has produced the first paper currency in history based on the "opium standard."

None of the foregoing is intended to suggest that Buddhism, the Viet Cong and opium smuggling are directly related. I am merely trying to show the confused background against which the shadow organizations of South Viet Nam operate, each one playing a part in the war in which America is so deeply involved.

Nor is opium traffic limited to society's backwash in the masses of poor people. More than one diplomatic passport has proved a boon to the smugglers. Several years ago, some Canadian officials of the International Control Commission were convicted of carrying the black, tarry liquid from one country to another.

The Indochina area is an essentially lawless corner of the earth, never more than a step or two away from complete anarchy. Successive governments in Saigon (including those of the French colonial regime) never have controlled the Vietnamese people in a very effective way.

There are no anticommunist political parties in South Viet Nam with any national backing. Against this background, the powerful Viet Cong political apparatus is in competition only with American occupation forces (of which the Saigon government is a part) and the amorphous potential strength of the Buddhists.

At this point, I would like to discuss the nature of relationships between Vietnamese Buddhism and the Viet Cong a little.

A Buddhist pagoda in Viet Nam is a good place to get your pocket picked. This is not to say the faith condones larceny, but the swarming, jostling crowds of poor people who pack the pagodas during festival days and in times of political crisis make an ideal setting for pickpockets, beggars, social flotsam in general, secret agents—and the Viet Cong.

In South Viet Nam, Buddhism is the faith of poor people, and the Viet Cong professes to be the party of the poor.

For those who have seen the richly ornate and graceful pagodas of Thailand, Burma and Cambodia, the pagodas of Viet Nam are a disagreeable contrast. Most of the pagodas in Saigon and elsewhere in the nation are starkly modern buildings made of concrete and faced with yellow stucco. They have almost no architectural adornments, and look a little like badly Orientalized versions of Spanish mission buildings. National Buddhist headquarters (Vien Hao Dao) is a rambling compound in a slum section of Saigon in which a steel hangar serves as the main pagoda and rows of one-story shacks provide offices for the monks. The ground is unpaved, unplanted and nearly always muddy.

All the shacks are fairly well furnished as offices for the top monks, and all are equipped with telephones, filing cabinets, typewriters, and—most important—duplicating machines.

The mobs of students, uniformed Buddhist boy scouts and other young people who congregate at this headquarters suggest more the atmosphere of a campfire rally than a religious shrine.

It is a far cry from the lone monk in brown robes, sitting

cross-legged before the idol of the Lord Buddha, chanting the sacred verses to himself and keeping hypnotic time to the cadences with the knocking of a stick on a hollow gourd.

The old Buddhist customs are still rigorously practiced. Heads remain shaved, and the average monk, who becomes a novice at the age of fifteen, maintains a strictly vegetarian diet all his life. This diet excludes even milk and eggs, but does not exclude soybean curd. Some monks are such clever cooks they can create remarkably close imitations of pork chops and other meats out of bean curd and various spices. The monks remain celibate.

The monks usually live in rathole cells that bespeak more real poverty than religious chastity. A high proportion of them have tuberculosis. Among those with advanced cases of tuberculosis are some of the top leaders of the Buddhist insurrection of 1963 which led to the ouster and death of President Ngo Dinh Diem.

A very few of the Vietnamese monks are extremely well educated by any standard. Some have studied in Japan, India and even the United States. The Venerable Thich Quang Lien, one of the younger monks, holds a degree from Yale University. He once greeted another Yale alumnus, an American reporter, by saying "Boola, boola!"

A few other monks currently are studying at American universities. One monk who lives in the Vietnamese countryside is entirely self-educated, but speaks nearly flawless English, French and German. He is fond of discussing the works of the existentialist writers with an American field official who stops by from time to time.

But in general, the educational level of Vietnamese monks is extremely limited. All have more or less read the basic Buddhist writings in Vietnamese, but scholarship at pagodas is undisciplined, casual and lacking in program.

In short, apart from a handful of fiery, intelligent and highly ambitious young leaders, the Buddhist monks of Viet Nam are not a distinguished-seeming lot.

Nevertheless, they have become a powerful bloc in their nation without whose active support the government itself is in extremely dangerous circumstances. The mere threat of a hunger strike is now enough to bring on a cabinet reshuffle. More serious threats by the Buddhist hierarchy can actually topple governments.

Newspaper columnists and political writers have argued for several years as to just what proportion of the South Vietnamese people is Buddhist. The Ngo Dinh Diem family (Roman Catholics) contended that less than a tenth of the nation was Buddhist. The U.S. Information Service, which tried to survey the situation, estimated that around three quarters of the population was at least nominally Buddhist, with large doses of ancestor worship, animism, Confucianism and other things thrown in. No real census of Vietnamese religious allegiances ever has been made.

The militant Hoa Hao sect, numbering perhaps as many as a million followers, counts itself a branch of Buddhism, although its priests often carry submachine guns. The Cao Dai sect, which also claims about one million followers, considers Buddhism a kindred faith. It has been said that most Vietnamese need the services of a Buddhist monk at least three times—at birth, marriage and death.

But if many Vietnamese take Buddhism as a faith or a way of life fairly casually, they still regard the Buddhist monk as an extremely prestigious individual, no matter what his intellectual shortcomings. When John Richardson arrived in Saigon in 1961 to take charge of the CIA mission in Viet Nam, he got a strong taste of this.

Richardson elected to live in an extremely comfortable and attractive villa on a shady street. The villa was occupied after Richardson's departure by Ambassador Henry Cabot Lodge, and has been used as the U.S. Embassy residence since. The CIA chief may not have known before he moved in that the site on which the villa stood had a dark and bloody past.

The site had once been occupied by a building of the dreaded French colonial *Deuxième Bureau*—the intelligence service. According to the stories, hundreds, or perhaps thousands, of Vietnamese political prisoners died of torture while being interrogated by French guards there.

During the Japanese occupation of World War II, the site was put to the same uses by the Imperial Army's intelligence organization.

After the war, during the brief period before the return of the French when communist leader Ho Chi Minh was president of all of Viet Nam, Ho's Viet Minh intelligence service used the same building for political torture. Then the French took it over again. After Viet Nam gained its independence in 1954, the torture camp was finally dismantled for good, and pleasant houses were built along the street.

But in the Vietnamese mind, many ghosts still stalk the site—the ghosts of men and women who died in agony, and who therefore are likely to cause all kinds of trouble. Richardson found when he moved in that he could not get servants to work for him.

In desperation, Richardson hired a team of Buddhist monks (presumably at CIA expense) to handle the highly specialized job of banishing ghosts. The team worked for about one week, chanting prayers, burning bits of sacred paper and incense, and hanging a set of octagonal ghost-repellent mirrors around the house. Servants were satisfied that the procedure was effective (although the precautionary burning of incense is necessary at the house to this day), and Richardson no longer had to wash his own dishes.

The important thing about this story is that while Buddhism as a doctrine has very little to say about ghosts and concerns itself mostly with freedom from worldly passions, Buddhism in Viet Nam is regarded as a bridge to the spirit world. And the spirit world is all-important. Dreams, signs and portents, fortune-telling, astrology and the phases of the moon, necromancy, and all the other trappings of spiritualism are close to the hearts of practically all Vietnamese.

Among the primitive tribes of the Central Vietnamese mountains, it is considered an offense to a river spirit to so much as throw a stone into the waters of his domain. To placate the spirit after such a misdeed generally requires the ceremonial sacrifice of a water buffalo, which in turn is a pretext for the ceremonial drinking of rice wine and a fine party.

But even for sophisticated, Western-educated Saigonese, the spirits hold sway. I know a young woman who, after her graduation from a leading American college, was given a new car by her wealthy family. The girl was eager to buy her sportster and take it on a spin to the beach resort of Cap St. Jacques about forty miles from Saigon. But the moon phase and spirit portents were just not right for it. So even the boisterous spirit of youth and a bachelor of arts degree were suppressed, and the purchase of the car was postponed.

Most Saigon newspapers are forced to maintain their circulation figures by running at least one serialized ghost story in each edition.

I doubt that there is a single family hut in rural Viet Nam that does not have its little family altar with a glass jar of burning incense sticks. On the altar there generally are a few mystical characters in Chinese, and one or more yellowed photographs of departed relatives—paper symbols of ghosts.

All this is obviously a highly fertile background for all kinds of charlatanism.

It also accounts for the enormous influence of the Buddhist monk.

As a faith, Buddhism is not much concerned with material matters. It teaches that man is chained to a wheel of life, death and rebirth which can be broken only by his attainment to the coveted "state of enlightenment."

It is not my purpose here to discuss the theology of Buddhism, but the one point I would like to make refers to the theoretical compatibility (or lack of it) of Buddhism with communism.

A book on the subject called *Buddhism Answers the Marxist Challenge* by Francis Story (published by Burma Buddhist World Mission, Rangoon) has been widely read by Vietnamese Buddhist monks. It contends that Buddhism and Marxism are not compatible. Story writes:

> Marxist materialism is scientific in so far as it follows the principles of causality, but it does not admit any causal process beyond that of matter and material agencies.
>
> It condemns religion because religion teaches that there is a process of causality based on moral principles. Every religion maintains that there is another life beyond the present one, and that this future life is in some way governed by the moral effects of what has been done, said and thought in this present life. This claim is nowhere made so strongly or logically as in Buddhism, with its rational teaching of Karma and rebirth, the two principles which are categorically denied by Marxism.

Vietnamese Buddhist monks in the past few years have often cited writings like that as evidence to refute American political writers who claimed they were communists.

The monks who advance such theoretical evidence are

no doubt sincere in their conviction that communism and Buddhism are incompatible. Many of the Buddhist monks leading the South Vietnamese movement are refugees from communist North Viet Nam, and know by personal experience of the atrophied state of their faith under the Hanoi regime. A few even have tried to organize teams of monks to travel in the countryside, denouncing communism as they preach.

But unfortunately for American policy in Viet Nam, the Viet Cong does not regard itself as at all imcompatible with Buddhism. The fifty-seven-member central committee of the National Front for the Liberation of South Viet Nam (Viet Cong) claims actual membership of several Buddhist monks and one Roman Catholic priest.

Buddhist monks have sometimes run into trouble with the Viet Cong, but as a rule, the orange- or brown-clad monks pedal their bicycles over the rice paddy dykes of Viet Cong base areas without the slightest interference. The inference drawn from this by a number of American writers is that the monks are phonies, or at best, religious dilettantes.

But I think this view is based on a general American misunderstanding as to what the Viet Cong really is.

The words "Viet Cong" in themselves are somewhat misleading. They mean "Vietnamese communist," and they were coined by Saigon's propaganda ministry as a kind of catch phrase, used in much the same sense as Hanoi's invariable reference to the Saigon government as the "U.S. Imperialist Lackeys."

Probably only top Viet Cong officials know how many of the National Liberation Front's members are Communist Party members. But Western intelligence experts believe the proportion of communists is probably extremely small—limited probably to the handful of foreign-educated intellectuals who pull the wires. In other words, the Viet Cong is a true "front" organization, appealing for the support of every social class, and every educational, religious and occupational background. The National Liberation Front is supposedly made up of many dependent fronts, such as the Farmers' Liberation Front, the Women's Liberation Front, the Writers' and Artists' Liberation Front, and so on.

Supreme leadership of the Front is openly described by Front leaders as "a Marxist-Leninist party," but this party does not appear in organizational tables used by the Front, nor is it often even mentioned.

In any case, there is certainly no requirement to be a communist to join the National Liberation Front. The fact is that even fairly high-ranking Viet Cong prisoners often show a surprising ignorance of the world communist movement. The ideological battle between Moscow and Peking is usually a matter of complete indifference to them, for example. They consider themselves first and foremost Vietnamese nationalists and patriots, "soldiers for the invincible cause of freedom against the American imperialists and their lackeys."

It is obvious to Western observers that the National Liberation Front is the creature of the Vietnamese Communist Party, and has strong but subtle ties to the Hanoi regime and even to communist China. But these relationships are not so apparent to Vietnamese eyes. For many, the Front is exactly what it purports to be—the people's struggle for independence.

Viewed in this light, the theoretical clash between Marxist-Leninist communism and religious dogma tends to blur or even disappear.

If it is possible for Buddhist monks to sit on the ruling central committee of the Viet Cong, there is no apparent reason why a member of the National Liberation Front could not become a Buddhist monk, or at least a Buddhist layman. The man himself might not even notice any contradiction in his allegiances.

A number of leading Roman Catholic laymen in Viet Nam have told me they believe even their faith has a number of adherents who belong to the Viet Cong. In 1948, a devout Roman Catholic was chief of Viet Minh intelligence. He later commanded a guerrilla regiment.

Without question, the Viet Cong is the most powerful political organization in South Viet Nam, and has by far the largest following of any nonreligious group in the nation. A major reason is the "underdevelopment" of the nation.

To most Americans, I think, the word "underdevelopment" evokes the picture of a child with a belly bloated by starvation. By inference, a CARE package of powdered milk is taken as the primary weapon against underdevelopment.*

---

*Nowhere has this view of the world been more explicitly stated than in a speech November 1, 1966, by President Johnson at Camp Stanley, Korea, before a group of American GIs. The President said:

Elsewhere in Asia, this image has some substance. But in Viet Nam, underdevelopment cannot be cured by bread alone. The fact is that South Viet Nam is one of the most agriculturally rich nations in Asia.

Even in bad years, the rich, green Mekong River Delta produces plenty of rice to feed the whole people, with a large exportable surplus to enrich the treasury. Fish are so plentiful in the sluggish canals and ditches of the delta they can actually be caught by hand. The pineapples, mangoes and other delicious fruits that proliferate in the area are among the finest in the world. Sugar cane and coconuts grow swiftly with little labor requirement, and ducks can be raised in huge flocks right in the rice fields. Feathers from the Vietnamese duck crop are prized as pillow stuffing, and are an important export item.

Very few people in South Viet Nam go hungry. This, of course, includes the Viet Cong guerrillas ranging over the delta. The abundance of food and warmth of Vietnamese peasant hospitality to all poor people give the guerrillas an almost free nationwide logistic network that would cost a Western army hundreds of millions of dollars to duplicate.**

The nation is rich in all kinds of salable commodities. The rich red soil that covers most of the central highlands is ideal for the tea, rubber and kenaf plantations which have been exploited by the French for the past century. Rubies

---

"The average fellow in the world doesn't ask for much. He wants an opportunity to have a job so he can earn enough food to satisfy the needs of his stomach and to cover his body. He wants a place where he can protect himself from the elements of the sun, the heat, and the cold, and have a roof over his head. He wants a chance for his kids to go to school to learn to read and write, to get as much education as they can take.

"If there is anything left over after that, he would like to have a little recreation for his family, a movie now and then, or to be able to load them all in the old jalopy and take them to see Grandma on Sunday."

In the same speech, the President noted that the United States already has these blessings and must guard them against a voracious outer world. He said:

"There are three billion people in the world, and we only have 200 million of them. We are outnumbered 15 to 1. If might did make right, they would sweep over the United States and take what we have. We have what they want."

**Pentagon experts estimated that even as late as 1966, the Viet Cong and North Vietnamese forces fighting in the South required only about twelve tons a day of supplies from the outer world. By comparison, the United States required many tens of thousands of tons each day, brought into the country by ship and plane, to keep its forces in Viet Nam going.

and even gold are sometimes found in or near this soil.

In peacetime, South Viet Nam could certainly attract an important share of the world's affluent tourists. Its cool mountain resorts, partly developed by the French colonialists, are near fine big-game hunting in the great rain forests. Elephants, tigers and water buffalo are the prime quarries. The coastal beaches are snowy white, clean and fairly free of dangerous fish. The gigantic lobsters of Nha Trang and Cap St. Jacques are certainly worthy rivals of those from Maine.

The Vietnamese farmer is lucky to earn $20.00 a year in hard currency, but this does not mean he is impoverished. His clothing, cheap, baggy, black calico blouses and trousers, is adequate for the tropical climate. Excellent supplies for housebuilding are no farther away than the nearest grove of bamboo and palm trees.

He may even have some savings—generally in gold or opium. Even the French recognize that opium was more highly valued by Vietnamese than their paper currency, and retiring civil servants often were pensioned off in opium.

Underdevelopment in Viet Nam, therefore, means something other than mere material hardship. It is partly the lack of technology. But much more important, it is a national state of mind.

The lack of technology means that communications in many areas are almost nonexistent. Few persons in Saigon have telephones, and outside the capital telephones are almost unknown.

Travel in South Viet Nam is an arduous and sometimes dangerous business. The one railroad line, which serves only the coastal towns, is ambushed or sabotaged once a day on the average by the Viet Cong, with frequently fatal results. There are only four or five first-class highways in the country, and most of the nation is served by rutted paths amounting to little more than trails. Many of these are permanently obstructed by the Viet Cong and even main roads are the target of incessant ambushes. Canals are also blocked or ambushed. The only sure way of getting from one point to another is by air, and this is too expensive for most poor people.

The result is that peasants of one district in Viet Nam may not have the remotest idea of what is going on in another district only a few miles away. A large proportion of Vietnamese have never visited the capital of Saigon, and know it only as the place where the king or his equivalent reigns. Every once in a while, raiding parties of troops come from Saigon to collect taxes, round up young men for the military draft, and look around for illegal weapons. That is about the total of contact with Saigon.

This state of affairs is obviously an excellent background for a semiclandestine guerrilla army. For one thing, a peasant is generally not much inclined to resist the ubiquitous guerrillas, even if he dislikes them, when he knows that there is no way of calling for help.

But the real nature of underdevelopment in Viet Nam has to do with education and a man's view of the world around him.

Most Vietnamese have a primary school education, and the great majority are literate, at least to the extent that they can read propaganda slogans.

Of the small Vietnamese professional class left by the French colonialists, large numbers remained French citizens and went back to France after Viet Nam became independent in 1954. Most of the remainder live in Saigon where they make money and dabble in politics. Provinces of nearly a quarter-million people often are served by only one or two doctors, who generally grow rich because of their huge practices, and become major landowners. Some provinces have no doctors at all.

Rural administrators generally are men with little more than a few weeks' training and salaries of only about $40.00 a month. It is said that when a man puts on a white collar in Viet Nam, he has the right to step all over his neighbors and take whatever he can get. Careers in the civil service too often are merely platforms for a lifetime of extortion.

This is a purely subjective judgment and perhaps open to challenge. But it seems to me that of the thousands of Vietnamese officials I have known, I can think of none who does not more or less hold the Vietnamese people in contempt. Many of these officials are loudly patriotic most of the time, and mouth the stock phrases about "the courageous and all-enduring Vietnamese people." But when they are occasionally induced to speak frankly, they speak of their nation not with pride but with contemptuous apology. Certainly, their attitudes in most cases bespeak contempt.

This feeling of suspicion and hostility is fully reciprocated by the poor people of the nation in their relations with their rulers. I think it is safe to say that the average Vietnamese views the only good official as a dead one.

When Viet Cong terrorists publicly behead some hamlet or province official and then disembowel the wife and children as well, Americans tend to assume that this will result in a powerful reaction by the people against the Viet Cong. Nothing could be farther from the truth in most cases. The Viet Cong often liquidates a government official precisely because it knows such an act will please the local people.

In passing, it is well to note that peasants often seem pleased when unpopular local Viet Cong commissars are rubbed out by government terrorists, too.

But if the Vietnamese people by and large are apolitical anarchists in tendency, most need some kind of higher authority toward which they can turn with a degree of trust. The humble, uneducated Buddhist monk meets this requirement. His organization demands almost nothing of the people, except enough rice and bananas to live. In exchange for the modest gifts of food solicited by the monks, the people receive powerful protection against the mysterious dangers of the spirit world, and are guided toward an afterlife that will be happier than this one.

Some, of course, turn to Catholicism. But, and again this is purely subjective judgment, I think the discipline and restrictions of Catholicism are more than most of the Vietnamese. people like to have imposed on them.

Buddhism is many centuries old in Viet Nam and fits the country like an old shoe. This, to my thinking, is the reason that, when Buddhism entered the Vietnamese political arena in 1963, its power shot up like bamboo. The potential was always there. It took the mistakes of the Diem government to bring it to realization.

Somewhat the same considerations apply, I believe, to the growth of the Viet Cong. Viet Cong forces are highly disciplined fighting units. But members are led to believe that the discipline is only a temporary evil. Once the imperialist bureaucrats are thrown out, there will be no more military conscription, no more taxes, no more interference by officials, just a happy life of private peace. If this image is exactly the opposite of reality in communist-governed nations, the

South Vietnamese farmer can hardly be expected to see the contradiction. He knows next to nothing about the outer world in general, much less its politics. So far, the Viet Cong has never raised the idea of collective farms, for example. It is difficult to imagine a Vietnamese farmer being forced to live on a collective farm without rebelling. The so-called Strategic Hamlets invented by the Diem regime, which had certain similarities to collective farms, were a notable failure and a cardinal propaganda benefit to the Viet Cong.

Generalities are dangerous, but to my mind the Vietnamese farmers who make up 85 per cent of the nation's population are people who loathe controls but who will exercise them ruthlessly on others if given the chance; they are men with little or no sense of identity with Viet Nam as a united nation, but the mistrust and dislike all outsiders; they are willing to unite and fight effectively only in the belief that they are overthrowing the controls they despise. When they are rich or educated, they generally prefer to live outside Viet Nam rather than in it.

Viet Cong propaganda takes all these characteristics into consideration and has proved highly successful.

The student who failed his examination would be delighted at the chance to burn up all the test papers, but cannot do it on his own. On the other hand, if he is a member of the National Liberation Front or one of the Buddhist youth groups that occasionally launch mass riots, he has a team behind him. The test papers get burned, and instructors are in grave personal danger if they protest.

One of the political rampages staged in the coastal city of Qui Nhon in late 1964 had its roots in exactly this cause. The student leaders of the riots all had flunked their examinations and were demanding a second chance at easier examinations. It was suggested by some of the teachers that the students might have passed if they had spent less time demonstrating in the first place and more in studying.

In summary, underdevelopment in South Viet Nam means social and political sickness. Many diplomats, politicians and other more or less qualified observers—both Vietnamese and foreign—have expressed grave doubts that South Viet Nam should even be considered a nation at all.

This view is of course academic, because South Viet

Nam is a nation, for better or worse. So are the scores of newly independent African and Asian nations that now dot the map.

Western colonialism is dead, and it has left a legacy of sickness.

Since 1954, the United States has sought to keep South Viet Nam alive by shoring up governments made up of anticommunist friends of America. Despite massive aid to these governments, it was a losing battle.

Since February 7, 1965, the United States has discarded the velvet glove that formerly concealed the mailed fist. It has sought to crush the insurgents by raw force, in hopes that somehow a new, pro-American generation of Vietnamese might emerge. But massive force has failed.

Meanwhile, the communists and their allies have gone on expanding their fronts and continuing the infiltration of the social bases of Viet Nam, including religion. By playing on existing hatreds and fears, the National Liberation Front can go on recruiting almost indefinitely. The best human pools from which to recruit are the few loosely organized but enormously popular mass organizations already existing in South Viet Nam, of which Buddhism is now one. Somehow the Viet Cong always manages to get its finger in pies like this, and does better than the anticommunists.

Their formula is a tough one to beat.

13

CREAM AND DREGS

In November 1964 Viet Cong strategists decided to try to encircle Saigon with an "iron ring," designed to strangle the capital's commerce and disrupt its contact with and control over the rest of the nation. They nearly succeeded.

Part of the strategy involved the movement of large Viet Cong forces that had been operating west of Saigon near the Cambodian frontier. These forces were to infiltrate around the northern suburbs of the city to the marshes and hill country northeast and southeast of the capital.

Once emplaced in their new base areas, the Viet Cong needed to outfit themselves. They had some weapons but they needed food, clothing, medical supplies and various supporting hardware.

They were able to get what they needed without difficulty because of the moral rot of the Saigon government, along with American unwillingness to do much about the situation.

The VC decided to get its cash and supplies by tapping Route 1, Viet Nam's only North-South road, which ran near their new jungle base. They picked a spot fifty-six miles east of Saigon, after ascertaining that the local government province chief could be corrupted.

The area is heavily wooded and sparsely populated. Local peasants make a living cutting wood and coverting it into charcoal, which is Viet Nam's main fuel.

The Viet Cong arranged a three-way deal.

Peasants were told they could go on cutting wood undisturbed, provided the peasants saw to it that government forces left the Viet Cong undisturbed. The commissars pointed out that this could be accomplished by paying a suitable fee to the local province chief.

Arrangements were made. The peasants paid the province chief, the province chief kept his local troops whitewashing rocks instead of chasing Viet Cong, and the Viet Cong set up their tollbooths.

Four Viet Cong checkpoints were set up within a three-and-one-half-mile stretch of Route 1, to make sure nothing was missed on the way through. They were made of concrete, and small buildings were set up to protect Viet Cong guards from rain.

The guards, who dressed in regular khaki uniforms, were given telephones connected to a jungle command post south of the road. They issued printed receipts for tolls exacted or cargoes seized from vehicles. The amount of tolls depended on the size of the vehicles and the nature of their cargoes.

Sometimes the guards would seize an entire vehicle and drive it down a trail leading to a camp in the jungle about four miles south of the road. Here, the vehicle was stripped of useful parts, and its tires cut up to make sandals.*

All kinds of goods were seized, including occasional loads of government propaganda magazines. During the two months the four checkpoints were in operation, they collected about $40,000 in cash.

Thousands of persons (including myself) knew the exact location and nature of the Viet Cong checkpoints on Route 1, but nothing seemed to happen to them. There was certainly no lack of complaints to the Saigon government and even to the American command.

Once, after telling a U.S. intelligence officer about the checkpoints, I was told, "Yes, I know, it's real bad out there. Shame so many of the roads are like that."

But the Viet Cong remained unhindered by any government ground operation, or even by air strikes or artillery.

Perhaps it was mere coincidence that the corrupted government province chief was related by marriage to someone at the very highest level of the Saigon government.

In any case, the Viet Cong finally had their fill. They had been able to steal all the supplies or cash they needed. Part of the cash was spent in Saigon, buying medical supplies that had come into the country under the U.S. AID program. By

*For sandals, Viet Cong guerrillas prefer tires that have been worn smooth, not new ones. Vehicles were often picked because of the poor condition of their tires.

the end of the year, two full-strength Viet Cong regiments had completely refitted themselves.

They struck near the hamlet of Binh Gia about forty miles east of Saigon, during New Year's week, 1965. Sucking Vietnamese government forces into a series of ambushes, they inflicted more than 500 casualties, including about twenty American advisors. It was the worst beating Saigon forces had suffered up to that point.

The use of corruption by communist forces in Southeast Asia as a weapon of war is nothing new. The interesting thing is that the Free World has never found an effective antidote.

Back in 1945, Ho Chi Minh acquired his organization's first weapons by means of a corrupted Free World army. Nationalist China had been assigned the job of taking over the occupation of North Viet Nam from Japanese forces at the end of World War II, at least until the French colonial administrators returned.

But Ho Chi Minh saw that Chiang Kai-shek's occupation troops were demoralized, sick of war, and eager to make money. Rather than fight Chiang, Ho decided to undermine him by buying out his troops. Thus, Ho invested much of his party treasury in purchasing more than 4,000 rifles and hundreds of machines guns—almost all American-made, by the way—from corrupted Chinese troops.

Later, Mao Tse-tung was to use some of the same tricks in smashing Chiang's army for good in 1949.

American servicemen and officials in Viet Nam have also proved highly susceptible to corruption, as I shall show in a subsequent chapter.

The social structure of noncommunist South Viet Nam is essentially a two-class system of moneyed aristocracy and peasantry, despite efforts by the United States to get a middle class going, along with some light industry. Even Saigon, a city of close to two million inhabitants, has only a tiny middle class.

From the air, Saigon looks like a sprawling village, with very few tall buildings, and main streets mostly covered by arching treetops. If you are rich (earning more than $200 a month), Saigon is a beautiful city.

Stately villas line the broad streets in the "nice" part of town, and each of these villas is shaded with tall tamarind trees. There are dozens of fine French and Chinese restaurants, and, if you're daring and don't mind the smell of fermented fish sauce, you might try one of the better Vietnamese restaurants.

Catinat Street (renamed Tu Do, meaning "freedom") and the streets near it are filled with expensive shops where you can buy fine tortoise-shell items, bronzeware and Vietnamese ceramics.

Hotels are air conditioned and comfortable. The Caravelle is the largest and swankiest of these, although getting rooms anywhere in town is hard. Most are occupied by American servicemen or officials. This has led to drastic reduction of service, inferior cuisine and rocketing prices at most establishments.

If you live in Viet Nam as a permanent resident, you will find it agreeable to spend the hottest months of April and May in Dalat, a cool mountain resort an hour away by air, where you will find all the comforts of Saigon. Your children will be having their vacation at this time, so you can take them along.

There are many profitable businesses in which you may engage, provided you have the capital to start. You can do contract work of every imaginable kind for the many American official agencies operating in the cities. You could open a bar or night club. You could start a loan agency, where you may collect 10 or 20 per cent interest a month. You might go into real estate, although investments in the countryside are a bit risky just now. Or you could open a factory, for which labor costs are remarkably low.

Best of all, since you have money, you will not have to worry about all the nasty government red tape involved in getting exit visas, in case you should feel obliged to leave the country hastily.

You may know the Interior Minister socially, and he will be able to get you fixed up. Most important, you can have a plane ticket to Paris any time you want to buy one, should the roof cave in.

Of course, there are occasional government crackdowns on racketeering, profiteering and black marketing. But there is no real danger for a wealthy Vietnamese. The Indian money-changers get jailed, and a Chinese businessman is stood up in the Central Market and shot. But Indians and Chinese are merely hated minority groups anyway, despite their business acumen.

If you are poor, of course, life in Saigon is less agreeable.

If you work in one of the white collar offices in town, you probably earn between $20.00 and $40.00 a month, and this won't go very far. Food in Saigon is cheap, but almost everything else is expensive. Your children will have to be satisfied with a trip to the zoo (admission: two cents) or a Sunday picnic at the side of the four-lane American-built Bien Hoa highway just outside town. You can get there by bicycle.

But if you are a Saigonese, you probably are among the masses who earn less than $20.00 a month, and you live in one of the vast slums that the visitors never see. You have no tall trees, no sporting club, and little more than your day's share of rice and fish and the thatched cubicle in which your family lives. Your cubicle is likely to be searched at night by police looking for Viet Cong, and your identification papers will be checked several times a day by someone in authority. If a fire happens to start anywhere in your neighborhood, your own dwelling will probably burn to the ground, because there are very few firebreaks in the slums, and the houses burn like the kindling wood they are.

Your children will go to primary school, but they won't get beyond that unless you have some money. Advanced education is expensive. Your family may never see one of the Paris-trained doctors who treat the rich and become politicians. You will have to settle for midwives and traditional medical practitioners.

If you have Parkinson's disease, you will tilt back your head while the practitioner introduces the head of a live gecko (the large insect-eating lizard) into your mouth. The savant will then snip off the lizard's tail, which will cause it to wriggle its way down into your stomach, curing your disease.

You can generally afford a ten-cent ticket in the weekly drawing of the national lottery, which could make you fabulously rich. You probably will buy one, even though you know that a former director of the lottery under the Diem regime once decamped with a half million dollars from the fund. For diversion, you can place bets on cricket fights. You can find the fighting crickets swarming in the streets during the hot season.

You can afford to drink. Local booze is awful but cheap.

If you are a man under thirty-five, the government will try fairly hard to draft you. You can probably dodge this, but if they catch up with you, you can always desert later, and you probably won't have further trouble.*

In or out of the army, you can make money with a motor scooter. Field grade army officers and officials in government ministries can no longer support their families on the $100 or so a month they are paid, and they must moonlight. One way to moonlight is to wait with a motor scooter outside the bars of Saigon for the GIs to come reeling out. They must get back to their bases by curfew, and will pay good money for scooter rides, since taxis are always scarce.

Thus, despite your position in the government, you must swallow your pride and cart drunken GIs back to their beds, even if it means you must report to work groggy from lack of sleep the following day.

If you have a flair for language, you could learn enough English to become a pimp.

If you are really hard up, you can probably join a *hui*, which is a kind of private credit union. You and as many friends as possible get together, each contributing a certain sum to the *hui* fund and then making loans from the central fund to the needy members of the group. Those who don't borrow anything draw interest from the others. It's a kind of shared risk investment, from which borrowers pay much lower interest rates than to banks or the professional loan sharks.

Chances are you are irritated almost constantly by the rich. Just pedaling your bicycle along you are apt to be forced off to the side of the street twenty times a day by honking cars. You probably dislike the drivers of these cars as much as they dislike you for loafing along in the middle of the street.

You can always get even with them by saving up enough money to become a taxi driver. As a taxi driver, your vehicle will be a banged-up little blue and white Renault *quatre chevaux*, in which you will find the shiny big cars give you a wide berth. They know that a collision with you will cost them a lot more than it does you.

---

*In 1967 an estimated 40,000 draft dodgers were wandering the streets of South Viet Nam. The annual desertion rate from South Viet Nam's armed forces is about 12 per cent, but it sometimes goes much higher. For instance, during one three-month period in 1966 there were 36,637 desertions from Saigon's forces.

In the army, as elsewhere in South Viet Nam, money talks. If you can scrape up about $500, you can buy yourself a reassignment from a dangerous combat post in, say, the 5th Division, to a desk job in Saigon. If you can't think of a legitimate way to get the $500, you can always rob a Saigon jewelry store, using one of the grenades the army issues you. You will find that Saigon police are afraid of grenades and will give you a wide berth.

With a little more money, you can stay out of the army completely. There are specialists who (for a high fee) will rub metal powder into the skin on your chest, which shows up on an X ray just like advanced tuberculosis. There are thousands of tricks, provided you have the money.

Getting the money somehow or other usually can be managed, if it's important enough. It almost always has something to do with the Americans, who have unlimited supplies of money.

If all this gets you down and you have a revolutionary bent, you can always join the Viet Cong. A recruiting agent is never far away.

Actually, the ruling class of Saigon—and, for that matter, of South Viet Nam—is pretty small. If you live in Saigon for a few years and are privy to the social elite, you probably know just about everyone who is anyone or is likely to become anyone in the event of a coup, election, or other upheaval. People change jobs, of course, and some people end up as odd men out, either dead or in exile. But as long as a member of the "cream" of South Viet Nam's society is alive he must never be counted out.

The political prisoners President Diem kept confined on the penal island of Poulo Condore (Con Son) sixty miles off the coast were all released after the 1963 coup. Many have held high office (one, Phan Khack Suu, became chief of state for a while). Many of the people high in the Diem government replaced their former prisoners rotting on Poulo Condore Island.

There are various ways to become one of the elite, but they all involve being born with a certain amount of money. To reach the top, you must have an education—preferably a foreign education, since you must speak French or English or both—and education is expensive.

Incidentally, this situation is just as true in Hanoi, the

capital of communist North Viet Nam, as it is in Saigon. The three most powerful men of the North, President Ho Chi Minh, Premier Pham Van Dong and Armed Forces Minister Vo Nguyen Giap, all must be classed as foreign-educated intellectuals. None of them was born into the really poor class, and each of them is as much at home discussing European art and literature in fluent French or English as he is talking Leninist dogma.

A great deal of nonsense has been written and said in the United States about preserving democracy in South Viet Nam. In 1967, there was even an election, rigged up as the result of American pressure for "democratization." But even if an honest election could be carried out, democracy is more than merely electing people. It implies a certain knowledge by the voters of how their country is run. It implies a little universal education. It implies a certain commonweal in moving the nation. It implies faith by the people in a central government of some kind. South Viet Nam has none of these things. With or without nominal democracy, it will remain a nation run by a small elite for a very long time to come, whether the government is communist or pro-American.

As a generality, if as a Vietnamese you have a really solid education, you are likely to rise to the top, regardless of which side you are on. It doesn't really matter what field of learning you choose, although doctors very often make out better than others. Very few Vietnamese doctors end up practicing their professions. They can do much better going into politics, or so they believe.

One case in point is Dr. Tran Van Tho, a southerner whose family scraped up enough money to send him to France to take a medical degree. He arrived in Toulouse without a sou in his pocket, but borrowed a fairly large sum from another student—a rich Cambodian—to get started. Tho made the academic grade and eventually returned to Viet Nam after 1954. He set up a private clinic in Saigon, and joined Diem's political party.

Tho let the nails on his pinky fingers grow long in the style of old-fashioned Vietnamese aristocrats and rose through the political ranks. Eventually, he became Diem's information minister. Tho was delighted with the empire he had built. He had a fine villa, he had two secret police bodyguards to follow him wherever he went, he headed a large and important organization, and he held a post in which he could give his anti-American feelings full vent.

He worked hard for the expulsion of various American reporters. At one point, he demanded and got the expulsion of John Anspacher, director of the U.S. Information Service, a man he cordially hated. That was in 1962, at a time when the U.S. Embassy was doing its best to humor the requests of Vietnamese officials no matter how shortsighted these requests were.

Tho's family was less than perfect. The French wife he had acquired as part of his meteoric social rise deserted him and took the children back to France. But there were lots of girls in Tho's ministry to pick from, and he could (and did) make life extremely unpleasant for them if they resisted his advances. None of them could escape by quitting their jobs, because in those days you couldn't just quit without permission of the minister. If you really wanted out, about the only thing you could do was get transferred to one of the remote, dangerous and unpleasant provinces. Such transfers generally were (and are) used as punishment within the Vietnamese civil service, and this is one of the reasons rural civil servants have so little enthusiasm for their jobs, by and large.

Tho turned out enormous quantities of propaganda highly flattering to Diem, and more important, to Diem's all-powerful brother, Ngo Dinh Nhu.

At one point, Diem became exasperated with the politician-doctors infesting his capital, especially those who were his political opponents. He rounded up some of them and sent them to the penal island of Poulo Condore. But he also passed a doctors' conscription bill, aimed at forcing doctors into government service to practice in the provinces, most of which had no doctors at all.

Naturally, Tran Van Tho was exempt from this draft and took delight in helping to draw up the list of doctors to be drafted. The list included all his rivals.

But Tho made so much bad blood with so many people that in the end he became too much even for Diem. He was fired as information czar. Of course, Tho was still left his seat in the National Assembly, which entitled him to a chauffeur-driven limousine, a nice house, and other amenities. But for financial reasons, he was forced to return to his practice at least part time, so he cranked up his clinic again. That is the story of one Vietnamese doctor.

Another doctor named Pham Huy Co was one of the outs during the Diem regime. Co never visited Viet Nam during the first nine years of Vietnamese independence, but maintained a practice in Paris. His practice was lucrative enough to support his political party and a flourishing anti-Diem propaganda apparatus he kept in operation. Co designed a new national flag (a red field with a yellow cross), announced himself as a staunch anticommunist friend of the United States, and, through agents, began a grenade-throwing campaign in Saigon. In 1963 quite a few of Co's grenades went off around town, one of which nearly blew the pants off a messenger of mine who happened to be near when it went off.

Each grenade was wrapped in paper and contained thousands of little anti-Diem, pro-Co leaflets. The low-power bombs were not supposed to be dangerous, but were merely intended to make a loud noise and scatter the leaflets. Actually, a number of people were hurt by the little bombs, which turned out to be more powerful than expected.

Co gave press conferences in Phnom Penh and Tokyo and attracted quite a bit of official American interest for a while. He seemed to be for all the things America was for. Shortly after the death of Diem, he returned to his homeland, presuming that a place in the sun would have been reserved for him. It turned out otherwise. Even his old fellow military plotters against Diem, all of whom now had good jobs, ignored him. Successive military governments also ignored him, and he couldn't even land a seat on one of the powerless civilian advisory councils. This was a bitter disappointment, and Co began organizing political meetings and press conferences. Co probably has fewer than 300 followers, all of whom have allegiances to other organizations as well.

He is one of scores of Saigon politicians doing exactly the same thing. He is not willing to join forces with any of them, because he knows he would probably be outmaneuvered politically and would again find himself on the outs. It is better to go on giving dinners for powerful people and talking up a campaign in the coffee shops. At least this way he can remain independent.

In a general way, this is the pattern with all Vietnamese politicians, and I mean that term specifically to include Vietnamese military officers.

Vietnamese military officers have always held roles completely foreign to the patterns of Western armies. Among other things, they command troops and run fighting campaigns. But they also administer about 85 per cent of all the people in South Viet Nam. When Diem came to power in 1954, he felt it would be a mistake to make too many changes in the French provincial administration system immediately. As it turned out, the system never was changed, and still functions essentially in the French colonial pattern, except that Vietnamese instead of French hold the top jobs.

Under the colonial system, the nation was ruled by a colonial governor through a number of ministries, most important of which was the Interior Ministry. This ministry appointed a province chief for each of the country's major subdivisions. Each province chief had his own staff and in turn appointed district chiefs at the next lower level. District chiefs and their staffs named canton chiefs, who named village chiefs, who named hamlet chiefs.

Under the French, most of the province chiefs were army officers. This, presumably, was because the main worry of each rural administrator was the war being waged in his own sector by the communist insurgents. It was reasoned that military men were better qualified than civilians to do this work.

Diem continued the pattern. Out of some forty provinces, only two had civilian chiefs, and the rest were regular army officers—majors, lieutenant colonels, and colonels. Nearly all of these officials were natives of provinces other than the ones they commanded and a majority were North or Central Vietnamese.

This geographical situation reflected the composition of the army itself, which is recruited primarily in central Viet Nam and the coastal cities. One rarely finds Vietnamese officers native to the Mekong River Delta where half the population of South Viet Nam lives and where the war rages hottest.

Currently, every one of South Viet Nam's forty-five provinces is commanded by a military officer, as is every one of the nearly 300 districts in the country. Communities that rank as cities generally have army officers as mayors. Each of these administrative officers is, of course, subject to military discipline and is part of the Defense Ministry. He is usually outranked by the regimental, division and corps commanders who wander in and out of his sector with troops from time to time.

Nevertheless, the rural administrative officer is the supreme government authority in his region, with sweeping powers of good or evil. He is so remote from Saigon he must generally work his problems out for himself, and he has basically exactly the same job that provincial mandarins of the Vietnamese civil service held for many centuries. The average Vietnamese citizen has a great deal of contact (mostly unpleasant) with his local district chief, but generally none at all with Saigon.

An ordinary army captain does not have an enviable job in South Viet Nam. If he has a job as commander of an operational company, there will be all sorts of unpleasant field duties, not to mention the danger of getting shot in combat with the Viet Cong. But if this captain happens to land a job as district chief he becomes a little emperor. As the chief tax collector, conscription officer, judge, county prosecutor, police chief, contract officer and everything else all rolled into one, he literally has the power of life and death over his subjects. If someone chooses to give him a hard time, that person is apt to be arrested as a Viet Cong agent, and no one is likely to be the wiser. That person may rot for months or years in some provincial jail without trial or further investigation, or he may be shot on the spot. Similar pressures can be brought to bear on entire families, even on entire hamlets.

If you are a Vietnamese army captain earning $40.00 a month, wouldn't you like to be a district chief?

In general, the requirements for the job are not too exacting. The main thing is dedicated loyalty to the officers further up the line who make the appointments. Military competence is apparently not a prerequisite. Discretion and political *savoir-faire* are.

It has been argued that in Viet Nam the military officer has had the best general training for administrative office. U.S. Ambassador Maxwell D. Taylor said, "We can't afford the luxury of discriminating against a man because of the color of his coat. You have to use administrative talent where you find it."

This is no doubt true.

But it also has been argued by various political writers that the Vietnamese rural administration service is one of the cleanest in Asia. If such is the case, Asia deserves the undying pity of the rest of the world. Vietnamese army officers serving as administrators are no worse and no better than you would expect them to be. A few are outstandingly good, and their provinces or districts always are used as showcases when visitors (especially foreigners) come around. A few are so bad that popular demonstrations erupt when the Viet Cong assassinates them.

Most manage to stay inconspicuous by keeping their extortion within limits, their love-making to the local girls reasonably discreet, and their vengeance arrests confined to a handful of enemies. It is most important to keep your nose clean with the Americans these days, but this is not too difficult, because they have so few qualified field men that they can't keep tabs on everything all the time. The main thing is to avoid alienating the official just above you.

There are lots of little things you can do to make a living. If one of your men gets killed fighting the Viet Cong, the government is now obliged to pay his family a year's salary, say, about $400. This payment comes down from Saigon and goes through you. You can charge certain "fees" without too much danger of being caught. You can charge something for providing a coffin (made free by a squad of your troops), something for "funeral expenses," something for your own expense account involved in seeing to all these matters. So you plit the $400 with the family, and that's that.

You probably are on friendly terms with a lot of American advisors, all of whom are anxious to stay on good terms with you (since their rating officer will have a close look at these relations before considering any of them for promotion). These friendly people generally will buy you all kinds of supplies at cost at their PX—transistor radios, ladies' hair spray, and so on. You can sell these things at 1,000 per cent profit locally, and it all adds up.

You may have been able to collect a nice haul of taxes from some hamlet one month, but there's no automatic need to turn this tax money in to your bosses, if you're discreet. You can keep it and claim that you couldn't get your tax-collection team into the hamlet because the Viet Cong was too strong there.

To make sure the hamlet makes no trouble about all this, you can always feed headquarters an "intelligence report" that a Viet Cong regiment has camped in the hamlet, along with the recommendation that the whole thing ought to be blown off the map immediately. Generally, this will be done, and the Skyraiders will be over in a day or two to bomb the town to rubble.

I lived in Viet Nam continuously for five years, and I have spent a great deal of time in all its provinces, returning time and time again to many districts, villages and hamlets. I have many Vietnamese friends who live in these places. If there are still those who doubt that Vietnamese national administration has ever been anything other than as I have just described it, I would invite him to accompany me on a two-week tour of the countryside to places not included in any of the official itineraries.

I do not mean to imply that all Vietnamese military provincial officers are corrupt and self-serving. Some military officials, especially those who served in the Viet Minh in the war against the French and later switched to Diem, are excellent officials by any standards. But they are exceptions. Unfortunately, most of the really intelligent, dedicated and patriotic men and women who form the stuff of sound leadership stayed with the Viet Minh.

Efforts have been made, of course, to develop an effective civilian administrative system in South Viet Nam.

In 1955, Michigan State University signed a contract with the Diem government to set up schools for a new generation of administrators. The U.S. AID Mission was working along similar lines.

Hundreds of American experts in accounting, taxes, urban renewal, public works, land development, agriculture and all the rest came to Viet Nam. A National Institute of Administration with American teachers was set up in Saigon and began churning out budding *fonctionnaires* by the thousand. A lot of combined talent was brought to bear on this project, and there were high hopes.

But from the beginning, Diem was much more interest-ed in the police and security programs than most of the other things. The various Vietnamese police organizations (includ-ing the dreaded "Bureau for Political Research at the Presi-dency") bloomed, and all of them were equipped with the most advanced American gadgets, including phone tapping equipment and other sophistications. As the Diem regime became increasingly rough on its political adversaries, one American police advisor remarked:

"I'm afraid we have unwittingly created a Frankenstein's monster here, a made-in-America police state."

Years after Diem's demise, the situation remained essen-tially the same, through a series of military dictatorships, with or without civilian façades. The various Vietnamese police forces remained enormously powerful and were used as much against political opposition as they were against civil criminals.

Some of Diem's police officials took a great deal of technical know-how with them when they were sent to jail themselves after Diem was overthrown. Saigon was treated to the spectacle of regular visits by both American officials and the new Vietnamese "ins" to get advice from former officials in their prison cells.

The style of successive secret police chiefs did change drastically, however.

Under Diem, the chief of the Bureau for Political Re-search at the Presidency was Dr. Tran Kim Tuyen (a medical doctor, naturally), who had most of the social graces. Dr. Tuyen, a very short man, attended most of the diplomatic functions of the capital and had a keen appreciaion of music. He played the violin himself.

Dr. Tuyen was a close friend of William C. Trueheart, deputy to former Ambassador Frederick E. Nolting, Jr., and of the CIA station chief, John Richardson. Americans regarded Tuyen as a relatively gentle and restrained man serving in a position of enormous power in which he could have acted like a latter-day Heinrich Himmler. The genial Dr. Tuyen went to prison after Diem was overthrown.

Dr. Tuyen was the temperamental opposite of Colonel Nguyen Ngoc Loan (later a general) who headed the national police establishment for a while under Premier (later Vice

President) Nguyen Cao Ky. Loan had been Ky's hatchet man in the air force, and assumed the same role when Ky took over leadership of the nation on the heels of a coup.

Tuyen had liked to trade secrets with diplomats in concert halls and at receptions. Loan sometimes went to press conferences carrying tomatoes in his pockets to throw, in case an incident needed stirring up.

During Tuyen's time, the secret police would come in the middle of the night to make arrests. In Loan's time, political assassinations were generally in broad daylight.

When Tuyen wanted to make a point to me, he made it subtly and in literary French, full of poetic allusions. On a similar occasion, Loan made a point to me in slangy English, accompanied by a fist in my stomach that doubled me up. Sic transit.

Diem also liked American ideas about land development and he had visions of turning the virgin jungles of Central Viet Nam into fields of golden grain. Unfortunately, most of the land in the populous Mekong River Delta already had long been reformed by the Viet Cong, which was prepared to fight to keep it from being re-reformed. And somehow the jungles never have turned into wheat fields.

But if Diem liked some of the new American techniques, he distinctly disliked many others. For one thing, the Ngo family was essentially a French-Vietnamese family, and in its eyes the old administrative system was not nearly so bad as the Americans were making out. Diem and his indispensable brother, Nhu, both found it easier to speak and write in French than in Vietnamese. The night they decided on the measure that was to bring about their deaths two months later, they summoned the cabinet to the palace. The two brothers, looking haggard and tired, had decided to crush the Buddhist rebellion by smashing the pagodas, arresting the monks and nuns, and clamping martial law over the nation. They scribbled the terms of their decision in longhand—in French—and passed the paper around the table to the assembled ministers. This according to Vice President Nguyen Ngoc Tho, who was there.

The thing Diem least liked about the Americans was their persistence about belittling existing systems and their constant introduction of revolutionary ideas, along with their open personal friendships with some of his foes.

Some of the Americans working for Michigan State University, the U.S. AID Mission and various other American education missions were pretty outspoken in their criticism of Diem. In a learned article one of them described South Viet Nam as "a permanent mendicant," and Diem was incensed. U.S.-Vietnamese relations went from bad to worse, and one after another the American civilian advisors were thrown out. The Michigan State mission was closed down in 1962, leaving the National Institute for Administration in Vietnamese hands. One American, Dr. Stanley Millet, was detained and questioned by police before being permitted to leave the country.

Millet had been teaching political science at Saigon University under a grant to Viet Nam under the U.S. Smith-Mundt Education Act. Millet spoke Vietnamese pretty well, was on close social terms with most of his students, and therefore was close to most of the Saigon intelligentsia, including leading political opponents of Diem.

Millet saw one after another of his friends disappear, and he began to conceive a deep dislike for the Diem government. He used to express his opinions fairly openly at cocktail parties and other places the secret police regularly wired with tape recorders, and the word was not long in reaching Nhu.

It happened that one of Millet's acquaintances was a man named Nguyen Van Luc, an intellectual with decidedly anti-Diem views. Luc had two sons in the Vietnamese air force, both of whom had been trained to fly in the United States and who had become star fighter pilots. On February 27, 1962, one of Luc's sons, Sub Lieutenant Nguyen Van Cu, climbed into his American-built AD6 fighter at Bien Hoa Airport fifteen miles from Saigon, took off, and bombed the presidential palace to rubble. Another rebel pilot who flew with Cu was shot down by palace antiaircraft guns, but Cu's bullet-riddled plane made it 145 miles west to Phnom Penh, the capital of neutralist Cambodia, where it crash-landed.

Mme. Ngo Dinh Nhu got bruised up by the raid and a Chinese governess was killed by a falling beam, but the whole presidential family managed to get to the palace bomb shelter in time and survived. Cu lived happily in Cambodia until the 1963 coup, teaching English to Cambodian students and dreaming of returning to Viet Nam. He did, after the coup, and was reinstated in the air force.

Father Luc, the other air force brother, and a lot of other people associated with the Nguyen family were arrested right after the palace bombing. And among the friends of the family was Stanley Millet.

Millet was finally allowed to leave Viet Nam, but Diem was never entirely satisfied that the American professor had not had something to do with the raid that nearly cost him his life. Nor was Diem alone in this feeling. Many ranking Vietnamese, including some currently in high offices, feel the American CIA is constantly active in Vietnamese politics and was responsible for the 1963 coup, among many other things. For the record, and there is no reason to doubt it, Millet said he had no advance inkling of the raid.

Luc got out of jail after the coup and was active on several governmental bodies that formed and were dissolved in quick succession. He remained a goad to various governments and kept his hand in politics.

The central fact is that despite all the power plays and reshuffles, the Saigon ministries, with all their red tape, favoritism, inefficiency and politics, have not changed in any important respect since French colonial days, and there are no prospects for any major change. The old forms in triplicate, the rubber stamps, the two-and-a-half-hour daily siesta and the ridiculous multiplication of bureaus and employees persist, war or no war, and the sheer inertia of Vietnamese administration is amply powerful to frustrate any innovator. Diem never changed it, and, after Diem, neither did the Minh-Tho government, the Nguyen Khanh government, the Tran Van Huong government, the Phan Huy Quat government, the Ky government, or the Nguyen Van Thieu government.

The problem is less one of mechanics and organization than it is of attitudes. The Vietnamese hated the French enough to rise up and destroy them. But after a century of colonial rule, patterns are etched into a society.

Colonialism is not all bad. It sometimes introduces efficiency, education and other desirable by-products. But these things are only by-products. The reason for having a colony in the first place is for commercial exploitation, not altruism, and the first job of colonial officials is to make sure that nothing seriously interferes with this exploitation. This immediately makes the colonial official a "have" and an "exploiter" among the "have-nots," no matter how benign and enlightened his social views may be.

Inevitably, a colonial class developed in the French community in Viet Nam that lived pretty high on the hog. The Vietnamese came to hate the colonialists, but at the same time envied them. In many cases, they imitated the French ways, just as a matter of prestige. French automobiles, night clubs, clothing, and all the rest were indelibly stamped into the texture of Viet Nam as status symbols.

The same mixture of hatred and envy was extended to the French colonial official, the little king who could have any girl he wanted, take anything he pleased, and spit on his constituents if they objected. It is a sad observation of humanity that many Vietnamese hated this kind of thing not so much because of what it was but because it was a Frenchman doing it. Now there are Vietnamese holding the same jobs and spitting on the same people, and too often it seems that nothing has changed but the color of the faces.

There is no accurate gauge of Diem's popularity (or the lack of it) since he was never exposed to a free election. But there are grounds for feeling Diem was genuinely popular with a lot of Vietnamese for a long time. For one thing, he rode the crest of a revolutionary wave, coming to power at just the time his nation became independent (largely because of the efforts of his arch enemy, Ho Chi Minh). For another, Diem had been a good provincial mandarin in his time and had a reputation for great personal honesty, stubbornness and courage. Many talented young Vietnamese returned to Saigon from France in the first years of Diem's rule, captured by the ideal of building an independent nation of which they could be proud. In the end, these same people were dancing and singing in the streets of Saigon the day after Diem was overthrown and quietly butchered inside an American-made M113 personnel carrier.

Many reasons are offered for the sweeping hatred of Diem that characterized his final years. One is that he was a Roman Catholic in a non-Christian country. Another is that he was a ruthless dictator. And so on. There is some substance to all of these. But personally, I feel the biggest factor in the disenchantment of the Vietnamese people with the

Diem regime was his failure to do anything to change the French colonial system of administration. And this fatal flaw appears to be no less true of Diem's successors.

The old attachments to the French colonial way of doing things show themselves in interesting ways not only in South Viet Nam but in the communist North, as well.

I know a Frenchman, for example, who used to be the manager of Hanoi's swankiest hotel, the Metropole. In 1954, when the French were finally beaten and the Viet Minh was marching into Hanoi, my friend was still manager of the hotel.

The crisply uniformed French army stood at rigid attention, tears streaming from the cheeks of some officers, as the "Marseillaise" sounded and the *tricouleur* was hauled down for the last time. The ragged, poverty-stricken Viet Minh army straggled into Hanoi looking much more like a defeated mob of guerrillas than a force which had just won a brilliant victory over a powerful European army.

The Viet Minh looked terrible, and its leaders knew and resented the fact. Hanoi was to be kept looking as shiny as possible within the wretchedly poor capabilities of the new government of the Democratic Republic of Viet Nam. And, if only as a place to entertain foreign dignitaries, Ho Chi Minh wanted the Metropole Hotel kept at its best. It was immediately nationalized, of course, but my friend was asked to stay on under contract to the Hanoi regime to maintain the hotel.

Some things had to change. Capitalist tipping was halted. The hotel staff was organized into political cells, but polite and efficient service was rated high as a political virtue.

So the Metropole still looked good. The trouble was, the management could no longer get the imported luxuries that make a European hotel what it is. One of the first problems was tomato juice. North Viet Nam grows some tomatoes, and the government insisted they be used somehow to replace the French canned juice demanded by hotel patrons. The Vietnamese tried hard to make juice for the Metropole, but all their efforts failed. Tomato juice is tricky to make without the right machinery. Supplies of other left-over imports dwindled, hotel linen and furniture began to wear out, and decent liquor for the bar was no longer available. The Metropole's days as a great hotel were over, and my friend finally left North Viet Nam forever. Friends who can still go to Hanoi

(Canadians and Indians) tell me the Metropole is now a dingy third-rate place frequented only by down-at-the-heel Albanian junior diplomats and their like. But it still tries to keep up an attractive face.

Face, especially the French kind, is something vital to Vietnamese, and no Vietnamese likes to have his country thought of as being in any way backward or inferior to any other nation. There is nothing Vietnamese hate more than slurring references to the state of their development.

It was for exactly this reason that in 1967, Premier Ky demanded and got Northrup F-5 jet fighters for his air force. As Ky said at the time, he had no real need for jets (he had plenty of highly efficient propeller-driven fighter-bombers), but they were essential to maintaining Vietnamese face. After all, neighboring Cambodia and North Viet Nam had jet fighters, so why not South Viet Nam?

In his memoirs, one of Viet Nam's top old Bolsheviks, Bui Lam, mentions an incident in 1921 that I think is quite revealing.

In 1921 [Lam wrote], the French government held a colonial exhibition in Marseilles with a view to inducing the capitalists to invest more in the colonies in line with the policy of systematic exploitation of the colonies put forth by Albert Sarraut.

In this exhibition, shame was brought on the colonies: Viet Nam was represented by a rickshaw. But the French organizers were unable to find any Vietnamese who was willing to hire himself out as a rickshawman. In a film on Viet Nam there were scenes of children easing their bowels on beds and grown-ups calling dogs to jump up and eat the excrement.

Meanwhile, King Khai Dinh and Pham Quynh, who were visiting the French cities, kept chanting "their gratefulness for the civilizing and protecting country."

We [the Vietnamese Communist Party] were very angry, and time and again were about to set fire to the movie house. Right at that time, we read the articles criticizing the colonial exhibition, the policy of racial discrimination and of exploitation of

French colonialism. All these articles, dear to our hearts, were signed by Nguyen Ai Quock.

(Nguyen Ai Quoc, meaning more or less "Nguyen the Patriot," was one of the aliases of Ho Chi Minh, a name which also is an alias. The venerated president of the communist North was born Nguyen Sinh Cung (or Coong), changed his name at ten years old to Nguyen Tat Thanh, lived in France, Russia, America and various other countries as Nguyen Ai Quoc, signed articles written in French as "Lin," was known in China variously as Mr. Vuong, Ly Thuy and Wang Shan-er, and returned to Viet Nam to take charge of the whole communist movement as Ho Chi Minh, or, more familiarly, as "Bac Ho"—"Uncle Ho.")

Despite Vietnamese insistence on maintaining face, most of South Viet Nam's civilian politicians rely abjectly on foreigners to make progress.

During the Diem regime, most of his noncommunist political opponents took refuge abroad, especially in France. They used France as a base for churning out anti-Diem pamphlets and interviews to newsmen.

But in the eyes of many Vietnamese, Diem was brought down in the end by America. It therefore behooved the Vietnamese politician to do his stumping among Americans— American diplomats, military officers, scholars, newsmen and CIA agents. These were the people who made and broke governments in Saigon, not the Vietnamese people.

Thus, one sees a growing body of Vietnamese politicians living in Washington, lobbying endlessly with various American officials. They believe, and with considerable justification, that their chances of becoming Vietnamese leaders are better that way than by campaigning in Viet Nam.

After all, Diem lived abroad (including several years in the United States) before becoming president, and all his successors owed their positions mostly to American support.

The politicians who restrict their campaigning to Viet Nam alone rarely get anywhere. The election of November 1967 confirmed that point.

Despite these realities, one cannot help but view with a certain contempt the wealthy politicians who abandon their own people and lean on foreigners to step to power.

What, then, of the young officers who ruled Viet Nam after Diem?

Among them, Brigadier General Nguyen Cao Ky stood out most prominently.

When small, underdeveloped countries undergo political upheavals and military coups, it very often happens that the man with a few airplanes wins the day. Thus it was that the CIA was able to overturn the government of Guatemala in 1954 with a few Thunderbolt fighters.

And thus it was that Air Commodore Ky, commander of the South Vietnamese Air Force, came to power as the result of a coup on February 19, 1965. Ky did not engineer the coup, but he was quickly able to control it because of his air force.

Ky was born in 1931 in North Viet Nam. (It is a striking fact that many if not most of South Viet Nam's leaders, whether they be politicians, army officers, Buddhist monks or Catholic priests, diplomats or whatever, are from North Viet Nam. This fact is keenly resented by many South Vietnamese.)

Ky joined the French army and was graduated from their reserve officers' academy in Viet Nam in 1952. During the Indochina War, the French sent him to Marrakech in North Africa, where they taught him to fly and to know the difference between good wine and bad. He grew a mustache.

After Viet Nam became independent of France in 1954, Ky rose rapidly in the new Vietnamese air force. He was sent to the United States for advanced flight training in jets. While there, he learned to speak the jaunty English of the American and acquired a keen taste for cowboy movies, a taste he never lost.

At the age of thirty-three, he found himself in command of the Vietnamese air force and in a position to dictate terms to governments. He cut a dashing figure in black or orange flying coveralls with lavender scarf. His wives were all good looking, and fit decoratively in the rear seat of his private T28 fighter-bomber.

After assuming power, he remained as casual as ever in his chats with diplomats and newsmen, and some of the remarks he dropped reverberated throughout the world.

Once, for instance, he told a British reporter that his biggest hero was Hitler. There was a generally unfavorable public reaction to the remark, especially in England. I asked him if he would confirm that he really had said it. Ky replied that his remarks had created a false impression. He did not admire Hitler the man, he said, but merely the methods Hitler had used in uniting Germany.

Ky also delighted in shocking Washington. When someone in Washington said the United States sought peace with North Viet Nam, Ky would say he wanted to invade North Viet Nam and bomb Red China.

Like most of the other young Vietnamese officers, Ky hated former U.S. ambassador Taylor and sought whenever possible to embarrass him.

Ky undoubtedly had to swallow a lot of youthful pride when he stepped into second place in the military hierarchy behind the dour General Nguyen Van Thieu. The latter was named as President in November 1967, with Ky as Vice President.

Ky is a very agreeable young man. But he seems cut from the same mold as the dashing General De Castries, the commander of the French bastion at Dien Bien Phu when it fell to the Viet Minh.

Ambassador Lodge took Ky under his wing after Taylor left, treating the Premier "like my own son" and visiting him several times each day with advice and guidance. Ky and Lodge became good friends.

But in many Vietnamese eyes, and in my own, Ky remained more of a cowboy than a statesman.

Another of the more prominent young officers was Subbrigadier General Nguyen Chanh Thi, who very nearly became premier himself before being forced into exile with the other odd men out.

Thi, four years older than Ky, is a nervous little man whose eye twitched frequently when he was waiting to give speeches. He used to wear a red paratrooper beret and carry a swagger stick.

I got to know Thi in Phnom Penh, where he lived in exile after trying unsuccessfully to overthrow Ngo Dinh Diem with a coup on November 11, 1960.

Thi, a colonel at the time, commanded the Vietnamese paratroop brigade in 1960, and got to thinking about what it would be like to throw Diem out and set up a more forward-looking, modern government. On November 11, he ordered four paratroop battalions and some odds and ends of armor, heavy weapons companies and so on into Saigon. Thi's coup caught even Diem's secret police completely by surprise, because it had been planned so hastily. Thi quickly seized control of the whole city and placed his forces in an iron ring around Independence Palace. The coup appeared to have been a resounding success, and a lot of people who by this time were fed up with Diem were dancing in the streets.

But Thi had not planned ahead very far. In the years preceding Thi's coup, a variety of the Saigon intelligentsia-politicians began holding conspiratorial meetings in coffee shops and bars around town and began to form a kind of loose organization. They agreed on only one thing—that Diem must go—and that was what held them together. The secret police kept an eye on all of them, of course, but Diem never bothered to lock them up because he regarded them as harmless. This group began meeting most often at the plush bar on the eighth floor of the French-owned Caravelle Hotel, where it was convenient to meet and entertain visiting American officials, journalists, and other supposedly influential foreigners. Hence, the organization came to be known as "Les Caravellistes." Activist Colonel Thi had got himself tied up with this bunch.*

And it was to this group that he turned for political guidance after his troops had seized Saigon and placed Diem under what amounted to house arrest. Chaos and confusion immediately followed; the politicians were unable to give Thi any effective guidance, and he decided to try a parley with Diem himself.

At that point in the coup, another young officer, Brigadier General Nguyen Khanh, had taken an interest in the goings on but was not yet sure which way the wind was blowing.

(Khanh was destined for the top spot himself. In January 1964 he seized power in his own coup, and held on until ousted by Ky in February 1965. Khanh went into exile in Paris, where he settled down quietly with his wife and children.)

---

*The spokesman and over-all leader of the Caravellists was politician Tran Van Van. Van survived the Diem era and returned to politics after the 1963 coup. He strongly opposed the regime of General Ky, and in 1966 someone gunned him down. Van's widow charged that Ky's agents assassinated him.

Khanh sneaked through Thi's forces around the palace and got in by a back entrance ("I wasn't sure whether or not Diem was being attacked by the Viet Cong," Khanh said four years later), and offered his services to Diem, mainly as a negotiator with the rebels. Negotiations came to pass, and Diem went on the radio, promising that he would step down immediately in favor of a military junta to which he would be attached temporarily as an advisor.

Thi, the rebel forces and the politicians were more confused than ever, but Diem's promise sounded encouraging. The tank crews stretched out for siesta and lunch to wait out developments.

Developments were not long in coming. A day later, army units loyal to Diem roared into Saigon from the Mekong Delta, and the bloodshed began. In bitter fighting throughout the city, the loyalists pushed the understrength rebels back and back, the siege of the palace was lifted, Thi and a dozen other rebel officers commandeered a transport plane and escaped to Cambodia, and the coup was over.

A lot of the Saigon intelligentsia were rounded up and shipped off to Poulo Condore after that, and some were badly tortured in Saigon's secret jails (one of which, unknown to any outsider at the time, was right in the middle of the Saigon zoo near the lion house. It was called "P42," and some pretty terrible things happened there. Confinement in P42 was a valuable credential after Diem was overthrown, and a number of old P42 inmates now hold important jobs).

While Thi was in Cambodia after his attempted coup, he was a beaten and impoverished man. I took him to dinner once in a while, and good food and beer made him more cheerful. He and some of the other exiled 1960 rebels lived better after young Lieutenant Cu bombed the Saigon palace and flew to Phnom Penh. Cu, who spoke excellent English, could at least make a comfortable living teaching. Cu's little English school prospered and was soon earning enough money to support some of the rebels who had arrived earlier, including Thi. It was obviously galling to Thi to have to accept charity from a man in his twenties, six military grades his junior, but there was no choice.

Somehow, all political figures in South Viet Nam seem linked in an endless chain.

While Thi and his paratrooper comrades were in exile in

Cambodia, the Diem government finally got around to trying them *in absentia* for treason and rebellion. Thi was sentenced to death—a sentence that obviously was dropped after Diem was overthrown.

But in that trial, eleven of the absent officers, including Thi, were represented by lawyer Truong Dinh Dzu. Dzu, whose office was down Rue Pasteur a few doors from mine, often used to talk to foreign newsmen and diplomats about his opposition to the Diem regime, and the trial attracted even more attention to him. Eventually he got into trouble himself, and was jailed on the charge of passing a bad check.

This same Dzu got back into politics after Diem was overthrown, and attracted international attention in September 1967 by running against Generals Thieu and Ky as a peace candidate. His ticket came in a surprisingly close second, and a few weeks later he was jailed on the bad-check charge.

At that, he was probably lucky. Another of my politician neighbors, dentist Hoang Co Binh, was driving home in his Volkswagen one evening (or, rather, being driven; dentists rate chauffeurs in Viet Nam, even if they own only Volkswagens) when a large car forced him off the road. As Binh's car stopped, the occupants of the large car blasted it with a submachine gun. Binh's driver was critically wounded, and he was cut up. The assailants were almost certainly not Viet Cong.

During his Cambodian exile, Thi plunged himself into political reading, plotting, and doing almost anything to keep his sanity. He got interested in the propaganda being sent from France by Dr. Pham Huy Co (whom I have described earlier in this chapter), and he helped set up the leaflet bomb campaign in Saigon. He also claimed to have regular contact with officers still in Saigon who were planning a new coup. But in fact, Thi had nothing to do with the 1963 coup. He came back to Viet Nam, and the man who had once served as mediator between him and Diem was now his boss. Khanh sent him as far north as possible, gave him a division to command (a safe 400 miles from Saigon), and eventually promoted him to subbrigadier general.

Thi took his command seriously and remained loyal to Khanh, making a show of supporting Khanh during several attempted coups.

But Thi, a Central Vietnamese himself, was establishing

himself as potentate of what amounted to an independent Central Viet Nam. He cemented ties with powerful Buddhist organizations in the frequently rebellious city of Hue. He made himself enormously popular with student groups and academic leaders at Hue University, a stronghold of political activity. He won the support of many members of the Dai Viet and the Viet Nam Quoc Dan Dang (VNQDD) parties, two of the more important splinter groups.

Most important, he made friends with Lieutenant General Lewis W. Walt, who at the time commanded the U.S. Marines in Viet Nam. Walt's headquarters was at Da Nang, a city in Thi's domain, and his friendship was important.

After Khanh was thrown out in 1965, Thi drifted rapidly away from the central government in Saigon and its new boss, General Ky.

Inevitably, antigovernment rioting broke out in Hue, Da Nang, Quang Tri, Quang Ngai and other Central Vietnamese cities.

Thi, who had captured the admiration of most of the people in the area with his sometimes hilarious and often moving speeches, became the natural leader of the insurrection. Da Nang's mayor, who had been appointed by Ky himself, rebelled against Ky and refused to move against the revolt. By the spring of 1966, Central Viet Nam was again a separate nation.

Once again, the U.S. cultural library in Hue was sacked and burned, and rebel troops actually shelled American military facilities at Da Nang. American civilians were evacuated from Hue, along with the U.S. Counsul there. In effect, America broke relations with the secession.

But General Walt, who had remained Thi's friend, prevented things from getting completely out of hand. At one point, Walt walked out onto a vital bridge in Da Nang that rebel troops were about to blow up. The bridge carried supplies for the Da Nang Air Base without which raids against North Viet Nam would have been hampered. The troops ordered Walt off the bridge. He refused. In the end, the rebels let the bridge stand.

Eventually, Ky was strong enough to undercut the rebels, and the Central Vietnamese insurrection collapsed. Thi's many American friends secured a safe-conduct for him, and he left the country for another long period of exile. He

moved to Virginia, which is conveniently close to the source
of Vietnamese political power—Washington.

I could draw many more profiles of Vietnamese officers
and their leadership potential, but I see no point in confusing
the reader with more names and chaotic history.

Suffice it to say that a number of Vietnamese officers
have proved effective and popular warlords in the regions
they commanded. This, unfortunately, has not qualified them
as effective national leaders. The sense of regionalism that
made many of them effective as local leaders worked against
them in the virtually impossible task of pulling the nation as a
whole together. It is hard for me to imagine a real Vietnamese
statesman emerging from the officer corps, and I make no
exception of the President elected in 1967, General Thieu.

As I have implied, the civilian politicians in South Viet
Nam are scarcely more prepossessing than the military.

One of the great problems is the lack of any party with
sufficient money and strength to form a real national organization. Without Western-style parties there can be no Western-
style parliamentary democracy.

Various American missions have toyed with building up
both the Dai Viet and the VNQDD as major parties, but
these efforts have led to little change.

Meanwhile, the elite kept one foot always abroad.
Vietnamese businessmen continued to invest most of their
risk capital abroad rather than develop South Vietnamese
resources; the sons and daughters of any family wealthy
enough to buy an exit visa and a one-way ticket continued to
leave the country in swarms. The mark of real success in
South Viet Nam was being able to leave it.

Prospects were that South Viet Nam's leadership would
continue to change by coup, not democratic process. Saigon
and the other large cities are not likely to be free of the stink
of tear gas and gunpowder smoke for many years to come.

Luckily for its residents, Saigon has learned over the
years to clean itself up rapidly after each eruption of violence.

When prisoners are shot by firing squad on the sidewalk
in front of the National Railways Building, a fire truck is
always on hand to hose things down the instant the body is
cut from its post. Within a minute or two, the hoses wash
every trace of blood from the sidewalk and post.

Within two days after the bloody 1963 coup, municipal

tree surgeons were out patching up the huge tamarind trees lining Rue Pasteur and Cong Ly Street. Many had been badly splintered by shellfire and bullets in the assault on the presidential palace. The palace itself, which was badly damaged, looked as fresh as new in a few weeks.

Unfortunately, statesmen cannot be tidied up as quickly as sidewalks, trees and palaces.

In discussing South Viet Nam's political and military figures, its "cream," so to speak, I have so far neglected to mention one Saigon politician who caused the United States more trouble by far than any other.

In himself, he seemed no more distinguished than the other dabblers in coffeehouse politics along the Rue Catinat (Tu Do) in Saigon. A lawyer, he got involved in anti-French peace groups in the 1950s, and was jailed for leading a demonstration in March 1950 against a good-will visit to Saigon by some American warships. The French kept him locked up for two years, without trial.

He may have been briefly jailed in 1958 in South Viet Nam's provincial capital at Tuy Hoa for getting a girl in trouble. In any case, the Diem government never regarded him as anyone to worry about.

Nguyen Huu Tho, born on August 10, 1910, in Vinh Long Province in the Mekong Delta, never impressed the outer world very much until they learned that he was Chairman of the Central Committee of the National Front for the Liberation of South Viet Nam—the number-one man in the Viet Cong.

There was one big difference between Tho and the other Saigon politicians.

The others, for the most part, had to rely on their own pocketbooks and personal attraction to keep themselves politically afloat. They chose to head their own tiny splinter groups rather than subordinate themselves to one or two really powerful parties.

Tho, on the other hand, chose to ally himself with the most powerful political organization in Asia. No doctrinaire Marxist himself, he nevertheless saw in the communists a force that could win. And he has not wanted for expert advice and every kind of assistance.

14

MAT TRAN GIAI PHONG

The four Vietnamese words in the title of this chapter are the name of America's enemy in Viet Nam. They mean Liberation Front and are a shortened form of the full and official name, which is *Mat Tran Dan Toc Giai Phong Mien Nam Viet Nam*, or *People's Liberation Front of South Viet Nam*.

Probably not one American in a hundred thousand has ever seen or heard the words *Mat Tran Giai Phong;* it is fitting that in a war in which we know very little about our enemy, we don't even know his proper name.

News writers often seek to enlighten us with a cliché explanation that "the National Liberation Front is the political arm of the Viet Cong." The errors embodied in this phrase are not the result of mere ignorance of the enemy's organization; they create a wrong impression of the entire character of the war.

In the first place, National Liberation Front is an inaccurate translation of the name. Secondly, Viet Cong is merely a propaganda name for the enemy, invented by the Saigon Information Ministry and generally accepted by Americans. To describe the one as "the political arm" of the other is a tautological absurdity.

But the real point is that "the political arm" of the enemy is the most important part of him; a more fitting anatomical analogy would be to describe the Liberation Front as the total enemy, with its political Central Committee as its head and nervous system.

The teeth and claws of the enemy are his regular soldiers, and these are what Americans generally think of as Viet Cong, forgetting that even the name Viet Cong, short for "Vietnamese communist," has a primarily political sense.

All this may strike the reader as quibbling over words. I think it is not. The key reason America has done so badly in Viet Nam is that it has insisted on dealing only with the enemy's teeth and claws, not its brain.

It is the total enemy that I shall describe here.

Americans tend to think of the enemy in terms of a handful of its famous leaders.

But the backbone of the Vietnamese communist movement is not Ho Chi Minh, Pham Van Dong, Vo Nguyen Giap, Nguyen Huu Tho, or any of the other worldly Bolsheviks of another generation. It is the Vietnamese peasant, sturdy and conservative in his ways, who is a courageous and intelligent fighter, provided he trusts his leaders.

Ho and the other top communist theoreticians have been saying exactly this all along, but neither their followers nor their enemies entirely believe them. To a Vietnamese communist, Ho is only a little lower than the angels. To many an American counterinsurgent, Ho is a fiendish genius sitting up in Hanoi, pulling the strings of a dirty war. To my mind, both these views fall short of the truth.

This is not to say that the reigning communist intellectuals are not important to the movement or do not control it. Regular visitors to Hanoi who also are old Moscow and Peking hands have told me that the degree of control the top communists of North Viet Nam have over their country makes even the regimes of Stalin and Mao look like "pseudo-liberal, counter-revolutionary deviationism."

I must pause here to inflict a little history on the reader. The Viet Cong, like all other organizations, developed from its historical forerunners, and did not hatch full-blown in 1959 to goad the United States.

Since the turn of this century various revolutionary Vietnamese groups have been active. For that matter, Vietnamese revolutionary tradition predates the time of Christ, and many revolutionary heroes still remembered in poetry, holidays, and by street names in Saigon date back that far. Vietnamese have at various times fought Chinese, Mongols, Khmers, Chams, Japanese, French, Americans, and, most of all, other Vietnamese. The history of the Indochina Peninsula (the two Viet Nams, Cambodia, Laos, Thailand and Burma) makes even the Balkans look peaceful by comparison.

The French colonized Viet Nam in the mid-nineteenth

century and thus inadvertently gave birth to modern Vietnamese communism. France provided at the same time a target of fairly universal hatred and a capital in which the revolutionaries could get organized. Paris itself became the cradle of Vietnamese insurrection. It still plays an important role.

There were several reasons for this. For one thing, while French colonial policies have often been extremely repressive, a much looser rein was kept on people from the colonies visiting France itself. A Vietnamese revolutionary was generally much safer from the hands of secret police in Paris than he was in Hanoi or Saigon. The same has been true to a large extent of Algerians and other French colonials.

A second and more important reason is that communism itself is fundamentally a European doctrine. First codified by Marx, a German, it spread in Europe and came to full bloom in Russia. Not until relatively late in the game did it make inroads into Asia, where it underwent some big changes from its original form.

Communism in one form or another was a big political force in the industrial cities of France from the early nineteenth century onward. After World War I, communism swept through Europe, and the great factories around Paris came to be known as "the Red Belt." Ho Chi Minh, the son of a rural doctor, had spent most of his youth drifting around the world doing odd jobs, such as serving as a cook's helper on the French steamship line Chargeurs Reunis. He arrived in Paris just after the war, joined the mushrooming French Communist Party, and earned a living as a photographic technician while learning the arts of party organizing and churning out communist propaganda.

Ho rose rapidly, and his history from then on is too well known to record here. But the point is, all his initial organizational work was in Paris, to which he generally returned after sojourns in the Soviet Union and China.

There has been a large Vietnamese colony in Paris for many years. Most of the Asians you see there are Vietnamese, and if you notice such things, several times a day you will see the Vietnamese *ao-dai* worn by women as you stroll around. There are great numbers of good Vietnamese restaurants in Paris, the only city outside Viet Nam I know of in which one can buy Vietnamese food.

Thousands of Vietnamese are permanent residents of

Paris, but the biggest continuing influx is in the form of students. For this reason, the largest Vietnamese concentrations are in the cheap student quarters of the Left Bank and around the various university facilities.

At one time, Vietnamese communist headquarters in Paris operated quite openly, with a sign on the door describing it as such.

Eventually, the *Deuxième Bureau* got around to closing this hotbed of revolution, so it had to go underground. The headquarters is now a floating operation, but most often is set up in a garage building of which the garage itself is the front. I have not ventured inside this building (I would not be welcome), but I have many Vietnamese friends who are or have been regular visitors there. Since this garage is currently the source of a lot of America's troubles in Southeast Asia, I think it is worth further description.

A Vietnamese student arriving in Paris is apt to speak rather imperfect French. He (or she) probably lacks adequate warm clothing for the bitter academic winter. He is almost always hard up, at a loss to find some place to live, disgusted with the fare served at third-rate French restaurants and eager for a bowl of good Vietnamese *pho*, and extremely lonely. Paris is a cold and lonely place for any poor stranger to the city.

But the student is not likely to remain in this predicament long. Within a few days, one or two friendly Vietnamese students who know all the ropes are likely to come calling on him. If he asks them how they happened to know he was here and why they are doing him this kindness, he is apt to get a rather vague answer. But these host-students and others he will meet will be to him the most solid friends he could want. They will help him find a part-time job, they will give him small loans, they will make sure he has a decent place to live and knows all the good Vietnamese restaurants, they will invite him to their homes to meet other nice young Vietnamese, and they will eventually suggest that he come to eat at the garage.

Having learned that the garage (or whatever place is currently in use) is a clandestine meeting place, the student may have some misgivings about going there. But he is in for a very pleasant surprise. There are no grim, bearded Bolsheviks inside, and no apparent conspiracy. The rooms are bright and cheerful and filled with young people like himself. There are reading rooms; there is a pleasant common room where there may be a pretty young girl strumming a guitar, two other students bending over a chessboard, and others chatting and laughing. Everyone treats him as an esteemed friend, and nothing could be less sinister. It is a joy to hear the singsong patter of Vietnamese instead of French for a change, and the whole thing is warming.

The big surprise comes in the community dining room, where the meal is cheap but tasty. The waiters themselves are all students, most of them advanced post graduates in medicine, law and letters—the very elite of students.

In Viet Nam, such a thing is unheard of. The student, or rather, scholar, has a special place in Vietnamese society, and it is unthinkable that he would lower himself by serving food to other people. In old-fashioned, cultured Vietnamese families it is still the pattern for the husband to spend his days over his books, learned articles and poetry, while the wife earns the living and tends the home fires. The Vietnamese husband does not generally help his wife with any household chores, except in very modern families. But here, the fledgling doctors, lawyers and poets are also waiters!

The student is at first thrown for a loss as to how to address these waiters. Obviously, you can't yell "Boy!" when you want another bowl of rice, nor does it seem quite right to yell "Please, sir." But one quickly learns from the others to call the waiters *Dong Chi*—"Comrade." The student has learned his first political lesson from the garage: There are to be no distinctions of class in addressing other people in the new club.

He will get to know the waiters later, and they will always be friendly and helpful to him, treating him as a complete equal, despite their elevated academic caste.

Time passes, and the student may become a regular part of the community house. He will be exposed to a certain amount of communist teaching from his comrades, and he will probably participate in the lively and interesting "discussion groups" and "cultural night." But no political pressure of any kind will be brought to bear on him, and the talk will be friendly, free discussion and argument. No badgering or hard sell.

If the student likes the way things are done here, and if

his studies (and political attitudes) mature, he may eventually find himself as one of the waiters or group leaders. He has been closely watched the whole time, and appointments like this are made carefully. When the student's education reaches a certain level of attainment, he begins to come under extremely close scrutiny by the permanent officers of the fraternity. Questions about patriotism and the belief in the golden future of Viet Nam (North) begin to come up, and the student is shown some very interesting pamphlets. It seems that a doctor enjoys a lot of privileges in Hanoi.

Besides the opportunity of serving a growing nation, he will be provided by the state with a comfortable villa, he will get liberal food ration allowances, his children, if they are worthy, will have excellent education facilities, and he may even be entitled to a motorcar (or, more often, a motor scooter).

For engineers, lawyers, chemists, and all the other professionals, there are other blandishments.

"You are Vietnamese, and your place is not in imperialist France, but in the Vietnamese fatherland," the student is told. "You don't want to go back to the slavery of South Viet Nam, do you? Do you want to be drafted into the army of the U.S. lackeys and have your fine education spent as cannon fodder in a dirty war against our patriotic compatriots? Of course not. Why don't you come to Hanoi and join the people? You can always leave, if you don't like it."

The student may or may not take up the offer. If he does, he is apt to find that he does have special advantages, and while North Viet Nam is pretty threadbare, he gets the best of what there is. He may also leave Hanoi to go abroad, but he is not likely to do so because he is fed up. He leaves because he has reached the degree of trust that he can be safely sent once again into the land of the Philistines. He may go to France as a recruiting officer or party organizer. Or he may merely pass through France on his way to South Viet Nam, for a very special kind of work.

The South Vietnamese embassy in Paris also has occasional dealings with students, mostly of an unpleasant character. The embassy there frequently poses problems involving red tape and restrictions on currency exchange that students find aggravating.

A number of students were stunned one day on receiving invitations to dinner at the South Vietnamese embassy on the occasion of the South Vietnamese national day. The Vietnamese ambassador was no friend of the students, and this gesture seemed like Scrooge sending Tiny Tim a turkey. But most of the invitees came to the dinner, dressed in their Sunday best and ready to bury the hatchet.

The ambassador arrived, got them together in the reception hall, and gave them the most blistering tongue-lashing they had heard yet. The themes included squandering their parents' money, wasting the resources of their government, and other related subjects. Afterward, they all went into the dining room, gulped down their food in silence, and hurried off—some of them for a friendly coffee at the good old garage. That dinner is still remembered with bitterness by a lot of former Vietnamese students. The next year, the ambassador sent out the same invitations, but almost no one showed up.

Ho began in the early 1920s by sharing his meager supplies of rice and salted fish with the Vietnamese sailors and students who used to visit him in his room in Paris. There was always a spare mat in the room for anyone who had no place to sleep. Ho's successors have continued this tradition. My Vietnamese-Parisian friends tell me that 90 per cent of the Vietnamese colony in France is sympathetic to the Viet Cong and helps the movement in little or large ways. This may be an exaggeration, and I have no way of knowing. But on the basis of what I have seen, it sounds not unreasonable.

This does not mean, necessarily, that the Vietnamese communist in Paris is ready to take up a machine gun against the American imperialists.

It is a long way from the cafés of Boulevard St. Germain des Pres to the jungles of South Viet Nam. I know a young married couple, for instance, who met and married as students in Paris, got interested in the garage, and talked the toughest Viet Cong line most of their friends had ever heard. They were regarded as among the toughest young revolutionaries in Paris.

But a few years after Diem came to power in Saigon, they both returned to the homeland—not Hanoi, but Saigon. The husband joined Diem's semisecret political party, became a good, solid "Personalist" (the political philosophy Diem ascribed to his regime), and got a post in a thriving government business in exchange. The couple rapidly prospered, and the old days (and talk) in Paris were forgotten in favor of more practical considerations.

This couple has been in trouble with the military governments that followed Diem, and the husband, under suspicion of flagrant corruption, has lost his job. But they have salted away enough to live for a long time with no further income, and they can always go back to Paris if things get too bad.

But Paris remains Uncle Ho's revolutionary garden, and he expects a certain amount of chaff along with the wheat. Paris is also the best of all possible rear bases for the Vietnamese communist movement, and is likely to improve with the current rapprochement between Paris and Peking.

Vietnamese are not always able to freewheel in Paris. After the French military collapse at Dien Bien Phu, a lot of my Vietnamese friends who lived in Paris at the time started carrying switchblade knives. There had been a series of wild Vietnamese celebration parties, and discharged French veterans of the Indochina campaign took to beating up any Vietnamese they came across in the streets.

But times like that are rare.

Let me change the scene to Phnom Penh, the capital of Cambodia, a picturesque and lively little city of 600,000, and a kind of exquisite miniature of Saigon. The absolute ruler of Cambodia is a hot-tempered and brilliant young prince of the blood named Norodom Sihanouk.

In 1953, a year before Ho's Viet Minh defeated the French in battle, Sihanouk drove his own bargain with France and won independence for his tiny country without ever getting deeply involved in the war.

America started pouring military and other aid into Thailand, Cambodia's western neighbor, and South Viet Nam, Cambodia's eastern neighbor. It happens that both these neighbors have been mortal enemies of Cambodia since the beginning of recorded history, and Cambodians still fear and dislike both the Thais and Vietnamese. Both have taken healthy bites out of the old Khmer (Cambodian) empire, which, during the Middle Ages, was one of the greatest and most powerful empires in Southeast Asia. The old Khmer capital of Angkor Wat was built at that time, and its ruins still are among the great architectural treasures of the world.

Sihanouk claims linear descent from the builders of mighty Angkor, and has tried hard to preserve what little there is left of his nation. Cambodia's colonial relations with France were much more cordial than those between France and the other Indochina colonies. A primary reason was that France prevented both Thailand and South Viet Nam from taking some more bites out of Cambodia. Sihanouk has not forgotten this historic fact. A highly cultivated man of parts who writes and acts in plays, composes music and captains sports clubs, Sihanouk sees himself as a combination Henry VIII and Charles de Gaulle.

He elected to keep his nation neutral after winning independence, and steadfastly turned down American overtures to him to join the Southeast Treaty Alliance (SEATO). Sihanouk wanted no part of an outfit one of whose leading members was Thailand.

Increasingly, Sihanouk has leaned ever closer to the communist bloc, particularly to China. While his main economic ties are with France (Sihanouk threw the American AID Mission out in 1963), Cambodia is now receiving a certain amount of military hardware from China. He also reminds the Western powers from time to time, "If Cambodia is invaded, we are small, but six hundred million Chinese stand behind us."

Despite Sihanouk's dislike of all Vietnamese, North or South, it is no longer possible for him to turn a cold shoulder to Hanoi. There are obvious political reasons for this, but there is also an interesting ethnological reason.

Only about one third of the inhabitants of Phnom Penh, the Cambodian capital, are Cambodians. Another third of the city is Vietnamese and the remaining third is Chinese. Only Cambodians can hold public office, and public officeholders may not marry Vietnamese or Chinese. But the Vietnamese and Chinese have the lion's share of economic wealth in the city. Just as in Paris, the Communists have been the most active in organizing the Vietnamese and Chinese. Nearly all the Chinese schools in Phnom Penh are run by Peking communists, and all the Chinese and Vietnamese newspapers are communist. (This despite the fact that the Cambodian Communist Party has been outlawed and practically wiped out by Sihanouk.) Therefore, Sihanouk has a powerful Viet Cong headquarters right in his front yard which could make terrible trouble for him if it chose.

All this means that Phnom Penh is now the major

forward base of operations for the Viet Cong. Less than a hundred miles from the center of the Vietnamese war, it is a good place to print leaflets and newspapers to be sent into Viet Nam.

There are continuing reports that significant shipments of arms and ammunition are reaching the Viet Cong through Cambodia.

The North Vietnamese legation in Phnom Penh now occupies one of the largest buildings in town and hums with activity. (It took the building over from the Chinese communist embassy, which needed larger quarters.)

Cambodia is geographically relatively large, but it has fewer than six million inhabitants, which gives it one of the lowest population densities in Asia. In simpler terms, it is full of wide open spaces (especially along its frontier with South Viet Nam) where unusual activities can be carried on without attracting official notice. These activities include Viet Cong operations.

At this point, I shall switch to Viet Nam and the Liberation Front proper, skipping over Laos, much of which is now openly controlled by the Viet Cong (or their Pathet Lao assistants) and which can no longer be considered a foreign base for the Liberation Front. It is part of communist Viet Nam.

In 1954, South Viet Nam was a nation in anarchy. Powerful private armies roamed the nation and even controlled Saigon. A band of river pirates formed a secret society called the Binh Xuyen, organized a formidable fighting force, took over Saigon's police, established a syndicate dealing in narcotics, prostitution and many other things, and turned Saigon into the vice capital of Asia.

In the 1920s, several Vietnamese religions were invented by local prophets—ostensibly to promote spiritual belief, but actually for use as covers for underground military organizations being used against the French.

One of these got started in a village named Hoa Hao not far from the Cambodian border. The new religion called itself a denomination of Buddhism and came to be called Phat Giao Hoa Hao, meaning Hoa Hao Buddhists, or Hoa Hao for short. Hoa Hao men grew their hair to their shoulders, preached the pure and simple life, and began arming themselves. One of their most prominent and colorful military leaders was Ba Cut, a Christlike-looking man who could handle a Tommy gun well, had a beautiful young wife he had kidnaped out of a private school, and who claimed he was immortal. The Hoa Hao movement grew like lightning and became the scourge of the upper Mekong Delta. In the early 1950s, Hoa Hao claimed a million followers, and this may not have been much of an exaggeration. The movement is still very strong.

Another faith called Cao Dai also got started in the 1920s. Its prophet, a colonial province chief named Ngo Van Chieu, was a French-trained intellectual. He used to sit each night in his home holding seances in which he claimed to be in communication with the departed spirit of Victor Hugo. The ghost of the French master would dictate mystical poetry to the prophet during these seances, which the prophet dutifully transcribed. Victor Hugo, Sun Yat-sen (the leader of the revolutionary Young China movement) and an ancient classical Vietnamese poet became the three leading saints of Cao Daiism. The religion merged elements of Buddhism, Confucianism, Taoism and Christianity, recognizing the teachings of all four faiths.

Grotesquely impressive pink and green Cao Dai temples went up in areas where the faith took hold, and followers worshiped before gigantic images of human eyes. The Cao Dai cathedral in Tay Ninh is something a sight-seer should not neglect, if he can manage to get through the Viet Cong checkpoints on the road from Saigon. There are huge plaster serpents with neon lights for eyes, exotic tableaus of the steps to heaven, and other attractions.

But the important part about Cao Dai was its army— several regiments in strength, and magnificently trained and armed. The Cao Dai army held complete sway in several populous provinces in the early 1950s, crushing both French and Viet Minh units that ventured into the Cao Dai Holy See. The French later succeeded in making a deal with the Cao Dais which kept the Viet Minh out of the Cao Dai area until the end of the Indochina War.

Besides the Cao Dai, the Hoa Hao and the Binh Xuyen, there were many other groups challenging Saigon authority when Diem took over. There was a large residuum of the Viet Minh organization itself which elected to stay in South Viet Nam rather than go north to the new Democratic Republic of

Viet Nam. There were intellectuals, professionals and old-time revolutionaries from the Dai Viet Party, the Vietnamese Kuomintang (VNQDD), and many others who wanted no part of Diem. Unfortunately for themselves, they wanted no part of each other, either.

Diem moved swiftly. He crushed the Binh Xuyen in a pitched battle between his fledgling army and its troops. He cracked down hard on the Cao Dai, and most of its leaders fled to Cambodia. He tried repeatedly to make a deal with Ba Cut, leader of the Hoa Haos, giving Ba Cut a regular commission in the army in exchange for his allegiance.

Ba Cut repeatedly double-crossed Diem, however, so Diem launched Operation Nguyen Hue against the Hoa Haos. Ba Cut was captured in 1957 and publicly guillotined.

Political parties opposing Diem were more or less outlawed, and a lot of their top leaders were locked up or exiled.

By 1958, Diem was in undisputed control of South Viet Nam. The private armies were gone, the dangerous political opponents were neutralized, the streets of Saigon were quiet and more or less free of grenades, and it looked as if Diem had won some peace for his nation.

But as it turned out, this was only a respite. None of the old fighting political organizations had been crushed completely, but had merely been forced to go underground. In later years, American advisors were to cross swords repeatedly with Hoa Hao guerrilla units, under the impression they were fighting Viet Cong.

My reason in going back over this history is to show that there were many groups in South Viet Nam in addition to a lot of peasants and, of course, the communists, who remained violently opposed to Diem. All that was needed to harness a lot of this revolutionary talent into a single channel was some overridingly persuasive new political organization. That organization was not long in forming. It was the National Liberation Front.

The Front began to take shape in 1959. It purported to be all things to all people and, from the beginning, was made up of many dependent front organizations. There was no mention of communism in any of the early organizational work done by the Front, and its leaders made a point of bringing clergymen of all faiths even into the central committee.

A parenthetical note on the relations between Vietnamese comunism and religion:

Ho Chi Minh and all his top deputies are old-line communist purists. Ho is currently the dean of international communist revolutionaries (he was born May 19, 1889), and he believes in the Marxist dogma that "religion is the opiate of the people." Nevertheless, he and the others have maintained a certain show of religious tolerance. Even the Roman Catholic Cathedral in Hanoi still stands, and Vietnamese priests officiate there at masses. The cathedral is kept locked up most of the time, and foreign priests are never allowed into North Viet Nam to see what really is going on. But for other visitors, the façade is still there.

At any rate, the fronts included one each for farmers, workers, women, students, professionals, artists and writers, journalists, soldiers (government), clergymen, each of the racial minority groups, and so on. Each front has its own specialized agitprop organization for recruiting and indoctrination.

For government soldiers, the propaganda was particularly interesting. As in all communist-front organizations, the very first precept is class warfare, and a close second is the battle against foreign imperialism. These two themes tie together neatly for use on Vietnamese soldiers. The line to the soldier is this:

"You are a man of the people. You have never had any money, and your family is poor. While you are out spilling your intestines, your commander is probably in Saigon, dressed in white dinner jacket, drinking champagne and watching a Paris fashion show at the Caravelle Hotel [this has happened] or playing tennis with the U.S. ambassador [this also has happened]. You are continually oppressed by your officers, all of whom were trained by both the French and American imperialists.

"As a Vietnamese patriot, you have two duties: to fight for the destruction of a feudal class system that keeps you chained to misery, and to throw out the foreigners and their lackeys who perpetuate this system.

"In the People's Army, there is no class. There is military discipline, but your officer is your comrade and your brother. What you must do and bear, he must also do and bear. We work and fight together, live together, eat together.

"If you cannot join us, your compatriots, you must at least not fight us. To fight the People's Army is a crime against your own flesh and blood."

This approach is not always successful, but it has demonstrated a powerful appeal.* It has done much to undermine the fighting spirit of Vietnamese units. American advisors are constantly exasperated by army units that fail to seek out the enemy, avoid contact, and break off contact if by chance it is established. Without conscription, the Vietnamese army would collapse, and the unwilling Vietnamese draftee does not make the most energetic soldier in the world.

All these fronts began to take form in 1958 and 1959, and the first flickering of guerrilla resistance to the Diem regime began to be felt. The Saigon government saw a familiar hand behind these troublemakers, and the propaganda ministry invented a new and presumably derisive name for them. They were to be called henceforth in all Saigon references as the "Vietnamese Communists," or, in Vietnamese, "Viet Cong." The name stuck, although the rebels themselves have never used it.

Front activity spread rapidly, recruiting heavily from all the anti-Diem factions and picking up as many peasants as possible.

The main leaders of the front movement were southerners, but they soon were joined by expert advisors in both political and military matters sent down from Hanoi. These advisors kept trickling in. At present, there probably are almost as many "advisors" from Hanoi working with the Viet Cong as there are American advisors working for the Saigon government. A key difference between these opposing groups of foreign advisors is that the overwhelming bulk of Americans are regular army men, while the advisors from Hanoi are mostly political organizers who may also be military tacticians.

Hanoi also sent regular guerrilla troops, of course, but for the most part they operated on their own, not integrated with southern Viet Cong outfits. The North Vietnamese fighting units, which began infiltrating into South Viet Nam

---

*The Viet Cong calls its propaganda campaign within the ranks of Saigon's armed forces "Binh Van." Douglas Pike, the leading official American student of Viet Cong organizations, described *Binh Van* as "the most deadly weapon in the Viet Cong arsenal" in his excellent study, *Viet Cong, The Organization and Techniques of the National Liberation Front of South Viet Nam*, M.I.T. Press.

only in 1965, fought mostly in the sparsely populated central highlands and the northern part of South Viet Nam. The heavily populated Mekong Delta and Saigon area were left mostly to the Viet Cong, and assisted by advisors from Hanoi.

From the first few thousand members, the fronts grew rapidly until on December 20, 1960, a national congress of front organizers was convened and formally proclaimed the *Mat Tran Giai Phong*.

The headquarters of the new national front had to be kept secret and floating because of the danger of Saigon raids. But from the beginning the front controlled certain "Liberated Zones"—the Do Xa region in the High Plateau, the D Zone jungles north of Saigon, C Zone in northern Tay Ninh Province along the Cambodian frontier, the U Minh Forest near the southern tip of Viet Nam, and so on. Big meetings could be held in these base areas without the slightest danger of serious interference.

The National Liberation Front quickly formed a central committee and a presidium (or politburo), of which lawyer Nguyen Huu Tho was chairman from the beginning. Another key member of the first presidium was a Paris-educated doctor named Phung Van Cung. A former executive of the old Vietnamese communist Democratic Party, Tran Buu Kim, sat on the politburo.

But Western intelligence specialist speculate that the greatest power in the Viet Cong politburo belongs to its secretary-general, a former mathematics teacher named Nguyen Van Hieu. Hieu is certainly the best-known Viet Cong leader outside South Viet Nam. Besides his politburo duties, he is a kind of shadow foreign minister and ambassador without portfolio for the Front, lecturing and attending ceremonies in Indonesia, Czechoslovakia, East Germany, the Soviet Union, China, and other communist or nonaligned countries. He seems to get in and out of South Viet Nam without difficulty, using the various standard infiltration routes, of which there are thousands. South Viet Nam's frontiers are leaky as a sieve, and probably always will be unless someone decides to station several mission sentries continuously along their vast length. Even then, I suspect the frontiers would leak.

Names of all the executives of the National Liberation Front are published and updated regularly by the Front, and there is nothing secret about them. The members of all its committees also are published. I won't bore the reader with a lot of meaningless names, but suffice it to say that each of the committees of the Front leadership is actually a shadow ministry, complete with secretariats, departments and all the other paraphernalia of communist bureaucracy. These shadow ministries function in the jungle, of course, but they still need some of the usual trappings. The Viet Cong makes a point of seizing government typewriters and filing cabinets in its raids.

Similar committees organized by Ho Chi Minh during the Indochina War emerged later as ministries in Hanoi, and this is the same pattern being applied in South Viet Nam.

Along with the development of the National Front committees came the extension of the organization downward, in the form of provincial and district committees. Each subdivision was given an administrative structure patterned after the national committees.

One of the most important of the national committees, the one with which America has been chiefly concerned, is the "People's Self-Defense Armed Forces Committee," or war ministry. It is really this committee and its fighting forces that most Americans think of when they speak of the Viet Cong.

The central army committee is directly in charge of the Viet Cong's "main force" guerrillas, their counterpart of the regular army. These forces operate nationally and are generally involved in the really big fights.

The war ministry is also linked with the Viet Cong's hundreds of thousands of "paramilitary" troops but does not command them directly. Each province also has its military committee, and this committee commands the "regional guerrillas" in its bailiwick. Below the province level, district military committees control "Hamlet Self-Defense Forces," at the lowest end of the Viet Cong's military totem pole.

All these military forces are coordinated from the top, of course, but local military leaders are given a large share of responsibility and autonomy in working out their local problems. This system is similar, incidentally, to the one used by Saigon, which also breaks down its forces three ways: regular army, provincial civil guards, and district and hamlet militia.

There are several reasons for doing things this way, but one of them is that communications in Viet Nam are so poor that local military units must be left largely to shift for themselves.

The main communist reason for the system is based on the idea that fighting forces must be "of, by and for the people," and should be immediately linked to local and presumably popular administrative commissars. Only a local leader knows enough about the situation in his area to command troops intelligently, the communists reason. Local units should be made responsible by headquarters for carrying out certain missions, but then left alone to work things out for themselves. If they fail, they will have to suffer the consequences, both from the enemy and from headquarters. The consequences may sometimes mean a beheaded district commissar.

A key part of the Viet Cong war ministry is its agitprop section, which is tied to all the other ministries. This section commands the 4,000 or more armed agitprop agents who travel in teams throughout South Viet Nam, raising all kinds of hell for government authorities. The agitprop teams are considered by the Liberation Front (and by growing numbers of Saigon officials and Americans) as the real cutting edge of the Viet Cong. All the teams are expert guerrilla fighters, the "special forces" of the Viet Cong. But their main object is not fighting but "agitation and propaganda." Viet Cong recruiting and growth in all fields owe most of their success to these teams. An American Army officer said of them recently that "they have done us far more damage than all the Viet Cong's main force battalions put together."

A complete communist organization normally must have a front which is open to all, an administrative system which is open to some, and a directing party which is usually secret and open only to the elite.

The Viet Cong had the front from the beginning, evolved the administrative system soon afterward, but gave outsiders no hint of the existence of a party for some time. Obviously, there must have been a party all along, because this is always the core of the whole thing. But it was not until January 1962 that the Liberation Front announced publicly the formation of the "Vietnamese People's Revolutionary Party." This party, the Front said, was "a Marxist-Leninist party" which henceforth would serve as the "vanguard" of the Front. At last the Viet Cong was an openly communist-run outfit.

It is well to note in passing that the average member of the Front and most of its branches is not a communist member. Party membership is reserved for the elite, who must establish their political credentials over a long period of time. Once they do this, they usually rise fast in the Viet Cong hierarchy. This fairly sharp distinction between party members and nonparty members of the front, coupled with conspiratorial techniques worked out over many decades of communist evolution, makes it fairly easy for an agent to penetrate the Liberation Front itself, but very difficult to penetrate the governing party.

It is safe to say that no one outside a handful of the highest echelon of Viet Cong leaders has an accurate idea how many members the Front has. Fairly good estimates have been made of Viet Cong fighting strength, and intelligence men feel confident about their charts on the Viet Cong order of battle. But the Viet Cong fighting arm is only a small part of its national organization. Guesses have been made that the Front may have something in the vicinity of five million members in South Viet Nam—a nation the total population of which is only around fourteen million.

There is no other party, religious organization, professional or student group or military force in South Viet Nam that can come anywhere near this figure in strength.

Ngo Dinh Diem had a kind of party called the National Revolutionary Movement, and his brothers, Ngo Dinh Can and Ngo Dinh Nhu, organized a secret society called the "Can Lao Nhan Vy Party" ("Personalist Workers Party"). But the combined membership of these two groups never approached anything like Viet Cong membership, and both parties died completely after the deaths of the Ngo brothers.

This leaves the Viet Cong as the only effective political organization in South Viet Nam.

In a war in which people and not real estate are the objectives, the political success the Viet Cong achieved brought them very close to total victory. America has yet to show that it can upset this victory with mere hardware.

15

AMERICA AND THE
NEW FACE OF WAR

In our minds' eyes we are always the good guys.

We Americans raise our families in peace and harmony.

We enjoy and preserve the democratic way of life, and we have built for ourselves what we consider the happiest, most successful society on earth.

Perhaps most important, we are virtuous.

We unstintingly give of our treasure to help the under-privileged of the world. We give our blood and our lives to help the rest of the world live as we do.

We send forth our young men in uniform to destroy the enemies of our way of life and to keep the world good.

Never, in our minds' eyes, could we be guilty of needlessly killing innocents; of torturing prisoners; of being ungallant to women; of cowardice; of making the poor people of another nation poorer still.

All those things are the domain of the wicked foreigner. It was the Germans who built death camps and the Japanese who conducted death marches; it was the North Koreans who butchered hospital inmates in Seoul.

Alas, Americans are human beings, in common with all other nationalities. We have our greatness. But we also have within us the animal.

Those who contend that our fighting men never feel the primeval lust for blood betray their ignorance of combat. I have seen bloodlust all too often in Viet Nam.

Jungle warfare rots the body and soul, and it looks romantic only on television.

The jungles of Viet Nam are so dense that a man can lose contact with his unit only ten feet away.

Vines catch one's feet, rifle and gear, making movement

torturously slow, sometimes less than a quarter of a mile an hour. Thorns up to two inches long rip through fatigue uniforms deep into the flesh. Most of the overhanging branches of trees are alive with small red ants called "fire ants." The sting of these ants is indeed like fire. When a soldier brushes against a branch, the ants come cascading down the neck of his fatigues, crawling over his neck and chest. A buttoned collar does no good.

The deep streams of the jungle are alive with leeches that crawl through gaps in clothing and stick like glue.

The jungle floor is stifling hot, and breezes rarely get through the foliage. It often rains, leaving troops and their equipment soaking wet, molding and rusting. Soldiers in the jungle rarely have air mattresses or shelter. When it rains, they awake in the morning with their skin whitened and wrinkled by water, and often so full of various fungus infections that toenails start dropping out.

On long jungle marches I have often seen soldiers retching up blood for one reason or another. Malaria is common, and there are one or two strains in Viet Nam that don't respond to the weekly pills GIs normally take in such areas. There have been deaths from malaria.

During operations, there is no relief at night. GIs merely stop in the jungle, set up a defense perimeter and wait out the night. They refill the two or three canteens they carry from plastic water jugs flown in by helicopter, and pass around canned C Ration. If they have any C-4 explosive handy, they heat their cans over it; otherwise, they eat cold spaghetti and meatballs, or the like.

The jungle would take its share of casualties even without a war. But in Viet Nam there also are snipers, booby traps, mines, and thousands of large and small ways the Viet Cong has devised to make life miserable.

As columns of American troops clank through the jungle, there is little energy for talk. The stony-faced kids, with toilet paper rolls and cigarette packs stuck in the straps around their helmets, plod along like a chain gang. Tempers sometimes fray very thin, and when arguments occur they are often ugly. Captains snarl at NCOs, NCOs snarl at the troops, and the troops just mutter.

One hot January day in 1966, Bravo Company of the 2nd

Battalion, 502nd Airborne (101st Airborne Division—the "Screaming Eagles") was painfully working its way through a jungle north of Saigon. Every once in a while, the columns of soldiers would come to the huge crater of a thousand-pound bomb dropped by a B52. All the trees around these craters were torn out, making walking easier for fifty feet or so. But apart from the craters, the jungle was mostly painful green monotony.

In the distance one could hear the crunch of air strikes, but only faintly above the gentle whistling of jungle birds. There were, of course, signs of other human beings. From time to time the column would find a small lean-to loaded with bags of rice, apparently left by guerrillas.

The troops would douse these with gasoline and set them afire. There were also occasional booby traps. One was rigged up with a dead guinea fowl hung from a branch, possibly with the idea of tempting someone to grab the tasty bird.

Each man carried a quartermaster-issue hatchet slung from his belt. Hatchets are not normal equipment for soldiers, and in the jungle are not as useful as machetes. But the battalion commander, Lieutenant Colonel Harry Emerson, had decided to name his outfit the "Hatchet Battalion," and to equip it accordingly. He also sent "Hatchet teams" of commandos in threes and fours into enemy base areas.

Emerson offered a case of Scotch to the first man in his unit to kill a Viet Cong with his hatchet.

The column was moving along unsuspectingly when there was a sudden flicker of movement and a Chinese-made grenade suddenly was lying on the trail near the troops, the fuse in its wooden handle spitting. A shattering crash followed in a second or two, and fast-moving bits of metal ticked through the trees.

Four GIs were hit, and one was screaming.

The whole column was alive with hate, and some soldiers were shooting. In the thicket, a man was running away. He dropped out of sight, and one of the Americans dashed after him, yanking his black-handled hatchet from its sheath. There was silence.

In a moment it was done. The American was back. He was grasping the hair of a freshly severed head, the eyes of which were already closed. The GI's face betrayed no expression as he raised the head, blood slowly dripping on the moss and rotting vegetation.

GIs took turns hefting the trophy and posing with it, but an officer finally came by and told them to bury it.

Bravo Company's commander was Captain Thomas Taylor, the son of General Maxwell D. Taylor, former Army Chief of Staff and U.S. Ambassador to Viet Nam.

The younger Taylor was concerned that newsmen had seen the beheading, and he snapped:

"I hope there is no misunderstanding about this. That VC threw a grenade at my men and he was killed in battle."

He was right, of course.

A few hundred yards away, a GI who had seen it was retching. "Jesus, I thank God I've only got forty-nine days left in this place. We're turning into animals."

He was right, too.

Americans don't like to torture prisoners, but in Viet Nam they have accustomed themselves to turning away when a nasty piece of work is about to be done by a Vietnamese counterpart.

In fact, Viet Nam may be the first war in history in which America has not taken charge of prisoners. Viet Cong captured by American units are turned over to Saigon authorities, no questions asked.

Despite our image of ourselves as gallant to women, the wife of General (former Premier) Nguyen Cao Ky has been moved to complain more than once in public about the behavior of GIs in Saigon.

Senator Fulbright once described Saigon as an American brothel, and I think the description was apt.

As I have mentioned earlier, Vietnamese loathe seeing their women with American men, and sometimes there is violence. Even when there is not, there is often bitter feeling at a high level.

For instance, Le Cang Dam, former Director of Immigration in the Saigon Interior Ministry, had a close relative who became friendly with a U.S. Marine guard at the American Embassy. This relative became pregnant, and the marine told her after the baby was born that he was sorry, but he didn't feel his mother would want a Vietnamese daughter-in-law. One must suppose that the Interior Ministry was not more disposed after that to friendship with Americans.

We like to think of our servicemen as having nerves of steel, holding their fire until they see the whites of the enemy's eyes, and then killing precisely.

Monday morning, May 9, 1966, the scorching sun rose into a cloudless sky over Saigon, and dust and exhaust fumes rose from the huge traffic jams in the heart of the capital, as usual. Military and civilian trucks clogged most of the streets, along with cars and motorbikes and scooters. In traffic jams, even the spaces between motor vehicles were filled with bicycles, pushing and squeezing to get to work.

Diagonally opposite the National Assembly Building (which was converted into an art gallery, there being no National Assembly) in the center of town was the Brink Hotel, a large L-shaped building of five stories used as quarters for field-grade American officers.

The Brink was bombed by Viet Cong terrorists on Christmas Eve, 1964, and ever after it had been guarded by U.S. military policemen in emplacements, by searchlights, barbed wire, and a rule that no Vietnamese could walk near the building.

Despite that, the area was generally jammed. Countless bars, tailor shops and souvenir stores sprang up in Hai Ba Trung Street running past the Brink down to the waterfront.

It was 6:30 A.M. when a small bomb exploded on the sidewalk of Hai Ba Trung Street in front of the "Susie Wong" Vietnamese tailor shop 100 yards or so from the Brink Hotel. The window of the shop was smashed, but there were no casualties. The man who had thrown the bomb dashed off and was not heard from again.

But the United States military establishment was aroused.

A civilian truck was moving past the Brink Hotel at that moment, loaded with men and women dockworkers on their way to work at the waterfront. The MPs at the Brink said later they assumed the truck was loaded with attacking Viet Cong. They riddled the vehicle and its load of occupants with machine-gun fire.

The noise of the shooting aroused another MP post farther up the block. Thinking they were being fired on, the

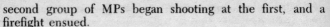

second group of MPs began shooting at the first, and a firefight ensued.

Meanwhile, officers living in the Brink began pouring out, some still in their underwear, carrying pistols and carbines and firing in all directions.

The whole thing was the most sickening instance of military indiscipline and downright cowardice many of us had ever witnessed.

When the Americans finally realized there were no Viet Cong anywhere and that all the shooting was coming from Americans, the battle subsided. The casualties for the morning were five Vietnamese killed (most of them workers in the truck), twenty-six Vietnamese wounded and eight Americans wounded.

Deputy U.S. Ambassador William Porter promptly apologized to the Premier, General Ky, and promised restitution to the victims of the incident.

The families of each of the dead were given by the United States one blanket, one mosquito net, one sack of rice and about $10 in cash.

Graves in good locations in Saigon are so expensive they are often rented for a few years, not bought outright. The bones are dug up and transplanted when the lease expires. Ten dollars does not go far, even in renting a cheap grave.

We think of ourselves as honest, and yet we bring our black markets with us wherever we go, corrupting the societies we touch.

Scandal even involved the former director of America's post exchange and commissary system in Viet Nam, Navy Captain Archie Kuntze. Kuntze, a genial man who used to call himself "The Mayor of Saigon," faced a court martial in 1966 for irregularities. He was acquitted of the formal charges, but dropped from the Navy promotion list.

Hundreds of tons of American goods pour into the Vietnamese black market each month, along with black market American money.

There is even a black market rate for American money bought with American money. Soldiers in Viet Nam are paid in Military Payment Certificates with which they can shop at the PX and other military establishments. Possession of regular American currency is illegal. But the GI who can get hold of a greenback (sent by mail from the States, for instance) can buy $1.25 or so of U.S. military money from Vietnamese money-changers, paying only $1 in greenbacks. With his $1.25 in military money, he can go back to the PX and buy $1.25 worth of goods, all highly salable on the black market.

South Korean troops sent to fight in South Viet Nam are paid their salaries by America and have PX privileges, so they too can make money with the black market.

Some Vietnamese grow very rich on a huge range of swindles, especially real estate deals with U.S. military procurement officers who need property for new installations.

On August 1, 1967, a U.S. Senate investigating committee was told about one of the more successful businessmen, La Thanh Nghe, who had received $896,258 in illegal kickbacks from American pharmaceutical firms. Nghe, by the way, was a cabinet minister in the American-sponsored government of Premier Ky.

One Vietnamese businessman told me he regarded Americans as the most easily corrupted nationality he had ever encountered, including French, Germans, Poles, Chinese and even Indians (the Indians are noted throughout Southeast Asia as dealers in black market money).

"For fifty dollars," he told me, "an American GI would sell me his mother."

As a former GI myself, I take strong exception to this view. But it is unfortunately a very common view in Viet Nam.

Vietnamese charge that Americans are ruining their children with gifts of chocolate and money, and by encouraging begging and scrounging.

"You Americans are turning our children as bad as your own," one Saigon lady said.

My object in writing of these disagreeable things is not to treat the reader to an anti-American diatribe. I merely wish to show that our ethnocentric view of ourselves as good guys is not necessarily shared by the outer world. For a Vietnamese, the greatest pleasure in life is not necessarily having a half-million Americans around.

There are Vietnamese getting rich, but they are the prostitutes, racketeers and low-lifers. For the others, the military occupation is a demoralizing scourge. All too many of my anticommunist Vietnamese friends have said, as the war wears on, "If only we could get rid of the Americans, then we could worry about the Viet Cong."

With all its brutality, the Viet Cong is way ahead in the race for the influence of people, and, as I have said several times before, that is the important part of the war.

We were ill-equipped to come into this war.

At home, our self-indulgence and acquisitiveness had become so ingrained that we brought them with us to Viet Nam. The men of the 2nd Brigade, 9th Infantry Division, spent their days on harrowing operations in the paddies, but could come home to a floating barracks ship on a Mekong Delta waterway called the "Penthouse." On the Penthouse were a PX, a dentist, a barber shop, a snack bar and so forth, all air-conditioned.

There's nothing wrong with making American servicemen as comfortable as possible. But Vietnamese government soldiers notice things like the Penthouse. They themselves cannot buy things in the PX, and, in many ways, they are second-class citizens of their own country.

It is no wonder that the Viet Cong *Binh Van* propaganda campaign amont Vietnamese troops has been so successful.

But this is only a trivial aspect of our lack of preparedness for the "new face of war."

As a nationality, we Americans are generally indifferent to the affairs of the outside world. We develop an active interest in Asia only when we have troops fighting there.

The children in our schools learn a smattering of some foreign language. The usual languages are French and Spanish, sometimes German and, rarely, Russian. The number of schools offering courses in Asian languages is tiny. For that matter, American children in history classes learn about the history of America and Europe, not Asia. At most, the average high school graduate recalls that Marco Polo visited Asia a long time ago and saw the natives making gunpowder and burning coal.

The children of China and Viet Nam don't learn much about us, either. But then, they're not fighting in our country.

American ignorance of Asian affairs has hurt our armed forces, our intelligence services, the Congress, and the White House.

At home, the Congress at this writing has largely turned

its foreign policy prerogatives with respect to Asia over to the executive branch. I have the impression from a number of congressmen that they share the confusion of the average American about Asia, and feel more secure letting the State Department worry over details.

On one of former Vice President Nixon's visits to Viet Nam, I asked him how he felt Americans were reacting to the war. At that point, I had been away for a number of years. His reply, essentially, was:

"I'm not sure, but I believe that in times of crisis like this, Americans will follow the flag."

It seemed to me that the observation was at the same time probably accurate and enormously disquieting. Very few of us cherish the notion that a citizen of our country has much say in foreign policy. But for Americans not even to have opinions of their own about these things seemed to me a terrible thing, if true.

Abroad, our ignorance and indifference have made of us a muscle-bound Goliath. Our intelligence services all too often rely on the intelligence outfits of our "friendly allies," who often are more interested in giving us red herrings than the truth.

At home, we read about and see images of a war in Viet Nam that is only half real. Our television screens are peopled by good and bad guys, and even our authentically dying marines are made by commentators to fit into stereotyped molds. In our air-conditioned homes, we watch Viet Nam in full color, spared of the stench of rotting flesh, the exhaustion, the pain, the hopelessness, the horror, and perhaps most of all, the loss of dignity. War on television provides the same pleasurable tingle as a rollercoaster ride—scariness without real danger.

We think of war as sport, and not only because it is presented that way to us on television and in the printed media.

Even our combat veterans think of it in terms of sport.

I got to know Marine Master Sergeant George Hurt from Bristol, Virginia, while he was an instructor at the Marine Corps sniper school near Da Nang. The school practiced on live human targets, and Hurt lectured on all aspects of the art of sniping. One of the subjects he covered was the psychological preparation a sniper must have. The sniper sometimes actually sees the face of the man he is shooting at and sees the expression of pain when the bullet rips in.

I asked Hurt whether he felt it helps to hate the man you are looking at as you kill him, and he said, "No, I don't believe so. It might sound a little glamorous, but I've always felt, and I think most the men think, that war is kind of a sport, and there's sportmanship to it. It's a thing you have to do. And you kill or be killed."

Another marine I talked with near Da Nang was Staff Sergeant Jimmy Howard of San Diego, who had just been evacuated from a hill nearby. He and all the other seventeen men in his platoon had been either killed or wounded, but they had beaten off the Viet Cong. He attributed the success to sports.

"Practically all of my people, I think, except for one man, have been real active in athletics all the way through school and career. It paid off."

But the Viet Cong are not sportsmen. They believe in dirty tricks to win at all costs. And there is no doubt that they hate their enemy passionately.

Meanwhile, at home, we remain turned inward, not toward Viet Nam.

A revolution of some kind is boiling in America's innards— something that moved Nixon to say:

"Why is it that in a few short years a nation which enjoys the freedom and material abundance of America has become among the most lawless and violent in the history of free peoples?"*

Certainly, there is no question in my mind of the spreading violence within the United States. In my five years in Viet Nam, I was wounded twice in combat but never robbed. In six months in the United States, my apartment was robbed twice (local detectives in New York City advised me to buy a shotgun for my wife), my father's apartment in another neighborhood was robbed and several weeks later bombed by a group of youngsters, and several close women friends were raped in their homes.

When we are as deeply concerned with our own illness as is the case these days, it seems a poor idea to send the

---

*Richard M. Nixon, "What Has Happened to America?" September 26, 1967, issue of the *Reader's Digest*.

legions abroad and expect them to accomplish much in the kind of war we have in Viet Nam.

I have no intention of selling short our youth. I have known many young Americans in and out of uniform who have attacked the problem of "people's warfare" with the passionate zeal of the Peace Corpsman, which is exactly the right way to do it.

They have served in the Special Forces, in CIA, in the U.S. AID Mission, in the U.S. Embassy, in the regular armed forces, and even as newsmen.

I would like to pay special tribute to Jerry Rose—a young and deeply dedicated newsman who accepted a request from former Premier Phan Huy Quat to serve as an advisor to the Vietnamese government. Jerry gave his best to analyzing such problems as the political indoctrination of refugees coming down out of the mountains to government camps.

But Jerry was killed.

There were young men who became students of Mao Tse-tung and North Viet Nam's General Vo Nguyen Giap. They studied and learned from the communist leaders in order to turn the tricks of people's warfare against the communists.

They strove to create an army of anti-Viet Cong Viet Cong.

They went alone into the countryside, sometimes carrying Tommy guns, but relying on their wits, their knowledge, and their learned ability to work and communicate with

B-52

Vietnamese at the lowest level. Some thought of themselves as a kind of fighting Peace Corps. Others went as volunteers for pacifist religious organizations. Either way, they shared the belief that "people's wars" are not won by B52s.

The energy and sparkling intelligence shown by some of these young people attracted the attention of the powerful in Washington, and Brigadier General Edward Lansdale was named to coordinate activities.

Lansdale, an Air Force officer who for years worked for the CIA, had helped establish a viable government in Manila after Philippine independence, and was one of the Americans who put Ngo Dinh Diem in power in Viet Nam. To Graham Greene, he became the model for "The Quiet American."

Lansdale is a man of highly unorthodox views who had many bitter enemies in the Pentagon.

From the beginning of his assignment in Viet Nam, he was up against formidable problems, many of which were the result of smoldering hostility from regular military people. Most of all, Lansdale's problem was the pool of ignorance and indifference from which most Americans sent to Viet Nam are drawn.

With some wonderful exceptions, America lacked the human raw material to wage a "people's war."

President Johnson had always been distrustful of the gray war of propaganda and secret operations. President Kennedy had been fascinated with it, but Kennedy was dead.

In 1966, President Johnson called for "some coonskins nailed to the wall" in Viet Nam, and made it clear to the people of Lansdale's ilk that if they couldn't win a victory quickly he would have to rely on other methods.

After a few months, Lansdale, Ambassador Porter (who had been in over-all charge of the unorthodox war) and most of the others were told they were through. Porter was appointed ambassador to South Korea as an apparent consolation prize.

And the President escalated the bombing of North Viet Nam.

In the first edition of this book, which was written three years prior to the current edition, I suggested that America was up against a new and dangerous challenge which it would have to face in many parts of the world, not just Viet Nam. I suggested that America should give its best thought and effort to the new kind of war in Viet Nam, which might well prove to be the forerunner of many similar future wars.

I still feel Viet Nam is a forerunner of sorts. Limited wars in which guerrillas model their campaigns at least partially after that of the Viet Cong are visible in the making in several parts of the world. Bolivia, for instance, is a possible Viet Nam in the making, allowing, of course, for major local variations.

But I no longer feel that America is capable of mastering this kind of war, at least in our country's present state of mind.

I have had the impression lately that we are doing both our imagined allies and ourselves more harm than good in Viet Nam, without in any way defeating the enemy.

In the second half of the sixth decade of the twentieth century, the word "isolationism" has a peculiarly attractive ring.

On October 19, 1966, Senator George D. Aiken, a crusty old Vermont Republican, suggested that the United States simply declare the war in Viet Nam was "won" and then de-escalate it.

Perhaps, after all, this is our only honorable answer to the agony of the new face of war.

INDEX

JOHNNY'S SONG
The Poetry of a Vietnam Veteran

Steve Mason
(05160 • $9.95)

A former Army captain and decorated Vietnam combat veteran, Steve Mason is a unique American poet. JOHNNY'S SONG, his magnificent epic, was born from a vow made to a group of veterans attending the dedication ceremonies for the Vietnam Veterans Memorial in Washington, D.C., also known as "The Wall." This book, then, echoes and amplifies their voices, for Steve Mason has written what they all saw, what they all felt, what they all dreamed.

His pen follows "a black blood trail across the page."

> *There is one other wall, of course.*
> *One we never speak of.*
> *One we never see.*
> *One which separates memory from madness.*
> *In a place no one offers flowers.*
> *THE WALL WITHIN.*
> *We permit no visitors.*

Relive the American Experience in Viet Nam

BANTAM VIETNAM WAR BOOKS

☐ 05160   **JOHNNY'S SONG** $9.95
           Steve Mason (A Bantam Hardcover)

☐ 25041   **THE 13TH VALLEY** $4.50
           Del Vecchio

☐ 22956   **FIELDS OF FIRE** $3.95
           Webb

☐ 24104   **A SENSE OF HONOR** $3.50
           Webb

Prices and availability subject to change without notice.

Buy them at your local bookstore or use this handy coupon for ordering:

BANTAM
SHOP-AT-HOME
C·A·T·A·L·O·G

Special Offer
Buy a Bantam Book
for only 50¢.

Now you can have an up-to-date listing of Bantam's hundreds of titles plus take advantage of our unique and exciting bonus book offer. A special offer which gives you the opportunity to purchase a Bantam book for only 50¢. Here's how!

By ordering any five books at the regular price per order, you can also choose any other single book listed (up to a $4.95 value) for just 50¢. Some restrictions do apply, but for further details why not send for Bantam's listing of titles today!

Just send us your name and address and we will send you a catalog!
